D1093570

A
Wayward
Quest

A
Wayward
Quest

◇◇◇◇◇

THE AUTOBIOGRAPHY OF

Theresa Helburn

WITH ILLUSTRATIONS

Little, Brown and Company
BOSTON   TORONTO

For permission to use unpublished material thanks are due the
following:

Mrs. Eugene O'Neill for several letters written by Mr. O'Neill
and by herself.

The Public Trustee and the Society of Authors for a number
of letters from George Bernard Shaw.

*Published simultaneously in Canada
by Little, Brown & Company (Canada) Limited*

PRINTED IN THE UNITED STATES OF AMERICA

Curtain Raiser

WHEN THE PUBLISHER first asked me to write my autobiography I was frankly appalled. It seemed to me that no one, however agonizingly honest he might attempt to be, could recapture the stuff of his own life.

But once I decided that I could not do such a book, I began perversely to try anyway. I've always been irresistibly challenged by whatever I felt was beyond my capabilities. Anyhow, I wanted to get the record straight in my own eyes. I became an author in search of her own character. Some of it seems new even to me, for only in retrospect have I seen clearly why I did the things I did, why I succeeded and why I failed.

I have not tried to strip bare my heart. Overly personal revelations in others either embarrass or bore me; the confessional belongs to the vanishing domain of privacy.

I have not attempted to write a detailed history of the Theatre Guild. Lawrence Langner has covered much of our work together in his autobiography, *The Magic Curtain,* and there are accurate listings of Theatre Guild productions, season by season, for the earnest scholar.

I have made no effort to follow chronology too slavishly. What interests me is the relationship of things, not the order in which they happened.

So it is of the theater I have written, for what has counted to me, first and last, has been the wonder and magic and undimmed enchantment of the stage; the incredible luck of being a person who earns his living at the thing he loves; the years filled to the hilt with excitement. While working on this book during the otherwise tiresome months of recuperation from a heart attack, I've learned a lot about myself, and I've had the fun of reliving some of the great moments of my life. But best of all, I've felt again the ever recurring thrill, the heart-rousing moment, when the house lights go down and the footlights come up.

Contents

Publisher's Note

WHEN THERESA HELBURN died on August 18, 1959, she was in the process of working on her memoirs with Elinore Denniston. Miss Denniston, who had full access to Miss Helburn's files, would arrange this material chapter by chapter and read the result to Miss Helburn for her approval. Thus this autobiography is as authentic as it could be; and our thanks are due Miss Denniston for her faithful labor. Our profound thanks are also due Mr. Lawrence Langner, Miss Helburn's partner in the Theatre Guild, and to Margaret Helburn Kocher, Miss Helburn's niece, to whom she was devoted, for their help in making many valuable corrections and suggestions.

A
Wayward
Quest

ONE

Cheesecloth and Magic

I WAS BORN on West Forty-fifth Street in New York City, in the heart of the present theatrical district. When I was four years old my family moved to a four-story house with a high stoop, on Ninetieth Street near Columbus Avenue, not far from Central Park.

The area was just being developed (my grandfather was a real estate speculator who bought houses on the perimeter of the growing city and moved on as he sold them), and there were still many vacant lots in which "squatters" — mostly Irish — had thrown up little huts and sheds in which they lived uneasily and impermanently. There was, I remember, more prestige involved in inhabiting the solid and uniform brownstone fronts on the side streets than the dilapidated tenements of the avenues, and I recall a certain amount of hauteur in my attitude toward the ragged youngsters from the avenues, who sauntered past — regarding us with assumed scorn — as we sat on the stoop on summer evenings.

Ours, I think, was a singularly united family. We shared

and fortified each other's interests; we talked endlessly together. My mother was vital, dominant, ambitious; my father was gentle, dreamy, philosophic; my brother was eager, intellectually curious, articulate. While I was young my grandmother, still beautiful in her old age, was the matriarchal head of the family. I remember her always surrounded by the lovely things her adoring husband brought her from his European trips, delicate laces and *objets d'art*.

We lived on Ninetieth Street because it was my grandmother's home. My father's business — he was a leather merchant — was in Boston, Massachusetts, and he was able to see his family only on week ends. Curiously, I can't remember that any of us ever realized that this was not a wholly satisfactory way of life for him, or that it was also hard on him when the annual chaos of "closing the house" took place, while we escaped the summer heat of the city for our four months' vacation. Children take a great deal for granted.

The house itself was dark and only half-furnished, although, when the annual upheaval of moving away for the long summer vacation came, there seemed to be countless things to be packed up and stored, and many pictures and high, ugly gas brackets to be carefully swathed in pink cheesecloth.

It was in the fall, on our return from our annual two months at the seashore and two months in the mountains, that I discovered magic in a piece of pink cheesecloth. It was an odd-shaped fragment that had fallen from one of the gas brackets and had acquired a peak. Idly I perched it on my head. There was a long mirror in the hallway from which the cheesecloth wrappings had been removed, and in it I saw the little girl with her peaked cap. Like a princess, I thought, strutting up and down before the mirror.

I tried it at a different angle and I became a court jester. Draped over my head, despite its gay color it was like the mourning veils women wore in those days. Just a piece of cheesecloth, but with it I could become anything I chose to be, something that was not myself. For most children, I think, the world of make-believe is the only reality. For me it became enchantment. The house on Ninetieth Street was furnished with all the creatures and the settings of all the fairy tales I had read.

Of course, it really wasn't as idyllic as that; I can see now with a kind of horror how inconvenient it was, how terribly hard those fresh, pink-cheeked Irish maids of ours worked, hauling coal up four flights, carrying meals from the kitchen in the basement, patiently trotting up and down all those stairs a dozen times a day. But for me those early years in New York were pure sunshine. There were no serpents in that paradise. The only cloud in my sky was that, of all the children with whom I played — my brother, my cousins and their friends — I was the youngest and always the littlest. There was no overcoming such handicaps, but I began to want intensely to be able to compete with them on a more equitable basis.

The first play in which I took part was given in the basement of our house, with an admission of two pins. Because I was the youngest, I was assigned the smallest part, which consisted of the single line: "Guard the door while I sleep." I was determined, however, to wring all I could out of my rôle so I emphasized my need for sleep by falling flat on my face at the end of the line. I did it with such enthusiasm that I was black and blue all over, but I learned to fall with a lovely sound, as though all the bones of my body were being broken, and with no damage to myself. My amused mother used to get me to do it at tea parties. The play was a melodrama with shooting, and we needed a gun. The only possessor of such a rare article was a boy from Columbus Avenue. So we sacrificed our social superiority for the sake of art and made him a member of the troupe.

But the basement was soon put to other uses, and there was no more room for an acting company, even one as undemanding as ours. My mother was a driving force in the Browning Club. She was a woman of ardent enthusiasms, a great hero-worshiper, a devoted neophyte while it lasted. There was nearly always some person, usually a painter, whom she admired fanatically. When she was young, her enthusiasm was for older painters; but as she grew older, she became interested in young painters whom she might be able to help. When she could afford it, she bought their paintings in order to encourage them.

Before her marriage she had been a teacher and she was profoundly interested in educational methods and theories. When I was not quite five, she determined to try out her theories on me and provide the kind of education she believed I should have. In the basement she established a little experimental school for me and a few other children of my age. By the end of the first year, she was so encouraged by the results, and the neighborhood women who had sent their children to the class were so enthusiastic, that her school went on to the primary grade, to the second, third and fourth years.

In time, the house was swamped. There were so many pupils in the thriving little experimental school that I was finally forced to sleep in a room converted from a bathroom, with the disheartening yellow-brown wainscoting that was so popular at the time. (Were people afraid of cheerful colors that would let gaiety into the dark houses or did they really consider the encircling gloom essential to respectability?)

Looking back, I can see that the money from the school was very useful around the house. We never lacked necessities, but we lived frugally. The spending of a penny for a banana or a pickle was a matter of much soul-searching and cogitation to us children. Pennies weren't lightly thrown away, and we expected our full money's worth from them.

During these early years I never saw a real play, not even children's performances. My education-conscious mother was determined that no time should be wasted on nonsense or on trivialities. But when I was nine — oh, when I was nine! — she took me to see Ada Rehan and her Broadway stock company in four plays. I have never forgotten them: *As You Like It*, *Much Ado About Nothing*, *The Merchant of Venice* and *The School for Scandal*.

From the moment when the curtain rose on the first play, I entered a world that was unlike anything I had ever imagined, but that I recognized at once as my own. The theater was not a dream, or a goal — it was home.

From that time on, I began to read plays, although, except for birthdays and holidays, I was not allowed to go to the theater. I read Shakespeare long before I had any grasp of what he was all about. Dialogue seemed to me the only natural and satisfying way of telling a story. I even read Plato at a preposterously early age, simply because it was in the form of dialogue and I felt that it had something to say to me. If I kept plowing through the dialogue, however undramatic, something was bound to happen, sooner or later.

But even at that early age I was unsatisfied with the *feeling* of the dialogue I read to myself. I needed to hear it. Today, I still find I get much more out of any prose, whether dialogue or not, if it is read aloud to me. I suppose that is the inevitable reaction of the born theater woman.

After the fourth grade, my mother sent me to the Horace Mann School, which I attended until my grandmother died; at which time we moved to Boston to join my patient father. I entered Miss Winsor's School, a fashionable and exclusive establishment, and I think I must have been admitted only because my scholastic rating was so high.

One of my classmates at Miss Winsor's School was Frances Parkinson Keyes. A friendship grew between us that has lasted all our lives.

I have been trying to remember my mind as it was during those first years in Boston, but without much success. I was one of those terribly bright children and I must have been impossible. I was not pretty, my hair and my clothes were all wrong, but I had a great deal of energy and ambition. I felt that I could do anything, and I seem to have had no inhibitions. In one way or another I simply had to excel. I was sure of that. Under my mother's influence, the obvious road for me was through education.

So upon graduating from Miss Winsor's I entered Bryn

Mawr. I majored in English and philosophy but I tried my hand at everything. My energy seemed to be inexhaustible and I hurled myself at each new thing as though there was not a moment to lose. I played basketball and hockey, I ran a couple of literary publications, I won prizes for composition, and I produced all my class plays.

At that time, Bryn Mawr was still strongly under Quaker influence. No dancing was permitted. We did not even have an organ in chapel. The only way we could entertain our young men — God help them! — was by inviting them to listen to the annual Glee Club performance. Whether I was typical of the girls of my class or not I don't know; I imagine the impact of that education on all of us was pretty much the same. I know I acquired an intellectual sophistication while remaining a Victorian prude. I was profoundly ignorant about everything that was real. I assumed that nice women had brains but no bodies. I did not know how to dress properly, how to use make-up or cope with my hair or make the best of what I had. As a young female I must have been a total loss.

The teacher I remember as being the most impressive was Katharine Fullerton Gerould, who taught English and wrote charming, polished essays for the *Atlantic Monthly*. Culturally, all this was beyond criticism. The only difficulty is that it left me shamefully ignorant in regard to all aspects of life outside of books.

Bryn Mawr frowned on the contemporary drama and there were no plays in the college library. The favorite subjects for sophomore papers were Stevenson and Ruskin. Frankly, they left me cold, so I decided to write my paper on Arthur Wing

Pinero. For three months, I went to the Philadelphia library to gather the material and read the Pinero plays; for me this was a daring and exciting experience. Why the college authorities allowed me to break with tradition I can't imagine.

But the most rewarding experience of my college years was producing the class plays. I knew nothing about producing, directing, casting, staging; but then, neither did any of the other girls. So, as I was to do so often afterwards, I rushed in where angels feared to tread.

At the end of my second year, I discovered that it was not enough to produce plays; I wanted to write one. I spent the whole vacation, long days of mingled delight and despair, grappling with a medium that requires so much experience and technique. On the whole, I was fairly well pleased with my play — actually, I was as proud as Punch — but when I returned to college and began to prepare for our next production, I discovered that Helburn was not as good as other material that was available and I put on Rostand's *La Princesse lointaine* instead. This was the first of many struggles I've had to make between personal vanity and detached judgment, and they never become less acutely painful.

The Rostand play deals with a long voyage in search of a faraway princess by a group of sailors who, during the journey, have become a shabby lot. The day before the play was to be given, the costumes arrived. We had ordered ragged sailors' costumes. What we got were the costumes used in *H.M.S. Pinafore,* in pristine condition, neat and clean, with fetching little round white collars.

At that first moment, I was ready to abandon the play forever. I wanted to die. But, like Madam Goddam in *The*

Shanghai Gesture, I survived. The next moment I got to work on a way of dealing with the situation. I ripped off the collars, messed up the uniforms of the Queen's Navee, and we got by. I played the villain, and I don't know whether I was good or bad. But I am sure that I was understood. For months, our English professor, Samuel Arthur King, had drilled us in diction, making us put a pencil between our teeth and then say:

Speak the speech, I pray you, as I pronounced it to you, trippingly on the tongue; but if you mouth it, as many of your players do, I had as lief the town-crier spoke my lines.

Later, I produced *Two Gentlemen of Verona,* which has always been a favorite of mine. Our performance was all we hoped for it, largely because of the delightful voice of Marjorie Young, the girl who sang that most enchanting of Shakespeare lyrics, "Who Is Sylvia?"

By the end of my four years at Bryn Mawr I had held almost every possible position in college and I was awarded a set of Shakespeare — later proudly displayed by my mother in a prominent position on a table — as a prize given in memory of May Helen Ritchie to the member of the senior class who showed "throughout her four years in college in the highest degree the qualities of joyousness, high courage, fortitude and faithfulness." It was better but less grandiloquently known, among the student body, as the "Sunny Jim" prize.

I finished college with éclat and all the senior prizes — and then I had a breakdown.

◇◇ TWO

Trial Flights

WITH THAT PHYSICAL COLLAPSE, I started the pattern of my life: a wild spurt of activity followed by total exhaustion. I have been doing it for fifty years, and I'm always just as surprised and annoyed when the day comes that finds me unable to move. Do other people learn by experience, I wonder? My trouble seems to be that though I know my faults I don't seem able to correct them.

All that winter I rested on a farm in Massachusetts, which my mother and brother bought for me, thinking that the quiet would do me good. For a long time I vegetated in a state of utter inactivity and then, little by little, my vitality came seeping back until I was completely restored.

With the return of my energy I found it impossible to rusticate any longer. I wanted to write, though I had not yet focused on the direction my writing was to take. Then, and all my life since, a free day, even a free hour, has meant that the rare blank pages of my diary or engagement books are filled with ideas for stories, articles, speeches, plays. The personnel of the Theatre Guild must shudder when there are free hours on my calendar. It usually means that I begin to bombard them with ideas and — heaven help them! — suggestions for improvements.

Like too many young people, I was filled with creative urges for which I had no proper outlet. I hadn't as yet discovered enough about myself to know where my basic interests lay.

I did have sense enough, however, to realize that "to want to write" is not enough. What I needed most then was intelligent guidance and time to discover myself. Producing plays had afforded me more interest than any other part of those crowded years at Bryn Mawr, so I decided on postgraduate work at Radcliffe, which would enable me to enter the famous 47 Workshop conducted by Professor George Pierce Baker of Harvard. This was one of the most important decisions I ever made.

It would be difficult to overestimate the effect that Baker's 47 Workshop had on the theater of the next twenty years. Several of my later colleagues shared that experience and all of them were profoundly influenced by it, whether they worked in the field of scenic design, of direction, of production, of acting, or in Professor Baker's own field — playwriting.

Professor Baker himself was far from being the innovator that many of his students became. He was limited entirely by the theater of his day; he not only did not attempt to progress beyond it, he could not imagine going beyond it. And the theater of his day — at any rate, that on which he concentrated — was the commercial Broadway stage. The playwrights to whom he devoted most of his attention were Arthur Wing Pinero, Henry Arthur Jones and Clyde Fitch. Lee Simonson, another 47 Workshop alumnus, later told me how he had failed to convince Professor Baker that George Bernard Shaw was worth more than a single lecture.

What made the 47 Workshop such an unforgettable experience for all of us who entered it was the fact that Professor Baker, a forceful and eager man, took us, for the first time in our limited experience, out of the academic atmosphere and thrust us into the electric excitement of the professional theater. He treated us not as students but as responsible adults to whom the contemporary stage was tremendously important. He talked not in terms of classical literature but in terms of Broadway. What he was discussing and sharing with us was immediate; it was actual; above all, it was professional.

We weren't there to fool around with pretty, "artistic" theories. We were there to learn to write for the living stage. And we wrote. How we wrote! The man inspired everyone who took his classes to try to write plays that could actually meet the competition of the professionals and make their way on Broadway.

Over and over, during the hectic years in the theater, I was to discover to how many young men and women Baker had given the decisive push that sent them headlong on the path that led to Broadway, in one capacity or another. I took the Baker course after Edward Sheldon had left it, and before Sidney Howard had entered it. Among the members of the Workshop classes with whom I was to work and who later were to distinguish themselves and make real contributions to the American theater, in one capacity or another, were Eugene O'Neill, Philip Barry, Lee Simonson, Robert Edmond Jones, and Maurice Wertheim.

But paradoxically, although innovation did not interest Professor Baker, among the young people who emerged from the 47 Workshop were innovators in almost every phase of the theater. They were directly inspired by a man who was an honest lover of what was, actually, a rather meretricious list of plays; for there were few, in the early days of the century, that rose, or attempted to rise, above the level of mediocrity. Here are the plays which, according to Burns Mantle's *Best Plays and Year Book of the Drama in America,* best represented the seasons between 1899–1909:

Barbara Frietchie by Clyde Fitch
The Climbers by Clyde Fitch
If I Were King by Justin Huntly McCarthy
The Darling of the Gods by David Belasco
The County Chairman by George Ade
Leah Kleschna by C. M. S. McLellan
The Squaw Man by Edwin Milton Royle
The Great Divide by William Vaughn Moody
The Witching Hour by Augustus Thomas
The Man from Home by Booth Tarkington and Harry Leon
     Wilson

The secret of Professor Baker's success lay less, I sometimes think, in what he taught than in how he taught. For he taught with love and fire and patience. For the rest, any student worth his salt can learn the content once the spark has been applied.

When I had finished the Baker course, I spent the summer on the farm, playing energetic tennis and applying my new knowledge to writing a play. What I overlooked was the fact that my knowledge of life was limited to what I found in the pages of books; with my theoretical sophistication, I built a plot on an unconventional relationship between a man and woman, and my feminine lead was supposed to be pregnant — for the Broadway stage of 1910!

This opus I sent for criticism to my brother, Willard, who was in San Francisco at the time. As any amateur knows, asking for criticism is simply a bid for lavish praise. It's one of the demarcation points between the amateur and the professional. Anyhow, what I got was criticism.

My brother wrote at length. Pregnancy on the stage, he pointed out, was rarely permissible. In fact, he seemed startled to realize that I had heard of the condition. Men, he informed me, did not travel with their mistresses masquerading as their sisters. It defeated the relationship.

He added severely, "Don't ask me why."

I should have been more grateful than I was for his painstaking destruction of my play, scene by scene, for he was having his own troubles. He was young — and he was alone. He was breaking off his letter at two in the morning, he wrote, to take a long walk up and down the San Francisco hills.

"Blister your feet," Willard wrote with the desperation of the young, "and you won't bite the pillow."

That fall, with my play forlornly shoved into the back of a drawer, I came to New York with my mother. I made my début on a small scale and, through her friends, my brother's friends, and my former Bryn Mawr classmates, I came to know a group of amusing young people, all of whom, as I look back now, were frightfully in earnest about something.

All, perhaps, with the exception of Horace Liveright and his younger brother Otto. I met Otto on a blind date and I remember him chiefly for his cheerful nonsense and the inexhaustible supply of calling cards, each bearing a most improbable name, with which he announced his arrival. The card of a Japanese nobleman or a Chinese caterer at once indicated that Otto was waiting in the drawing room.

Most of us were fledgling creators who had not yet found our proper niches, and most of us were solemnly intellectual. I frequently hear contemporary scorn cast at the frivolous youth of pre-World War I days, who presumably fiddled while Rome burned, and are summed up, for reasons that escape me, in the person of Clara Bow. We, to my stunned surprise, are grouped with Flaming Youth. We who burned with a hard gemlike flame and were stupefyingly grim in our earnestness! But there's one thing they can't call us: the beat generation. There wasn't one of us who would acknowledge defeat while we could stand on our two feet and fight back.

I smile now when I think of the rather priggish morality and unsuspected conventionality with which we condemned the Double Standard and upheld Free Love and all the shibboleths of the day with a rather humorless determination to back good causes and generally enlighten the world. But we were not, I realize, socially conscious, as are the young today. A war and a depression in which they were involved up to their necks have aroused young people to a vital interest in questions that were almost nonexistent to the majority of my generation.

All of us were doing something or trying to do something, and on the whole nearly every member of that group eventually found the right niche and made a genuine contribution in his or her field. Among them were Arthur Hays Sulzberger, who was a great friend of my brother; Claire Raphael, who ultimately became the head of the League of Modern Composers; Walter Lippmann; Philip Moeller and his lovely cousin, Josephine Meyer; and Edward Goodman, who stood out from his friends by his spectacular appearance at evening parties, complete with opera cloak and silk hat, which he wore with an air.

There was also Lawrence Langner, an attractive and alert young Englishman, who was by profession an international patent attorney and by avocation a kind of Benjamin Franklin with ideas about everything under the sun. He not only had ideas, he was prepared to implement them. When he saw something that should be done, he brushed aside obstacles as though they weren't there, and set out to do it regardless. Sometimes, when I think how often I've been the bulldozer to push aside obstacles in the path of Lawrence's ideas, I think I would have been wiser to take to my heels. But what a lot of fun I would have missed!

A writer I had expected to be, a writer I was still hell-bent on becoming. But it took me a fantastically long time to recognize my own field, even after I had done rather well in it. I think I've waited longer than anyone I ever knew to have my own plays produced, and even so they were not successful. At this time Eddie Goodman and I had plunged into collaboration on a play called *Other Lives,* which was not produced until nearly twelve years later. And another play of mine was produced twenty years after it was written.

I was also working hard on short stories, a number of which were published, and I began to write verse. In those pre-T. S. Eliot days, there was less snobbery and more direct excitement about poetry. There were fewer schools of poetry and more people reading it for refreshment and delight, perhaps because we were naïve enough to believe then that the purpose of all art was primarily communication. The poets were not attempting to stun the reader with their erudition or to baffle him with their symbolism; they were sharing with him their vision of beauty.

But, thank God, they were, as up to then all poets had been, on the side of life. It was not just an abstract beauty they acclaimed but man himself and the living substance of existence. Only later were the Hollow Men to attempt to make the world as emotionally sterile and empty as an atomic bomb. Only later was man's essential dignity in the face of the gigantic problems of life and death to be reduced to the ignominy of a whimper, degraded to the point of view which Melville called "snivilization."

There were several flourishing poetry journals and nearly all the good magazines — and how many there were in those dark ages! — carried verse in every issue. Editors had not yet come to the conclusion that it exhausts a man's mind to read anything longer than a quatrain.

I sold my first poem to *Century*, and when my work had been published by *Harper's*, the *New Republic*, *Poetry*, the *Bellman*, *Smart Set*, the *Poetry Journal*, and various anthologies, I joined the Poetry Society, which met at the National

Arts Club. There was no particular program planned for these evenings. They simply afforded opportunities for people interested in poetry, and practicing it as an art, to talk to each other.

And what good talk it was! There I met and in most cases came to know well the representative poets of the time: Amy Lowell, Sara Teasdale, Vachel Lindsay, Edwin Arlington Robinson, Zoë Akins (whom I knew much better later on as a playwright), Jessie Rittenhouse, Harriet Monroe, Conrad Aiken, Mary and Padraic Colum, Margaret Widdemer, Louis Untermeyer, Richard Le Gallienne, Percy MacKaye, Hamlin Garland, Robert Frost, John Wheelock, Corinne Roosevelt Robinson, Allan Nevins, Witter Bynner.

Often they read their new poems, the readings followed by a general discussion and occasional, rather tactful, criticism. Sara Teasdale was the quietest, the most retiring; Vachel Lindsay, who was then exchanging poems for bread on his tramps around the country (a tremendously romantic thing to do, in our eyes), was the noisiest — chanting his poems, with his famous Billy Sunday delivery, at the drop of a hat.

Practically all the members of the Poetry Society were, by contemporary standards, fairly conventional in their techniques, with the exception of Vachel, whose poems were meant for muscular delivery, and of Amy Lowell, who was beginning to follow the French experimentalists in free verse and "polyphonic prose."

My own verse, I see now, belonged simply to the lyric period of youth when, if ever, one will sing. The following, I think, is fairly typical of the verses to which I devoted several years during my trial flights, when I was still looking for the right direction.

> The shutters of my soul are closed
>   And yet within it is not night;
> The fire flames upon the hearth
>   And all the candles are alight.
>
> So many times you pass my door
>   And never pause! Does not one ray
> Of urgent brightness filter through
>   To bid you stay?
>
> The shutters of my soul are closed;
>   In vain I try to fling them wide.
> How should you know — who scarcely look —
>   The bars are fastened from outside?
>
> How should you guess I sit alone
>   Where it is neither night nor day,
> Watching the candles burning low,
>   Hearing your footsteps die away?

While I was enjoying my first New York season, becoming involved with a group of poets, writing short stories, and collaborating with Eddie Goodman, I met a former classmate of mine from Bryn Mawr, Margaret Franklin, daughter of Fabian Franklin and cousin of Amy Loveman, who later for many years was a brilliant editor of the *Saturday Review*. Margaret was teaching at Miss Merrill's Finishing School for girls at Mamaroneck. She asked me whether I would be willing to give a lecture there on the drama. I'd be paid six dollars an hour.

This was an unexpected bonanza, to be paid for talking about something I liked! I had never lectured in my life, but I rashly agreed at once to do it.

When I got there, I found a group of some twenty girls who were being "finished" in the approved style of the time. Here the drama was not the living excitement it had been in Professor Baker's course. It was "culture," respectfully approached.

That first day, I asked the girls, "Have you read any plays?"

"No," they said.

"Have you read any Shakespeare?"

"Oh, yes, of course."

"Someone," I remarked rather heatedly to the head of the school after that lecture, "should teach those girls that there is a connection between Shakespeare and plays."

She took me aback by saying promptly, "Why don't you do it?"

Well, after all, why not? Early in the fall I went out to start my course. I looked down at the polite, passive faces, at the notebooks and pencils, at my captive audience waiting for its daily dose of culture.

"We are going to turn this class into an acting company," I told the startled girls. "We are going to produce *Twelfth Night*. I want you to read the play and then write me a note telling me which part you would prefer to do."

It was no surprise to receive twenty notes asking for the part of Viola. There were, I pointed out, other rôles that were even more rewarding to the actor than Viola. Their next assignment was to tell me why they wanted to play the part, what they saw in it. This, they discovered, was not so easy.

For three months, we worked on six or seven scenes from *Twelfth Night,* reading them aloud, discussing the meaning of every phrase, arguing — it was an informal class — every word, from the point of view of the actor. What does this mean? How should that be read? By the time we had finished, the girls had learned the intention and meaning of every line, and they had found the learning process an exciting one. So twenty girls discovered that Shakespeare was not an assignment; not simply "a part of every cultivated man's heritage." He was a playwright — a man who knew, better than any other man had ever known, how to write plays that kept audiences glued to their seats.

I, too, had made a discovery. One of the girls in that class had a memorable kind of beauty that made the eyes follow her wherever she went. Her name was Katharine Cornell. Tall, slim and lovely, and at that time wearing mourning for her mother, she walked across the campus in a black dress, spectacularly escorted by her white Russian borzoi.

Kit was hipped on the theater; even then she revealed the feeling and the emotion that make an actress. And she was a worker. When she was not studying the script of *Twelfth Night* (she was cast as Malvolio), she organized her classmates in a study of pantomime, in which she usually played the romantic lead, and when they had prepared new rôles they would do them for me. She stood out from her admiring classmates like a moon surrounded by satellites, and yet she

23

never presumed on what she was or what she had. She was then, as later, lovely, modest and unassuming.

Though I was at that time an amateur in the theater, I had learned enough to be distrustful of encouraging anyone to go on the stage, because for the great majority it is a heartbreaking business. But Kit not only had the beauty and the temperament for it, as well as the patience to plug away doggedly at her part until she had mastered it, she was also prosperous enough to be unaffected by the misery and fear caused by being out of a job. She was, indeed, one of the few amateurs whom I have ever deliberately encouraged to attempt a career in the theater, and I have always been glad that I was enabled to provide her with her first opportunity.

I wanted to leave for France a few weeks before the end of the school year, but I had to find a substitute to carry on my lectures. I asked Edward Goodman to replace me.

Eddie came up, was impressed by Kit and later offered her a small rôle — actually it was an offstage scream — in one of the first plays put on by the Washington Square Players. And so she started on one of the most distinguished careers in the theater.

THREE

Springtime in Paris

LATE IN MAY I reached France. It wasn't my first trip. I had been taken to France when I was nine and again when I was thirteen; but this time I was alone, without the guardianship and restraints of older people, free to see and experience with my own eyes, not on a guided tour with a strong cultural bias.

This was an important step toward growing up, which took me an awfully long time. Because there was so close and warm a relationship between my parents and me, I was in my middle thirties before I ever managed to become a completely independent person. My parents loved me, they babied me, they guided me, they determined my major decisions, whether for good or ill. It took me years to realize how much harm this overprotection did me. It was years before I found my own feet and learned to see through my own eyes — abilities rarer than a lot of people realize.

I have never experienced such a sense of freedom and exhilaration as I had in Paris. Not that I abused my freedom,

25

heaven knows, or that I had any desire to do so. But I was happy, profoundly happy.

Happiness heightens all one's senses, I think, and I was sharply aware of everything around me, all the small scenes that have their own delight. There was, for instance, the man who ran the little merry-go-round in the Luxembourg Gardens. He had a drooping mustache, a sweet merry face, and he loved children. Even the tiniest little girl he called "Mademoiselle" with grave politeness, and I can still hear the gentleness in his voice when he would call out, *"Attention aux petits pieds."*

And there were the old men who played croquet, surrounded by a solid wall of spectators, all old like themselves, all looking as though they spent the whole day every day on the same spot and were content to do so. Why is it that age seems to have so many more compensations for Europeans than for Americans, where the cult of youth makes the aging process a thing to be dreaded?

And there were solitary walks — though one was actually never alone in Paris, for there was always the sound, regardless of how late it was, of market wagons rumbling slowly down the Boulevard Sébastopol, each with a man and wife atop the vegetables, the woman usually nodding as she slept beside her husband. And the little cafés were never entirely deserted, for two or three customers were always seated at the small tables.

The beauty of that enchanting city had time to sink in and really get me. I arrived in Paris "as corny as Kansas in August" and I found everything tremendously stimulating:

the great avenues, the fascinating streets, the lace balconies, the architecture.

I had gone to France at the invitation of a Bryn Mawr classmate, Margaret Lewis (later Mrs. MacVeagh), who was studying architecture. She had written to suggest that I spend the summer with her; we would take a bicycle trip through Brittany and Normandy to see the cathedrals and châteaux. She warned me that she was down to twenty-five francs a week so we would have to travel cheaply.

Peggy was living, to my delight, in a typical French pension on the fifth floor of the Boul' Mich'. There was a strange lot of boarders in that place, and the landlady frankly terrified us both. I'm not good at names but I have never forgotten hers: she was Madame Constantinople, and her first husband had been a Monsieur Baghdad. She was such a threatening character that Peggy and I shivered in our room, which opened on a balcony running all around the place. For self-protection we tied our shutters together at night with string; the only time I've ever felt protected by a piece of string.

The bicycle trip through Normandy and Brittany was sheer delight, but it's a wonder our health was not undermined for life. Because we were each living on twenty-five francs a week we breakfasted on hot chocolate and croissants — and there's nothing better than that. Whether we bought or just appropriated extra rolls I don't recall, but we lunched on more rolls and a bar of chocolate, sitting close beside some romantic château and imagining ourselves the glamorous ladies who had occupied it so long ago. I can't imagine how we managed about dinner. Perhaps there wasn't any.

That summer with Peggy Lewis I discovered architecture. I really began to see it, and I came to realize that for me it was the most satisfying of all the arts, that I found more spiritual food in it than in the new paintings and music which were so exciting to most of my contemporaries.

Yet I did not accept my personal response to art as valid, at least for me; and for years I went on doggedly trying to discover in paintings what other people did, finding the air thin to breathe and drawing my real life-giving oxygen from the magnificence of the great cathedrals. The week I spent at Chartres, morning, noon and night, absorbing the wonder and grandeur of line and mass, of color and light, was the high point of that summer.

Thinking of it now, I wonder how much of my spontaneous response was to the sheer theatrical quality and dramatic lighting that a great cathedral provides.

Since then I have visited Europe countless times, seeing plays and playwrights, but no visit has had the enchantment of that first summer.

Before returning home, I went on to England, Brussels, Bruges, Ostend, but I knew already that I'd be going back. I had to go back. I boarded the ship reluctantly, but my trip home was enlivened by a Texan who talked to me about Southern women: "They have liberty," he assured me in his slow drawl, "but it is very circumcised."

Back home again, with Paris still bright in my mind and a return to it the most desirable thing I could imagine, an opportunity came up unexpectedly. I met Mrs. Christian Herter, whose husband, a scientist, was the uncle of the present Secretary of State. She was, I think, the most completely enchanting person I have ever known, a woman of irresistible charm, gentle and distinguished, a member of the then fading New York aristocracy. Mrs. Herter wanted me to teach English literature and French to Polly, the youngest of her three daughters (Mrs. Creena d'Youngh) as well as to tutor her in Life with a capital L. At that time I knew nothing that did not come out of books, so I can't imagine what I was able to teach her.

Polly was tall, somewhat spare and attractive, with a handsome sculptured face; she was also intelligent, sweet and earnest about learning not only English and French literature but Life with a capital L.

This was my first introduction to girls of great wealth and I was continually staggered to realize how completely they were protected and shielded from all contact with reality. I still recall my surprise when I was strolling across Central Park with Polly one day and remarked that I must go to the post office.

"May I come with you?" she asked. "I have never been inside a post office."

Christine, the oldest daughter, was studying art, but all the Herters gave their first love to music. At that time, the Kneisel Quartet was the best chamber music organization in New York and they used to play at the Herter house. This was my earliest experience with chamber music; but then, and for many, many years to come, I was to have evenings of great quartets at the Herter house.

When Christine went to Paris to study art, Mrs. Herter suggested that I take Polly over to join her, and spend the winter. With one of those odd, self-conscious quirks a girl sometimes gets, I refused a salary. I suppose I felt that it would make me into some sort of governess. Anyhow, I went along to look after Polly, to continue to tutor her, and to take courses in philosophy at the Sorbonne.

That winter in Paris was one of the happiest of my life. As it turned out, I never studied at the Sorbonne beyond taking a single course in philosophy with Henri Bergson. After spending a great deal of time matriculating — proving that I was born, that I had parents, that my parents had been born, and all that — I had to give it up because the ventilation was so bad that the stale air made me ill.

But if I didn't have the Sorbonne, I had all Paris for my university and I was plunged knee-deep among creative people in music, in painting, in dancing, in the theater. Best of all, I met a group of young people who were willing to argue endlessly on aesthetic matters. So I began to supplement the theoretical education I'd had at Bryn Mawr by a more immediate knowledge of the people who were currently creating in the arts.

I had an insatiable curiosity at that time, a tireless drive, a need to try out at first hand these new theories. Endlessly as life stretched before me, it did not seem long enough to hold all the experience that was crying to be known. It exasperated me then, as it does even now, to see young people seemingly more willing to do without the stimulus that does not lie at their doorstep than to go in search of it. I am sorry, often, that they find just enough provender to keep them from being hungry; I'd like to see them starved with eagerness.

I plunged into an excited exploration of every art form that I could. And how lucky I was, with Isadora Duncan as my guide to the ballet, and Gertrude Stein my mentor in painting!

Kitty Herter had a charming studio apartment near the Avenue de l'Observatoire, which had the unusual advantage of a real bathroom — a magnet that drew all her friends, equipped with sponge bags.

Almost next door was the famous café, La Brasserie des Lilas, where, on Tuesday evenings, a group of poets gathered to read their verses and become vociferous about them. Among them was a young Frenchman, Jean du Roy, with whom I promptly fell in love. As I recall, it was a matter of poetry and moonlight and springtime, a welter of literary emotion. More of printer's ink than my heart's blood went into it, but it helped round out that winter in Paris, and give it a zest it would otherwise have lacked. What a waste it would be to spend a winter in Paris and not fall in love!

At the center of the group that gathered at La Brasserie des Lilas were the Mowrer brothers, Paul and Edgar. They were not poets but they were in touch with everything that was going on in Paris, because Paul was head of a big press service. For the first time in my life, current events became something more to me than news items. They were the stuff of life itself. And so they should have been, for this was the winter of 1913, and the rumblings on the horizon were warnings of a storm that was to destroy the Europe we had known and to change the geography as well as the history of the world.

And yet there was little talk of war at the time. Paul

Mowrer believed in fairies, "ethereal beings," he assured me
solemnly, "visible only to those who are particularly sensitive." Aside from this peculiar aberration, Paul taught me
to question some of the comfortable clichés that I had assumed to be true.

"American optimism," he told me, "is rooted actually in
pessimism. An American says, 'All is for the best. Everything
is coming out all right. But don't give us sad books or plays.
There's enough of that in life.' That is a confession of pessimism, an underlying denial of all his bright words."

I don't remember now who introduced me to Gertrude
Stein, taking me to the big bare studio in which she lived.
The walls were covered with paintings that, to my baffled
eyes, seemed to be largely geometrical designs, rather ugly,
and completely meaningless.

There were few comforts in that room, as I remember.
There were practically no chairs, and we spent the long evenings standing around, as one does at that barbarous institution, the cocktail party. This resulted in such acute fatigue —
because of a bad back I have always found standing difficult
— that it is a wonder my tiredness did not blot out every
other impression. Certainly there was no aesthetic quality
about Gertrude Stein's studio. There, indeed, I got my first
inkling of the deep gulf between the words *artist* and *artistic*.

Gertrude Stein, enormous in a red corduroy wrapper, was
direct and blunt, a no-nonsense sort of woman, solid and
earthy. Her inseparable companion, Alice Toklas, was a kind
of toothpick, providing the most extraordinary contrast I
have ever encountered. Gertrude, the patron saint of young
painters, kept open house on Saturday nights; and at one

time and another I met all of them — first and foremost, of course, Picasso. Because these men were authorities in a field about which I was completely ignorant, I was too shy to talk to them, and so missed a unique opportunity to know them and to understand and appreciate the kind of thing they were painting.

Not that I didn't try. I went doggedly to the exhibits and stared earnestly at the paintings and came home — empty. I can remember especially one Cézanne exhibit in which the center of attention was the artist's portrait of himself. I stood before it until my feet gave out, trying to whip myself up into some synthetic excitement, to convince myself that I was a part of the modern art movement, as I believed I ought to be. But I've never had any faith in synthetic excitement, and so I got nowhere.

Color? Yes, of course. Cézanne was a great colorist. But what was the nameless thing the moderns lacked? For me, they lacked the unself-consciousness of the masters. These new men painted *at* a picture rather than *in* it. That was how they had damned themselves with the epithet "clever." Cleverness just wasn't enough. There had been a humility in the attitude of the older men that the moderns lacked. For them, the picture was the thing. For the moderns, the painter was the thing. It seemed to me that I was always conscious of the painter's ego in the picture.

One thing, however, I did discover for myself. Some of the new painters were being acclaimed simply because they were new. They were using new methods to conceal the fact that they had no new vision. Often enough, they could not even draw. Vitality will often cover a lack of art, and art, some-

33

times, a lack of vitality. But without either art or vitality, what have you?

At that time I was too uncertain of myself to stand up to this position. But Gertrude Stein strengthened my convictions. One afternoon she and Alice Toklas came to tea. Outside my apartment a little organ was playing stridently, so out of tune it must have ached to hear itself. Miss Stein, wearing a brownish shirtwaist and a dark skirt that made her look like an enormous two-toned sack, looked around the room, seeking a chair that would be sufficiently sturdy to bear her weight, and then settled herself cautiously. She smoked incessantly, drank hot water, and talked. And talked.

I said timidly, "Miss Stein, I wish you would tell me what I can do to learn to understand this geometrical stuff, these new paintings everyone is so excited about."

"You have enough in your life, Miss Helburn," she replied.

That wasn't much help. "But — " I began.

"I don't see," she said, "why people should try to cultivate an interest in everything. They should be satisfied to follow their own bent. You aren't really interested in the Cubists."

She checked me before I could interrupt. "You aren't really interested in the Cubists," she repeated. "If you were, you would be haunting the galleries; you would at least be able to distinguish the work of the different men. And you aren't able to. Why should you try to whip up this interest?"

I always remember Gertrude Stein talking. Whether at her studio or at my apartment or at the theaters and concerts to which I occasionally took her and Alice Toklas, she talked on tirelessly. Sometimes I found her stimulating and sometimes unintentionally funny. When she demanded the value of simplicity in art and in life I could sympathize; when she declared roundly that her own personal scandals were inconspicuous, I wanted to laugh.

But she was right about following one's own bent, trusting one's own reactions, if one is to find honest joy in the arts. The new painting wasn't for me. Neither was the new music. Perhaps I had heard too many Beethoven quartets at the Herters' and had learned to appreciate a certain kind of music. At any rate, it still seems to my untutored ear that one must be either tone deaf or stone deaf to enjoy most of the contemporaries. My appreciation of architecture was also based on the classical. I found the same satisfaction in structure there that later I came to seek in a good play.

I was not the only one who preferred the classics. Mary Cassatt had graciously agreed to criticize one of Kitty Herter's canvases and I went with Kitty the day she took her painting to Miss Cassatt's.

The door was opened by a tall, thin, angular old lady, as straight as a ramrod, with a strong low-pitched voice. She led us into a room where two or three barking dogs kept up a din over which we could hardly hear ourselves, but which did not appear to disturb Miss Cassatt in the least.

She set up Kitty's canvas and for a long time considered it, examining it carefully through a lorgnon.

"You paint pictures," she said at last reprovingly. "You must not do that. Keep at studies. You won't be a painter of pictures until you are forty. You must be more naïve in your lines. Study the Primitives. Study the old masters, especially Rubens."

35

"But I don't like Rubens," Kitty confessed.

"I am sorry to hear that," Miss Cassatt commented with some severity. "Rubens is a great painter. Beware of Whistler. He is full of tricks you must not imitate. He was not original, you know. He did not hesitate to take my lines for his mother and children."

She turned away from the canvas. "You have nothing to learn from the moderns," she concluded. "Go back to the old masters."

A few years later, when I was spending a month alone at the Ritz in Paris, I drifted into a museum to see an exhibition of impressionist paintings. For the first time, modern painting became meaningful for me. I had all the shock of delight that comes with great music or a fine play. From then on, every morning I spent two or three hours delighting in paintings which I had assumed were a closed world to me. But I have never learned to respond to the abstractionists.

While I was trying to persuade myself that I was a part of the contemporary art movement, I was also learning about the new revolution in the dance. One of the most brilliant evenings I ever spent in Paris or anywhere else was the electrically exciting opening of the Russian ballet, which took Paris by storm. Paris, in those prewar days, had reached a spectacular pinnacle of glamour that Vienna at its most sumptuous never attained. The opening of the Russian ballet was a brilliant affair. There was a positive plague of coronets. One woman, I remember, wore a gown of beads and practically nothing underneath it, and jeweled sandals on her bare feet. From where I sat with the Herters, high up in the fourth tier of boxes, I looked down on what seemed to be naked acres of half-moons, because of the multitude of low-cut dresses.

Stravinsky revealed new tonal values in the *Firebird,* and that night, Bakst orchestrated color, a riot of reds, scarlets, pinks, and purples that showed, for the first time on the stage, that there is no more color clash in design than there is in a brilliant bed of multicolored flowers. Nijinsky, dancing with muscles seemingly made from steel and music, exemplified through the Fokine choreography that the human body had an unexplored potentiality for power and grace and for communication of meaning. The terrific strength and masculinity of that graceful body I will never forget.

After the opening of the Fokine ballet, I became really interested in the dance; so one of my friends took me to Isadora Duncan's studio, a large high room with yellow plaster walls and a cement floor. (It was, I think, the coldest place I've been in in all my life.)

When I walked in that first day, there was no one in sight but a little Japanese man sitting on a low stool, sewing on some yellow material. But little by little the dancers arrived, and presently they reappeared in their hand-woven togas, yellow and orange, brown and tan. How lovely they were! Isadora must have chosen her young dancers because they were such beautiful people, with slim lovely bodies that moved like poems, and a quality of freedom and joy and exultation I had never encountered before.

Now and then, I went there for dancing lessons. Why I wanted to study ballet I can't remember now. Later in New York I continued with it for several years. Like Bottom, I guess I just wanted to play all the parts, a characteristic I've not entirely outgrown.

I couldn't keep up the lessons with Isadora Duncan: my feet got too cold. The members of the class finally clubbed together in self-protection and bought a little coal stove, but I doubt if it ever succeeded in heating that barn of a room.

In time, I came to know the Duncans well: Isadora, her brother, Raymond, and her sister, Elizabeth. Raymond floated around, in his toga and sandals, like something out of a fantastic dream; it was Isadora who dominated, who filled the place with her personality. She had great dignity and a statuesque quality. In the light of her autobiography and the scandals that still cling around any mention of her name, it is curious to realize that the strongest impression she made on me was one of austerity.

I think it was because she was so absorbed in the dance, so devoted to it to the exclusion of all other phases of life and experience, that she had acquired very genuinely, very profoundly, a quality of dedication. She lived what she believed. Anyone with the strength to do that is bound to be impressive, whether for good or evil.

There was one terrible moment in my acquaintance with her, which I have never forgotten. I had taken a boat up the Seine to the country house Singer had given her. After she had welcomed me, she went striding down a corridor and flung aside a heavy curtain at the end, revealing a picture of her two children who had recently been killed in a motor accident. There was nothing I could say, nothing I could do. After a silence that seemed to last forever, the curtain was drawn again.

There was also music, always an element inseparable from any association with the Herters. For me, the most memorable musical event of that winter in Paris was the first time I heard Pablo Casals, who played one night with Alfred Cortot, long before political differences ended that magnificent combination. Casals played with such sweetness, sureness and richness of tone that his music was like a revelation. I heard most of it with my eyes closed, because of the disparity between the utterly undistinguished-looking man, who looked to me like a small Irish coachman, and the beauty he created.

Along with grappling with modern art at Gertrude Stein's, studying ballet with Isadora Duncan, hearing music with the Herters, writing short stories, verse and a novel in the mornings, tutoring Polly, and talking excitedly over the little tables at La Brasserie des Lilas, I was also exploring the French theater. Paris had two state-owned theaters, the Odéon and the Comédie Française, where the classics were played; there was almost no time when Racine and Molière and other classics were not available in fine productions.

There was a system of matinées for the younger students and evening performances for the older ones. In France, the theater was regarded as a part of education. It was unthinkable that the finest and richest of French drama should not be within reach of French youth.

Someday I hope that America will provide a similar opportunity for the young of this country. There is no substitute in classroom reading and scholarly analysis for the experience of seeing fine actors present the great plays of the past, which are often the great plays of all time; to have the words walk off the printed page and catch fire; to have the meaning brought to light through fine acting and emotions quickened and communicated to a group as they cannot be to an individual reading alone. Not that the productions were always what they should have been. There was one Racine tragedy which was ruined for me because the heroine's black wig kept slipping and showing a good portion of blond hair underneath, destroying the tragic illusion.

That winter I explored French plays as much as I could. One theater I had reason to remember later was the charming little Vieux Colombier, founded by Jacques Copeau. Here I saw his production of *Twelfth Night,* in which Olivia was played for comedy. To me Olivia has always seemed rather a drippy character, but when, without doing violence to the tone of the comedy, she was played as though she were sharing with the audience her amusement in putting over her preposterous grief, the play acquired an unexpected tang and sparkle. For once, Viola had a run for her money as the feminine center of interest.

Almost no modern plays were produced at the two state-owned theaters at that time. The only one I can recall seeing was Claudel's *Dance Before the Mirror,* in which Madame Simone appeared. I wanted to do an article on the French theater and asked for an appointment with Madame Simone.

So far as I know, that was my first excursion backstage in any theater. The dresser ushered me into a little dressing room papered in gray with pale pink curtains, a settee and armchair on which a little white dog was curled. There were bacchantes and a *scène d'amour* on the walls. From an inner room came the low sound of voices, one of them a man's voice, barely distinguishable. Just what one would expect in a French actress's dressing room, I thought in delight. The dresser held the curtain aside and Madame Simone appeared, not in the extravagant negligee I had conjured up, but in a chic brown taffeta dress and a fetching hat.

That day she told me something that it took me nearly twenty years to absorb — not because I didn't understand it, but because I didn't want to understand it. French plays, she told me, were foreign in spirit to American audiences. Their irony was alien to our point of view, which was actually much closer to German sentimentality.

When I think of the money I could have saved the Theatre Guild over and over if I had not been stuck with this particular blind spot of mine — if I had only been able to learn that French ironic comedy does not appear comic to Americans — I know I should be more tolerant of other people's errors all the rest of my life. I probably won't, but I ought to be.

"Do you ever play comedy?" I asked Madame Simone before I left. (*The Dance Before the Mirror* ended with her lover shooting himself in her arms.)

Madame Simone shrugged. "What," she demanded, "do you think this is?"

Yes, French irony is difficult to impose on American audiences.

All this had been during the spring of 1914. As the months passed, the whole atmosphere of Paris changed. The gaiety which had been so fresh and delightful took on an uneasy

41

and frenetic quality. Talk of art gave way to talk of survival. Rumors of war were an ugly undercurrent to everything. The French, who had seen this thing happen to them generation after generation, who walked always in its shadow, had a kind of weary fatalism.

Late in the spring, my father and mother reached Paris and I set off with them for Italy. I was free to do so because the Herters' great friend, Mme. Alexis Carrel, had descended on Paris to look after the girls, prepared for all contingencies, with a pistol in her pocket.

Perhaps the fact that war loomed on the horizon waiting to pounce made the impression of Italy a gloomy one. In my diary I wrote of Naples: "The streets were narrow, close-pressed, burrowed with alleys like a beehive and as swarming with creatures, misshapen and deformed, some with that most hideous deformity of all, faces without features. And children in the dirt of the gutters, scratching, scratching."

And again about Pompeii: "Not the mere melancholy of ruins but a sense of death without nobility, without a past and without a future."

Through June and July we traveled with increasing difficulty, for both my parents were unwell, my father seriously ill. Pisa, Rome, Naples, Amalfi, Sorrento, Pompeii; back to Rome, Venice, Milan, Bellagio. In the latter part of July we reached Bolzano, in the Austrian Tyrol. We stopped there, where war was something in a comic opera, with military band concerts, officers in gay uniforms, mountains spread like a theatrical backdrop against the night. And music everywhere. Tyrolean companies marched past in bright costumes — that's what they appeared to be, not uniforms but costumes to match the colorful stage setting: short knickers, bare knees, tall flaring feathers in their caps.

Then, in a period of two weeks, the curtain went down on musical comedy and was raised on the grim unadorned face of war. Russia declared war on Austria, Germany on Russia, France and Germany were at war. Germany violated the neutrality of Luxembourg and Belgium. England declared war on Germany. It is embarrassing to recall that, at the moment, my greatest excitement was due to the fact that a hot-water bottle had burst in my mother's bed.

As for my mother, she received the war news in unexpected fashion. "That's not possible!" she exclaimed indignantly. "They can't declare war without giving American tourists time to get home first."

The holidays were over now, over for everyone. We were given two days to leave the Tyrol, and there seemed to be no place to go. As my father was seriously ill, I took his place at storming the consulate along with hundreds of tourists. Already the face of Bolzano had changed. Officers strutted down the streets. Hot, dusty peasants trailed into town, with packs on their backs, coming to join up. Only women were left to bring in the grain from fields ripe for harvest.

At length, with much shuffling around, we reached Zurich, where we were held up for weeks by mobilization. Our consul there, like too many of the men who misrepresent us abroad, knew neither French nor German. No one had any idea of what was occurring beyond the borders. There was nothing to go on but rumors — conflicting, melodramatic and improbable, and much worse than no news at all. At last

43

I asked for permission to translate French and German cables and do a column in a local newspaper so that the tourists would at least know what was happening in the world.

Finally, we reached Paris, where we were told that we couldn't possibly proceed to London. The *chef du gare* suggested that we try Boulogne, instead. Our railway car was filled with people, some of them sitting in the aisles on suitcases, and all of them carrying as much food as they could handle. The idea seemed to be that the train would be held up indefinitely somewhere and there would be no food obtainable. Actually, we got through without any trouble at all.

I remember one man, sitting on his suitcase in the aisle, lamenting, "When I get home, no one will believe this."

It reminds me of the proposition that a tree makes no sound when it falls if there is no one to hear it fall. Many people feel that unless their experiences have been shared with someone, they have no existence, no validity.

But if the lamenting man on the train was typical of the refugees I encountered later, he had a much better story to tell by the time he got home. In fact, the development of refugee stories became one of my chief sources of entertainment in the next few weeks. The moderate account of the train with only two empty seats developed to a train with people hanging on outside. The discomforts and inconveniences, trifling in themselves, grew to horror stories. The imaginary fears became real experiences.

By the time we reached London, the first bandaged wounded were already being helped off the train at the station. *They* didn't talk. They just grinned.

Winter of Our Discontent . . .

BACK IN THE UNITED STATES, the war was a long way off, unreal, remote. "It doesn't concern us," was still the general point of view. And the kind of moral utterance that makes it so hard for foreigners to like us was rampant:

"The war," declared one of these self-appointed protectors of the public morals, "is caused by women smoking."

A woman told me cheerfully that the war would benefit the whole world by bringing it down to the realities. It had already accomplished something. Much of the sex news was being eliminated from the newspapers.

"I have always thought," I told her incautiously, "that sex is extremely real."

"Real," she agreed sadly. "But such news is erotic and unpleasant."

"And war news," I snapped, "is pleasant, of course."

That's the sort of reaction that has always been my undoing. If I had learned long ago to be tolerant of fools and to accept the fact that there's not much of anything to be done about them, I probably wouldn't be laid up now with a heart attack and too much enforced leisure in which to contemplate the errors of my ways.

I wanted desperately to be doing something useful, to be making a concrete contribution to the war effort. Before leaving England I had investigated nurses' training in a London hospital so that I could return to France and be of service, but my father collapsed when he heard of it and I had to bring him home. All I could find to do was making bandages and knitting.

Later, I got involved up to my ears in an insane sort of project with two women from Belgium who were worried about the future of the lace industry and feared that the women who made the lace would be driven out of Belgium by the invading Germans. I suggested bringing them over here and letting them work at their lace-making on my farm.

In some way or other, the project fell through and the farm was left on my hands. I went up for four months every summer, though I didn't attempt to do farming. I rented that work out to a man who knew how to handle it.

Each summer I would write plays and short stories frantically all morning, play frenzied tennis in the afternoon and fill in time as best I could.

The projects that had satisfied me before the war no longer held my interest. I had, for a time, been much excited about the Woman Suffrage Movement. Before my first spring in Paris, I had followed Mrs. Pankhurst's lectures at Carnegie Hall and had been prepared to march in the first woman suffrage parade. I had a VOTES FOR WOMEN sign and was about to step out when I met Beatrice Hale, a big buxom Englishwoman, a friend of mine and an ardent suffragist. She was carrying a large banner, holding it before her by two standards. I soon saw why. She was acutely pregnant and trying to conceal her condition while she marched up Fifth Avenue.

"I am expecting a baby at any minute, my dear," she told me cheerfully. "At any minute."

I chose discretion as the better part of valor and watched the parade from the side lines. I had had no experience at delivering babies.

Now, I didn't know what to do with myself. It was hard to remember how happy I had been a few months before. Certainly I was discontented now. Everything fed my discontent. Nothing seemed worthwhile when weighed against the war in Europe. I marked time and hated it.

I took courses in dressmaking, I studied ballet dancing, I was on the board of the Bryn Mawr Club and the Drama League. In the latter, Elsie Ferguson served on the same committee with me. She was always put on committees as a show piece because she was so beautiful. I remember her best as a fine and enthusiastic bridge player with whom I spent many evenings.

I continued to attend meetings of the Poetry Society, but even that was different now. Instead of Vachel Lindsay thundering away as General Booth entered heaven, boom, boom, boom, we read Rupert Brooke and talked about Joyce Kilmer turning Catholic and going to war. Lincoln Steffens told us didactically, "Mexico has more chances of civilization than we because it is not hampered by our virtues." He also expected, he said, that the war would provide a great comic poet. Like Dante, he added.

47

Between my two trips to Paris I had lectured for a winter at the Tuesday Afternoon Club in Westchester. The members of the Tuesday Afternoon Club seemed to have varied fare that season: one week I would talk about Shakespeare and Webster, about Ibsen and Shaw, and on alternate weeks a woman discussed minimum wages and the interpretation of wills.

Lecturing to people who knew nothing about the subject made me feel tremendously knowledgeable. It's the kind of feeling that probably constitutes the chief danger both in lecturing and teaching, a feeling of infallibility that needs to be cut down to size.

The chief advantage I got out of lecturing was a self-confidence that helped me through the sort of situation that had always stymied me in the past. For instance, I had never known how to cope with the person who prefaces what he has to say with, "As any person of good taste would agree . . ." That gamut left me wordless and abashed. After I had lectured for a season, it didn't impress me in the least.

But still I was restless, discontented, uncertain of what I wanted or how to get it. And I had arrived belatedly at the painful moment that comes to every person sooner or later, the moment when he realizes that his dreams are only dreams. Up to now, they have been fact, a clear blueprint of the future, which has loomed enormous, endless, big enough to hold anything, everything. Sometimes I think growing up simply means that one gets acquainted with his future. It may come in a flash or take a long time. But it always comes.

God knows it came late enough to me. I was twenty-eight. What added to the encircling gloom of that dark birthday was the fact that I lunched with a group of my former classmates, a reunion, with the discussion limited to their marriages and their children.

What did I have? A drawer full of rejected short stories. Mr. Phillips of the *American Magazine* had summed them up for me succinctly: "Good, one-sided, unpublishable." Even if they had been better, I would not have been consoled on that dark day. One thing about a manuscript, however good it may be, however promising: you can't run your fingers through its hair.

But I was still going to be a writer. That was about the only thing I was sure of. All those hours of work, ten years of it, all the notebooks filled with ideas and plots and sketches and character studies, all the manuscripts piling up . . . somewhere in that mass of words lay my future; otherwise, there was no future for me that I could imagine.

I was writing one-act plays like mad. Everyone seemed to be writing one-act plays. Lawrence Langner says it was because none of us knew enough about the theater to get through a three-act play. Some time before, Lawrence, who wasn't, even then, a man to be bogged down in frustrations — if there wasn't an outlet for his ideas, he made one — had inaugurated informal evenings of play reading. A group of us met at each other's houses, though most often at Josephine Meyer's, to read aloud interesting plays that were appearing in Europe and had not been performed in America, plays by Shaw and Maeterlinck and some of the Russians. In time, plays we had written ourselves.

49

There were only a few of us: Lawrence Langner himself, of course, the originator of the idea; Philip Moeller, who was also writing plays; Lee Simonson, who was editor of *Creative Art* and a former 47 Workshop student; Edward Goodman, with whom I had written *Other Lives* the previous summer; Louis Untermeyer, whose chief love was poetry but who was interested in all forms of literary expression; Walter Lippmann for a time, plump, quiet, important, and not greatly interested.

There were several groups in the Village who were all churned up about new ideas: the Liberal Club, the Socialist Press Club, the Arts Club. There once had been a sharp line of demarcation between uptown intellectuals and downtown, or Village, intellectuals. I had had no contact with the Greenwich Villagers, of whom I disapproved on principle, but what the principle was I'd be hard put to it to define. Now the groups began to merge, with Lawrence acting as the catalyst. At the Socialist Press Club, where he took me one evening, I heard Floyd Dell arguing hotly about whether propaganda drama can be true art. I didn't know the answer to that then. I do now. It's art only if you are careful not to say what the propaganda is.

At one of those evenings of play readings, Lawrence and I did a one-act play of Shaw's, entitled *Press Cuttings,* and later gave a private performance at the Socialist Press Club, leaving the state of the drama about where we found it.

One evening, Eddie Goodman came up to help me get supper for a party I was giving and to tell me about a project of Lawrence's. He planned to start a little art theater of his own, which he was calling the Washington Square

Players, because it was at the Boni Brothers bookshop on Washington Square that the plan had been developed.

Later on, another group started, the Provincetown Players, with Eugene O'Neill as its bright particular star, and George Cram Cook and Susan Glaspell its founders. The Provincetown group was a nonprofit, nonprofessional organization, which wanted to put on the plays of its members and give them a hearing.

The idea behind the Washington Square Players was somewhat different, and foreshadowed what the Theatre Guild was to be years later. They wanted to present plays which could not, at that time, obtain a hearing on Broadway; better written, more intelligent plays than the public could find in the commercial theater, but plays which they believed the public would be eager to see. And they were determined to put them in direct competition with the commercial theater.

There was one other factor of the Washington Square Players that anticipated the Theatre Guild. Lawrence had picked up in Europe, at the *Volksbühne* theater in Germany, the idea of a subscription theater, and he decided to run the Washington Square Players on that basis. His group acquired the little Bandbox Theater off Third Avenue, a few hundred dollars, still fewer subscribers, and a group of young people, nearly all of whom were amateurs; and they launched this theater with Eddie Goodman as director.

Lawrence came up to read me a one-act play he had written, called *Licensed,* which he was going to produce on the first bill of the "new art theater." This was the story of a girl whose fiancé dies on her wedding day and who reveals that she is going to have a baby. The play was a plea for birth control.

Lawrence offered me the rôle of the mother. Rehearsals were going beautifully and I was having a lot of fun when my parents inquired about the play, read the script, and had a collective fit. Their daughter in a play about birth control! The subject was immoral, the part was unladylike, and anyhow acting was no career for me.

The curious thing is that I can remember feeling no rebellion. My brother, who was a fine pianist, had wanted to be a professional musician, but had given it up without a struggle and gone into business when our parents reasonably pointed out to him how much more sensible he would be. I informed Lawrence, in some embarrassment but without tears, that I would have to withdraw from the cast.

I suspect that one reason why I relinquished the part without a struggle was that, while I loved the theater, while I wanted to write for it, I did not particularly want to act.

Lawrence, who never wastes energy in arguing against irrational attitudes, acquiesced. "But," he suggested, "why don't you write a play for us? Your parents won't mind that."

I didn't write a new one; instead, I dusted off a one-act play I had written several years earlier, called *Enter the Hero*.

This, my first play in any form, had never been produced, but it had been published. Unexpectedly, and to my great delight, I had received a letter from the eccentric stage designer, Gordon Craig, who was living in Italy. He had read the play and assured me that he had "shuddered at its strange green fire," though I hadn't the faintest idea what he meant by that.

"What is your theatrical ancestry?" he asked. "You must have the theater in your blood."

This was a shot in the arm, and I asked my parents at once about my theatrical ancestry. They assured me that I hadn't any, unless I wanted to count a family black sheep who had, in the course of a spotted career, served as advance agent for a ten-twent-thirt road show.

Craig and I corresponded for a long time before we ever met. His letters, in broken phrases, follow no conventional form. The words are scattered across the page like those of a Marianne Moore poem, with a haughty disregard for punctuation; and while they are often bewildering to read they are lovely to the eye because he seemed to design a letter rather than to write one. I often used to wish I could paper a room with Gordon Craig's letters; but, alas, he wrote on both sides of the paper.

These communications were like an absent-minded sort of conversation where a person rises abruptly from his thoughts like a flying fish from the ocean, tosses out an idea, and submerges again.

As if [one letter began abruptly] an artist ever had *intentions* . . . that's what I love in the artist: that he, or she, works conscious only of his duty & *unconscious* of the reason behind the order he has received — & not inquisitive as to those godlike reasons.

My one-act play, *Enter the Hero,* had had another adventure. Al Lewis, who was then leaving vaudeville to produce

in legitimate, looked it over and said I'd need a collaborator
to help me turn it into a three-act play for the Broadway
stage. He sent along a man named Sam Shipman who set to
work with me. Sam wasn't a very impressive man but he had
very impressive ideas. He wanted to write fine plays.

At length a three-act play emerged. There was only one
thing wrong. It bore little or no resemblance to my play.

A few years later, when I was drama critic for the *Nation*,
I reviewed Sam Shipman's play, *East Is West*. What had happened to his brave dreams of writing great plays?

"Plays like *East Is West*," I wrote hotly in my article for
the *Nation*, "make us wish for a congressional investigation
of the theater [I didn't know much about congressional in-
vestigations then], an exposé of the difference between theatrical shoddy and real wool. *East Is West* is a comedy, its
success . . . a tragedy."

When I talked to Sam about his play, sometime later, I
asked what had happened to his ambition to do great plays.

"Why try to do great plays?" he asked cynically. "We are
doing twenty thousand dollars a week."

The Washington Square Players decided to produce *Enter
the Hero*, and in the leading rôle they cast Edna St. Vincent
Millay. She was an exquisite creature, small, dainty, like a
pantomime Columbine, and the brightest light of the Village
at a time when Greenwich Village still had glamour. She
was as famous for her impulsive and fleeting love affairs as
for the memorable poems that celebrated them.

For some reason, though we had many friends in common,
Edna and I never seemed to hit on common ground, never
to be able to talk to each other below the surface, never to

find out what was real in the other. Our relationship remained on that shallow level all the years we knew each other.

Unhappily for my play, Edna proved to be a better poet than an actress, and *Enter the Hero* was withdrawn during rehearsals. It has, however, been produced regularly since then and not a year has passed but it has brought in royalties from amateur performances.

Nearly thirty years later, I received a letter from a very young lady whose grandfather had been my father's cousin. Her school in Toledo, Ohio, was going to do *Enter the Hero,* and she wanted some "inside" information about it. I was delighted to find that a play of my youth was being kept alive by the young.

Meanwhile, the war news fluctuated from bad to worse and at last the United States declared war on Germany. I wanted desperately to be doing something real, so I applied for a job as an ambulance driver and learned to drive a Model T, careening down Sixth Avenue around the old supports of the elevated tracks. But when I announced at home what I had done, my father promptly had a heart attack, so that plan, too, went by the board.

Instead, we went out to Santa Barbara. There it rained for a solid month; I had a severe attack of facial neuralgia, and wrote a three-act play in an attempt to keep sane. It was a wartime comedy, and this time I stuck to material with which I was at least reasonably familiar, introducing what little I knew about farming, and betraying my predilection for France by making my hero a French soldier.

Then I returned to New York, started my play on a round of producers and began to review books of verse for various periodicals. And one day I got a letter from B. Iden Payne, who was planning to open a repertory theater backed by Otto Kahn, saying that he would like to produce *Crops and Croppers* (the title was afterwards changed to *Alison Makes Hay*) as his first play.

I was more of a greenhorn than anyone I have encountered since. I read his letter up on my farm and came down to New York in a daze, partly accounted for by the July heat, as it was the first time I had ever been in New York City during the summer months. Riding down on a streetcar to the Empire Theater I thought, "I am going to have a play produced but no one in this car would guess it. They think I'm just an ordinary human being." The fact that they weren't thinking of me at all never entered my silly head.

Mr. Payne was nice to me and told me how much he liked my play. He paid me one hundred dollars, which was all I ever had out of it. But I had been paid! I'll never again feel as close to the pinnacle of success as I did at that moment.

An actress friend, my only acquaintance in the theater, who lived near my Berkshire farm, told me that authors were an awful nuisance around the theater.

"Don't go near the place for the first week of rehearsal," she warned me.

Of course, I stayed quietly at home. I didn't know that the author had only one week then in which to make any changes in the casting. So I was in for my first shock when I reached the theater. My idea of the hero was a kind of Leslie Howard with a French accent, slim, svelte, charming.

Mr. Payne had selected instead a plump middle-aged Frenchman. My heroine was a New York society girl, what today
would be a Katharine Hepburn type, smart, sophisticated,
cultivated. He had cast in the part an Irish girl who still
spoke with a rich brogue and would have been better cast
as a peasant. So I got my first baptism of fire. But this is the
theater, I thought; of course, it's bound to be different from
what I expected.

Another member of that cast was Helen Westley, an unforgettable woman, individual, striking and Bohemian. I had
never known Bohemians and I was frankly scared to death
of her.

Helen was continually yawning during rehearsals and one
day Payne complained, "You are always sleepy."

"Not at night, Mr. Payne," Helen assured him.

On the night of the first dress rehearsal I saw the stage
décor for the first time. The play was set in an old New
England farmhouse. The design had been turned over to
a favorite student of Payne's at Cornell. She had done it in
pale pink and green, like a boudoir.

"This is the theater," I told myself; "you mustn't complain."

Anyhow, I had already had a new kind of fulfillment, the
thrill of hearing the lines I had imagined at my desk spoken
by real professional actors. I wasn't like the author — Joseph
Conrad, I think it was — who went to rehearsal, heard his
lines spoken, fled from the theater and never returned. I was
grateful for everything. And there was one thing for which I
had cause to be grateful, though I did not realize it for years.
I was never asked to do any rewriting.

That first night of dress rehearsal there was an outbreak of artistic temperament when the leading man threatened to resign, then and there, because he had not been given enough billing.

"Resign if you like," Payne retorted. "I'll do the part myself."

The second night of dress rehearsal, the Irish "society" girl offered her resignation because the leading man was getting more billing than she was. I half expected Payne to offer to put on falsies and do that part himself. But he soothed her and the play opened.

On the opening night, Payne went to the hospital with ulcers and his idea of repertory was abandoned. The play got a mixed bag of reviews: "A series of laughs," one paper said. "The comedy is not so tiresome as it is just negative," said another. "There are bright lines everywhere in it and some cleverly managed situations. The appeal is to an intelligent sense of humor," said a third. "The predominant note was amateurishness," said a fourth. "One might wander up and down Broadway for blocks without finding a better two-hour round of amusement than the Belmont's new bill has to offer," said a fifth.

Well, the second night it played to an empty house and it closed in two weeks. I had had my first experience in the writing, casting, directing and producing of a professional play.

Encouraged by the interest Gordon Craig had shown in *Enter the Hero,* I wrote him about *Alison Makes Hay* and got a characteristic response:

"I am not really old & bitter at heart," he wrote, "but one

can write sometimes to the wrong people. One looks for friends — lovers — disciples — what you will & finds a pack of apes enchanted with their own tail."

Switching abruptly to the theater he said:

The prevailing taste (not only *this winter* & not alone in America) has always been "spies and thighs" — the theatre must recover itself — by itself — it is useless to wait for an audience . . .

Don't be conceited because someone older than yourself praises you . . . Never grow conceited . . . because you have work before you.

Some months later he answered a letter of mine, beginning with his usual abruptness:

I have been 10 weeks in Roma, the only great city left on earth over here. London & Paris both being prisons. Where old & most unmoral ladies are the warders . . .

You write to me in a queer strain . . . you must be in love — what else would put you in a "wretched state of mind" — "unable to work" — "unable even to be unhappy" . . . you turn to me as though I could comfort you. I will. Be comforted at once or I shall consider you too charming for words . . .

All is a little difficult over here now. No one of course attends to the artist unless he will work for no pay — as I'm tired of no pay — I've worked for that rather too long . . . One either has to beg ones bread from Dives or one has to devote 2 months out of 2 months selling old work — both situations are damnable . . .

The only real people are those who work. I love them. The only friends of ones spirit those who create: and that's how I feel . . . & that's all I care — all else is accident — that *not*. . . .

I must have written of my disillusionment with the failure of my first play, for Gordon Craig answered, quoting from my letter:

"How long did it take you to despair of the stage — & how long again to regain enough illusions to go on?" You ask me this . . .

My dear Miss Helburn I loved the stage when I was first in the heart of my father & mother — oh, but I loved — then, appearing the year after the 1879 war & feeling a bit warlike I swore to fight for what my father & mother had felt to be more than the stars, the moon, the seventy-seven seas & the like of the sun.

I have been doing that ever since. I have never for one moment despaired of the stage & so I have never had to chase illusions.

After this correspondence I finally met Gordon Craig, a handsome shaggy white lion of a man, a little old, a little cranky, a little bitter with the new artists. He represented the beginning of modern stage design. His *Hamlet* must remain in the memory of all who saw it. But he had been superseded, and he could not bear it.

"They all took my stuff," he complained, for, more egoist than artist, he was not content to have provided the spark, to have made the beginning.

In a sense, his good looks were his undoing. He was so extraordinarily good-looking that he had not had to be anything, to do anything. He expected too much of the world. He was conscious of his beauty and demanded more of it than he demanded of his art, and yet he and Adolphe Appia not only reformed theatrical design, they transformed it. Before Gordon Craig's day the stage had been literal and cluttered. He created in big lines with little detail and built a new dimension of beauty and significance into the theater.

For that we owe him much. We have, I think, given him much in gratitude and recognition. But he wanted more: more fame, more money. He was one of those old men who retain to the end the child's idea that the world owes him something. Or, in this case, everything. I still remember him: so handsome, so bitter, so irresponsible, with his wild spate of words, his brilliant perceptions and insights, his grievances; and the quiet young wife in the background who worked like a dog to provide his creature comforts.

When my first Broadway play was behind me, it seemed like a sound idea to learn something about the theater, and I did it, as my betters have done before me and will do after me, by writing about it.

I became the *Nation's* drama critic. That was a plum if there ever was one. I wrote only one article a week and I was allowed to choose for myself what plays I would review, what I would say about them; and, so far as I can remember, my material was never cut. I also got tickets for everything that was appearing on the Broadway stage at the time.

I rarely or never went to the *Nation's* office, which was rather stupid of me. My sins of omission probably account in part for the fact that I kept my amateur standing so long. I acquired little or no technical knowledge. When I was finally plunged into the theater, I had nothing to bring it but excitement and love.

◇◇ FIVE

. . . Made Glorious Summer

IN 1919, when I was thirty-two, the two most important events of my life took place. Neither of them was in the least what I had expected. Neither of them, at the time, was in the least what I wanted. But between them they changed my life and gave it all the meaning and value that it has had — and the best happiness I have known.

Up to that time, I had been floundering, without any focus or any goal, hell-bent on becoming a writer. No one could have been any more surprised than I when I finally discovered my destiny.

It was on April 8, 1919, that, at a dinner given by the Authors Club, I met John Baker Opdycke (known to his intimates as Oliver), a teacher and lover of English, a big laughing Frans Hals of a man, and we fell in love that first evening. Just like that.

I was scared to death. I had never really believed the protestations of men who said they loved me unless it came right down to a proposal of marriage. I was no beauty and I was keenly aware of it. I could see no reason why any man should love me. So I was never willing to accept love with complete belief.

Whatever I had expected love to be, it hadn't been like this. I think I retained for an indecently long time a kind of adolescent picture of an adoring man who was a flattering reflection of myself. Well, Oliver wasn't. It's hard to imagine two people more completely different. I was an extrovert, Oliver an introvert; I lived with a crowded calendar of lunches, teas (there weren't cocktail parties then), dinners, always the theater or music in the evenings, and people — people — people — all day and every day. To Oliver the thought of more than three people in a room at one time was horror.

I was excited about the theater, the countless activities in which I was involved, the personal difficulties and problems of the people I knew. Oliver, aside from his passion for the English language, reserved all his emotion for the big things, for the great causes, for the impersonal ways and injustices of the world; mine seemed to him trivial, his seemed to me remote.

I was conventional, snobbish, priggish and reserved. Oliver wanted people to be themselves, to be honest and real and courageous. He came into my life like a high wind that blew away everything that was artificial.

No wonder I was afraid. We were so different that I could not imagine being able to build a marriage while two diverse people tugged in different ways. Anyhow, I felt about marriage as I felt about the theater. No one should enter it unless he can't help it.

63

So I put up a fight. And a lot of good it did me. Oliver crashed through all the synthetic barriers I had built up as though they were made of tissue paper. He helped me get rid of what he called my Victorian furbelows and taught me the value — the essentiality — of honesty and reality.

Nevertheless it was a long time before I knew, as Oliver had known from the beginning, that we couldn't get along without each other. A love affair, it seems to me, either cools or it becomes a marriage. After three years ours became a marriage, one which lasted for nearly forty years and was the core and center and meaning of my life.

I used to say that the only reason I fell in love with Oliver was because he never made me go on the long strenuous walks that were so fashionable in those days. In fact, we never walked farther together than from the house to a taxicab.

He was a comfortable man with a penchant for comfortable furniture built for his heavy frame. No antiques would do. Once, I recall, at a dinner party at Lawrence Langner's, he leaned back in a fragile Directoire chair and broke it. From that time on, we had solid upholstered furniture, not only in our New York apartment but later at Terrytop, the country house we rebuilt at Westport, Connecticut.

Oliver had started his career as a press reporter, covering the Olympic meet in Athens in 1904. He had traveled from England to Siberia, China, Japan and the Straits Settlements. But when I met him and until he retired he taught English with love and devotion and wrote some twenty-five books on his chosen subject.

I have never been able to believe the statement that sorrow and unhappiness help make a better person and have an ennobling influence. It is happiness that not only fills the heart but opens it. The fulfilled person is not tangled up in his own feelings, he is free to concern himself with others. It is probably true that the unfulfilled person makes the real creator; but it is the person who is deeply happy who is able to go beyond himself and his own needs.

Certainly, I became a better person when my personal life was full and warm and complete. I began to see how many kinds of friendship there are, all of them, it seems to me, like lights in one's life. There's the one like a flickering candle, there's the one like a dark lantern, there are others like a warm lamp diffusing radiance. To be in touch with them is to be in touch with a hundred other things at the same time, a continuous kind of growing.

One of the nicest things that has happened to me is that I have found some of the best of these friendships among the people with whom it has been my privilege and my joy to work for the past forty years. But I set out to get the record straight so I do not want to build any misleading picture of myself. Loving Oliver made me a better person; it didn't turn me into a woman chockful of sweetness and light. It didn't make me accept mankind with any particular sentimentality. I really think I'd rather have the entire love and understanding of one person than all this constant reiteration of the value and necessity of loving and serving the human race.

I may as well confess that I've never really loved the human race. Some of it I have heartily disliked. If I have served it, my service has been a by-product of living in accordance with my own values, helping to bring them great theater.

65

Because I had vitality and good health up to the moment of my periodical collapses, I did not feel the need of anything outside myself, perhaps not even God. And if I could not accept the love of my fellow men, even as individuals, because I did not feel I deserved it, how could I accept the love of God, for which I was certainly less worthy?

A few months after I met Oliver the other important event took place: I became a minor part of the new Theatre Guild. A year later, I was made executive secretary *pro tem*, a job that not only I didn't want but that no one wanted. So started a career of theater production to which I had never given a moment's thought, which had not interested me, and which I would have regarded in any case as beyond my capacities.

But for that story I'll have to go back a little bit, not only back to the start of the Theatre Guild but to its reason for being.

In the early years of this century and in the last years of the nineteenth century, theatrical managers in New York had assumed, as so many advertisers were to do later, that the American public had a low common denominator and that its ideas of entertainment could be summed up in the apparent needs for amusement of the Tired Businessman, though he has never really been as tired as all that. For one producer, at least — Al Woods, who had come into the theater by way of burlesque — there was only one hard-and-fast rule: the play had to have a bedroom scene.

To make the situation more difficult, a couple of theatrical syndicates, controlled respectively by the Shuberts and Klaw and Erlanger, had practically taken over the theaters of the United States, so that road companies played at their theaters or at none at all. Under the circumstances, few producers were going to stick their necks out and risk violating accepted conventions on the chance of finding a new, untapped audience, or giving the old audience new fare.

Then, to worsen things for the stage, particularly for the road companies, along came the silent pictures where, first for ten cents and later, when motion picture "cathedrals" were built, for seventy-five cents (if you were elegant and sat in a loge) you could experience all the fairytale dreams that attracted the matinée audiences.

In the face of this new competition, the theatrical managers were trying to give the public what they believed it wanted. After 1914, this was summed up in "the play with a punch." This was partly, of course, a normal wartime reaction. At the same time, there was a completely unscrupulous disregard for the ownership of foreign material. Comedies from Europe were not only lifted without so much as by your leave, but they were changed and adapted for Broadway, "made American," and even put on as home-grown products, with no credit of any kind to the original author.

Lawrence Langner had long believed that there was an audience, a large untapped audience, for plays of real value, plays with something to say, plays that were literate and assumed literacy in the audience. He believed, as Molière once said, that "a playwright might make of an idea food for a crowd."

Lawrence and the people who gathered around him took

67

the theater seriously. Surprisingly few people did that, even among those who were active in it. People of any cultivation took an interest in literature and opera, in chamber music and sculpture. But the theater? That was "show business."

What Lawrence and I and a handful of others had in mind was an art theater, in its best sense. But we wanted to take the curse off the word "artistic" and provide something real and beautiful, not merely the trappings of culture or the pseudo-cleverness and the exotic unreality that are attached like barnacles to the word "artistic."

The Washington Square Players had been started to prove that well-written, intelligent plays could compete with Broadway, that there was an audience for the stirring and beautiful drama which the commercial theater had been afraid to attempt. But the Washington Square Players had necessarily drifted apart during the war, when all but one of the men entered the armed services. A month after the Armistice was signed, Lawrence encountered at the Brevoort Helen Westley and Philip Moeller, both of whom had been active in the original company. He told them he wanted to start another theater, this one to produce three-act plays and be professional in every respect.

"When do we start?" they asked promptly.

It wasn't as easy as that, of course. To begin with, they had to have a theater and pay rent. They needed actors and actresses, they needed scenic designers and stage sets and costumes; they needed directors; they needed plays. And, above all, they needed money for production and salaries and stage hands and electricians and . . .

Easy as falling off a log, of course.

But what Lawrence had from the very beginning was a small group of people who shared his vision, who believed with all their hearts in what he wanted to do, and who then, and in all the years that followed, put the common objectives ahead of personal inclination. So far as I know, that is a record, for they — and why leave myself out of this? — for we were all people with strong convictions, creative impulses, considerable personal ambition, and noisily articulate about these things.

In the long run, what made the Theatre Guild the most powerful art theater in the world, what raised the artistic standards of the Broadway theater and Hollywood motion pictures and later of radio and television, was the fact that for every one of us the theater was bigger than any one of us. From the beginning, all of us set aside our desire for personal self-expression for the sake of the basic idea: the play was the thing, and the play came first.

That first meeting ended with plans for another. And another. For several months a somewhat fluctuating group met. People kept appearing and disappearing, ready to participate and then swallowed up somewhere in the maelstrom of New York City and never heard of again.

These groups finally dwindled down into the small nucleus that launched the new theater, but only after hours and weeks of excited talk, discussing objectives, pondering over problems of financing and operation. At length, we decided that the plan was feasible.

This was not, like the Washington Square Players, to be an amateur group. It was to be professional; though I can say, here and now, that with the exception of Helen Westley and

Augustin Duncan, we were all amateurs and remained so for years, until experience turned us into professionals.

Europe had its art theaters. The Moscow Art Theatre and the Abbey Theatre in Dublin were both flourishing. But they were endowed. The Theatre Guild was to be something new in the world, an unendowed art theater. This was probably just as well, because the Guild was then literally rushing in where angels feared to tread and would have had an awful time trying to persuade any of the Broadway angels to back it.

Instead of an endowment, we should, Lawrence thought, follow the same plan the Washington Square Players had adopted. That is, we would build up a subscription audience, not only making our audience, in a sense, a partner in the whole enterprise, but providing us with enough money to put on our plays.

Actually, the first play the Theatre Guild did was produced with a capital of $1100; $500 was put up by Lawrence himself, the rest of the group chipping in $100 apiece. There were just 135 doughty subscribers. By the time the second play was to be presented, there was a lump sum of nineteen dollars in the treasury with which to stage it. But it got done! That nineteen-dollar play put the Guild on its feet and started it on its career. The only other capital we had was enthusiasm for our idea and faith in the public.

But I've jumped ahead of myself again. The Guild founders had an idea; now they had to implement it. First, they needed a home. Lawrence and Rollo Peters looked over the possibilities and decided on the Garrick, a small theater on Thirty-fifth Street once owned by Harrigan and Hart, and later leased by Richard Mansfield. William Gillette had played there, in *Secret Service*, and so had William Crane, in *David Harum*. And for one night, which shocked New York to its foundations — and apparently shocked even more deeply the New York police, who must have been learning about brothels for the first time — George Bernard Shaw's *Mrs. Warren's Profession* made its brief and sensational appearance.

This theater had been placed by Otto Kahn at the disposal of the Copeau Players, whom he had brought to New York from Paris as an international good-will gesture, with the enthusiastic approval of Clemenceau. Lawrence went to see Mr. Kahn and told him his problem; Mr. Kahn generously said that he could use the theater and pay rent when and if possible; otherwise, he need not be concerned about it for the rest of the season or even for the next season.

So there was a theater. The next need was to find actors. How do you get actors when you can't pay them? And, more serious, when you won't star them? For there were to be no stars. At that time the commercial theater slavishly followed the star system. A play was literally built around the star. He or she got all the best lines, even though at times this distorted the meaning and values of the play. He or she was usually surrounded by minor players so that nothing would take attention away from the star for a single moment.

What we wanted to do was to star the play and feature the players. And for over twenty years we succeeded in doing this. The whole structure of the art theater was to be built on a co-operative basis. We hoped to obtain the services of the best actors, directors and designers in their respective fields, all to share the risk of the experiment, coming into the organization for a minimum wage; all to share in the gains by having a percentage of the profits.

So far as the non-starring angle of the plan was concerned, almost all the really good actors and actresses were enthusiastic about the idea. Instead of being narrowed down to a type that was henceforth exploited, they had a chance to expand the range of their characterizations, to enlarge the scope of their acting, and to find in it a satisfaction they had not experienced before.

Helen Westley summed it up when she said: "The popular play presents the actor; the actor of the art theater presents a play."

What we had in mind then — and continued to have in mind, for as Lawrence says feelingly he has "fought and bled for the idea" — was a permanent acting company, so trained, so flexible, that its members could cope with any part, tragic or comic, in verse or colloquial speech, classic or experimental, and so become, in its finest sense, fully rounded players.

The idea of co-operation was to go even farther than this. There was to be a Board of Managers, instead of a one-man show; a board which was to determine policy, choose plays, conduct the business, supervise casting, rehearsals, publicity, and every one of the multiple phases of theatrical activity. The decisions of the board must be a result of its combined points of view. Here, too, there was to be no starring; here, too, a basic minimum wage. (Actually, it was thirty dollars a week.)

The members of that first Board of Managers were Lawrence Langner, Philip Moeller, Helen Westley, Lee Simonson, Rollo Peters and Augustin Duncan. The latter was a brother of Isadora Duncan and a good down-to-earth director.

While the Theatre Guild was learning to take its first uncertain steps, I was still acting as drama critic for the *Nation*. Although I sat in on some Guild board meetings, it was only by courtesy. My function in the Guild was a minor one. I was the play reader.

The first play which the Guild selected for production was *Bonds of Interest,* written by the Spanish Nobel Prize winner, Jacinto Benavente. When I asked Helen Westley once what the title meant, she replied, "It's what holds us all to the theater."

The Guild Board worked like dogs on that play, trying to substitute ingenuity for hard cash and to create a lavish set and splendid-looking costumes out of bits of this and that. Rollo Peters, who was a painter in his spare time, and Lee Simonson refurbished the scenery that the Copeau Company had discarded as worthless and had left behind in the Garrick to be sent to a junk yard. They patched and painted and eventually achieved an amazingly effective stage set. Together, the two men designed and made stunning-looking costumes out of the most unlikely scraps, which they reshaped or dyed or, in the case of a "cloth-of-gold" dress, actually made by painting a piece of oil cloth to get the effect they needed.

The cloth-of-gold dress came to grief in a spectacular way on the opening night, when the perspiring lady who wore it stuck to her chair. Dudley Digges, seeing that she was walk-

73

ing off the stage with the chair firmly attached to her, hauled it away, leaving a bare white spot.

The play was directed by Philip Moeller and in it appeared Rollo Peters, Dudley Digges (who had come over from the Abbey Theatre), Edna St. Vincent Millay, Amelia Summerville (the actress who had the catastrophe with the linoleum dress), Helen Freeman and Helen Westley. Today, it would be impossible to produce the play as Rollo did it for less than thirty thousand dollars.

The play owed what success it had to glowing beauty in the stage settings of Rollo Peters and Lee Simonson and to the costumes they had created. In itself it was a failure. The critics damned it with faint praise. Like so many Latin plays it lacked heart; it had no warmth.

The Guild had promised its subscribers four weeks of performance so it had to go on, even though the general public stayed away. Later, Helen Westley remembered the disheartening apathy of playing night after night to rows and rows of soldiers, sailors and Marines who came in gratis. Not that there was anything wrong with the armed services *per se*. But, as a rule, there's no worse audience than the one that doesn't have to pay.

One evening, Lawrence Langner was standing in the lobby, watching the meager audience with somber eyes, when Maurice Wertheim came up to him. Maurice asked how the theater project was going. Personally, he had liked *Bonds of Interest,* and the idea of an art theater appealed to him.

Lawrence shrugged and said he was losing five hundred dollars a week on the play.

"Let me lose the next five hundred dollars," Maurice suggested. "We'll take turns."

And the Theatre Guild Board got a new member.

Well, the Guild thus began with a failure, which was probably the best thing that ever happened to it. In some ways, there is nothing more fatal than an immediate success; it builds an unjustified self-confidence and often leads to taking foolhardy chances.

At least, there was one advantage in having no money. Literally, the Guild had nothing to lose, so it was not afraid of failures. Because it was without overhead and without debts, and free of all the restraints and obligations — of every kind — that come with being endowed, it had the freedom and the courage to experiment. If it had to eliminate nonessentials, at least it learned that the elimination of nonessentials is what creates beauty.

But the Guild was down to nineteen dollars and it had promised its subscribers two productions that first season. It was Lawrence who found the second play, picking up in Brentano's bookshop a copy of St. John Ervine's *John Ferguson*. He wrote Ervine, who asked George Bernard Shaw what the Theatre Guild was. G.B.S. had never heard of the Guild either.

"Better get your money first," he warned Ervine, so the latter demanded an advance of one thousand dollars. Clearly, the Guild and the playwright weren't seeing eye to eye.

But Lawrence explained the situation and the purpose of the Guild and Ervine agreed to the production, waiving an advance. Again Rollo Peters and Lee Simonson pitched in

75

gallantly, undismayed. They had found one thousand dollars little enough for producing the first play. They had to stretch nineteen dollars for the second one.

They patched together and repainted the battered scenery from *Bonds of Interest,* which had already earned retirement after its service with the Copeau Company. They bought a little paint and mixed it with the old paint that was left.

It's a good thing that *John Ferguson* was set in a poverty-stricken cottage, for the paint peeled off the walls in a most realistic way. The backdrop was patched from old cloths that Lee managed in some way to repaint. How the stuff held together I can't imagine. The sofa was made up of broken springs stuffed with cardboard and covered with cretonne Rollo had generously brought from his own home.

Howls went up on Broadway over the announcement that the Guild was going to produce *John Ferguson.* It was nearly the end of May, and, as the professionals knew, only the frothiest of musicals could survive a torrid New York summer — that was, until air conditioning changed the situation and lengthened theatrical seasons — and the preposterous Theatre Guild amateurs were putting on a heavy, tragic, religious drama!

But with *John Ferguson,* the Theatre Guild began its real life. The play was a great success. Opening night, critics praised it. Next morning, the lobby was stormed by ticket buyers while we looked on, beaming. Here was a play that could run without being papered.

And then the Guild struck a real piece of luck, one of those utterly unforeseen factors that shift all the odds in producing a play. That summer, the famous actors' strike took place. The Garrick was the only theater that was not affected, because it was co-operative. All the theaters in New York were closed — all but one. For weeks the playgoers had one choice: *John Ferguson.* I've always wondered what some of the visiting firemen, who came to New York once a year for a spree of girl shows, made of it.

So the Guild had paid its way at the end of its first season and even had made a little money — actually had money ahead! — to start its second season. It was on its way.

Six Characters . . .

How THE THEATRE GUILD appears to those on the outside I don't know. To those of us who have nursed and tended it from the beginning, it often seems like one of those cliff-hanging heroines of the old silent serials. Over and over, catastrophe has hung on a slender thread over our collective heads. And then, at the last moment, often in a totally unforeseen way, something has happened to save us and start us on our way again, stronger than ever.

This is a fairly nerve-racking situation. But there is one thing about it — you don't get bored. We knew from the beginning that we would either make a go of it or we would go broke; but either way, we would have fun.

The first dive off the cliff occurred before the second season opened. One Monday afternoon, an emergency meeting of the Board of Managers was called and, as usual, I was allowed to attend in my capacity as play reader. That meeting, like most of those that followed until we built the Guild Theater, some years later, was held in a little cubicle in the dim dusty attic of the Garrick Theater. This served not only as office and board room, but, with a few partitions tacked on one end, as rehearsal room as well.

Getting there was quite a feat. You went into the theater and climbed the stairs. You went out a fire door and down a wide-barred fire escape, from which you could look into the windows of dressing rooms and catch a glimpse of men's faces to which grease paint was being applied. You went inside again, into the blackness of a theater where you were met by a blanket of stale, warm air. There was the rustle of an audience. From the unseen stage a voice spoke and a voice answered, and you felt the tingle that goes along the spine at the sense of live theater. You went up more stairs, softly in the dark, onto the balcony and opened another door. You saw the dim lights outside a yellow-curtained box. You pushed open a heavy door and found yourself in a gloomy bare hole of a makeshift office, with a scarred rolltop desk, a few chairs and a green shaded lamp. The only other light came from the window, almost opaque with dirt, which opened on the fire escape in the narrow alleyway. In one wall there was a small square opening through which you could see what was happening down on the stage.

That day, there was more than the usual discomfort of the room. There was tension and unrest and a feeling of malaise as recognizable as the thick warm air in the theater below. There was a constant, uneasy shifting of position on the uncomfortable chairs. In short, there was trouble.

What had happened was inevitable. The problem of group or individual control had raised its ugly head and had to be fought out, once and for all. Rollo Peters and Augustin Duncan felt that group management was all right — up to a certain point. Beyond that point, however, they claimed that each individual should be allowed to go his own way, without dictation from anyone.

The other members of the board had tried sweet reasonableness; they had set forth their point of view with tact and patience. When these didn't work, the Queensberry rules were discarded, and the whole board plunged joyously into the melee — hammer and tongs, no holds barred — and fought it out.

When the storm died down and the dust settled, Rollo Peters and Augustin Duncan resigned. The group system had won — and the board was still licking its wounds, for it was in a state of chaos. Lee Simonson had gallantly if reluctantly taken over the work of active executive left vacant by Rollo, though he did not want the job and he was unfitted for it by nature. The result was that this artist, whose major interest was stage design, attempted to run the Guild by the only executive method he had ever experienced, the army system. He issued directives, and the shorter his temper got, the longer and more confusing the directives became.

At the same time, an actress became acting business manager. She was as badly miscast as Lee. Mutual tension and irritations mounted; there was an outburst of temperament and a stormy scene. By this time, they weren't even speaking, which did little for harmony and smooth operation. Lee, goaded beyond endurance, blew his top and resigned, not from the board, thank heaven, but from his executive position. And when the actress-business manager found she was not to be allowed personal control of a one-man show, she bowed out of the whole affair — board, Guild and all.

For the time being, it seemed as though the infant Guild was being strangled practically at birth.

Both Lawrence and Maurice Wertheim, aside from the fact that their days were filled by their professional activities, were scheduled to leave soon on long business trips. Helen Westley's chief energies had to be devoted solely to acting, for she appeared in almost every Guild production. Philip Moeller was a director and playwright — not, he said firmly, a businessman. And Lee Simonson, the stage designer, had already thrown in the sponge as an executive.

Who was left? There were a few possibilities under discussion but nothing had been decided upon. The immediate need was for someone to take over during the interim.

In a moment of desperation, you grab what you can get. Eyes turned questioningly to me.

"Will you take over?" they asked. "Only two weeks. After that, we'll be able to lay our hands on the right person. Only fourteen days. All we need is an executive secretary *pro tem*. Someone to take charge and handle anything that may come up while the rest of us are away or busy with production."

A temporary expedient, that's all it was to be.

This situation is probably duplicated over and over in any new organization. If you show the slightest indication of being able to do a thing, you're more than apt to be given the opportunity. A new group has to feel its way, and the chances are that it will follow the lines of least resistance. But there's one thing I am sure of. If you want to do anything badly enough, you will find a way to do it; the overcoming of obstacles is often important to the result.

It was a job nobody wanted, including myself, for I still

thought I was a writer. I knew nothing whatever about running a theater and I didn't much care. The theories of art interested me; I was ignorant about the technique by which art is created on the stage. I was even more ignorant about the behind-the-scenes activities that make such creation possible or impossible: sordid details like finance, like the renting and running of theaters, like arguing with unions and fighting over contracts, like supervising . . .

Well, all I had to give them was my inexperience.

I looked around that bare ugly room with its dirty windows — and it was mine! I think I rarely looked at the place again. From then on I was too busy. Surely there's no more lucky person than the fortunate one who earns his living at the job he'd rather do than anything in the world! Somehow, the two weeks lengthened to four and the situation drifted along. Now and then, there would be some half-hearted comment about finding a permanent executive. Now and then, a name would be suggested tentatively.

And then one day I was made Executive Director of the Theatre Guild. That was forty years ago and I've been there ever since, sharing the job with Lawrence Langner for the last twenty-odd years.

Of course, running the Guild was not then, and it has never been, a one-man job. The Guild's whole theory and practice was based on the idea of joint control by its Board of Managers, so from the beginning I was committed to majority rule. The situation was complicated by the fact that we were all amateurs. We became professionals only after years of experience, of trial and error, of hit or miss. Actually, my inexperience not only made me welcome the idea of group control, it made me dependent on it. There was not a single phase of theater management about which I knew anything. I had to learn everything, and a large part of my learning had to come from my subordinates when, later on, we had enough money to hire them.

Naturally, a situation like this could hardly have developed in the commercial theater but, for all six of us, the idea of profit was irrelevant. We had only one guiding principle: we wanted to produce fine plays. For that, like Lawrence and his permanent acting company, we were prepared to fight and bleed. Of course, our attitude toward potential profit was staggeringly naïve. We treated it with sovereign contempt. Sometimes I think all that kept us going was sheer ignorance. We ignored the hazards, the odds against us, and went ahead as though we couldn't fail.

The curious thing is that I, who had been diffident about what I mistakenly took to be my own field, sailed into the field I assumed to be alien, with a zest, a self-confidence, almost a kind of brashness that were new to my experience. I started my career as a theater executive with an assurance that appals me now, learning humility only as I grew older.

In general, the idea was that the Board of Managers would thrash out ideas, which it was my function to carry through; I was to serve as a kind of co-ordinator. On the whole, that's the way I saw my job for many years — a sort of filter for ideas, at best a kind of catalyst — until I went through that skin-flaying experience known as being the subject of a *New Yorker* Profile.

Here I found myself reported in terms I still don't recognize as applying to me, but, as they are part of the record, here they are:

Theresa Helburn . . . the power behind the throne . . . the terror of actors, the bane of playwrights, and the thorn of agents, managers and kindred mortals.

As I look back, I try to fit that "power behind the throne" image and another favorite term of a few years ago, "the Czarina of the Guild," into the actual picture. There were, as I have said, six of us: six opinions, usually widely different; six voices, uninhibited and often noisy; six personalities, utterly unlike. If any one of the other five was ever bulldozed into anything he disagreed with and submitted tamely, I don't remember the occasion.

Once, indeed, Lee Simonson said in exasperation that I had established a "dictatorship of the Executariat," but as, at the time, he was screaming his head off over some suggestion I had made, and stormily refusing to have any part of it, the democratic system didn't seem to have cracked at the seams or to have been strained, except for verbal exchanges, at which we all became expert.

In fact, our board meetings grew so noisy in time that we found it expedient to give up our early system of holding our weekly meetings over dinner at Henri's French Restaurant, and go instead to each other's houses, where we could argue vociferously to our hearts' content without disturbing or alarming outsiders, who seemed to look upon our free-for-all discussions as a prelude to imminent battle and physical violence.

What made it possible for six highly articulate and pas-

sionately partisan and opinionated people to work together
for nearly twenty years without one serious quarrel though
a thousand disagreements — and to accomplish by our joint
efforts far more than we had ever dreamed — was the fact that
from the beginning we operated on a give-and-take basis of
complete honesty. Under all the flying verbiage, under all
the hotly disputed points, under all the different points of
view about plays and actors, about production and direction,
there was a solid foundation, a rocky promontory, with the
words and the disagreements blowing over it like flying sand.
That foundation was our unquestioned trust in each other's
integrity and our common faith that the Guild mattered
more than any single one of us. Because that foundation was
never shaken, the six members of the Board of Managers
were able to fight it out like gentlemen. Our methods were
many, but we always had a single goal.

It's about time for me to introduce the *dramatis personae*
of the Theatre Guild. Because no one can discuss the Guild
without discussing Lawrence Langner, I had better stop right
here to say more about him.

The Theatre Guild, like the Washington Square Players
before it and the Westport Country Playhouse and the
Shakespeare Festival Theatre after it, was his brain child.
(Not his only brain child.)

While he was pouring out creative ideas for it, and they
will appear in their place, he was devoting his days to his foreign patent practice. During the Second World War this was
complicated by work for the government in Washington, as
well as on the National Inventors Council, which he initi-

ated, fostering many new ideas and inventions of value to the country's defense. In fact, for every member of the board — except me — the job on the board was not the member's only job, not even his most important job. That is one of the reasons why it seems incredible that we ever accomplished what we did.

I have worked with Lawrence Langner for forty years and we've never had a real quarrel. Lawrence claims that this can be accounted for by the fact that we are tolerant of each other's lunacies; I claim it is because we have had only differences of opinion. The fact that we are extremely unlike in character has enabled us to supplement each other well.

Lawrence is patient and gentle and concentrates intensively before making up his mind. My tendency is to be quick and impulsive and probably to jump to conclusions. He is dispassionate and able to see both sides quite clearly. He has an amusing philosophy which he calls "leapist," that is, to jump ahead in his mind nine years and realize how unimportant the issue will be by then or how easily solved. I take everything as demanding an immediate, final and correct decision.

Lawrence's powers of concentration are amazing. There are times when I try to talk to him and discover that he is somewhere in outer space. I have learned not to try to pierce that barrier and to wait quietly until he returns. Sometimes, however, I say plaintively, "Lawrence, where are you?" and then he comes back with an answer to my question, which he has been pondering during his flight.

He is both kind and generous, and, perhaps because of his legal training, much more aware of the other person's point of view than I am, much less insistent on forcing his own. Also, he is never happy in the present unless he is planning constructively for the future. Mrs. Langner (Armina Marshall) and I sometimes dread periods of comparative leisure because we know that he will then hatch a lot of new plans for the Guild of which we may or may not approve. From this you may gather that he is an extremely stimulating and delightful person to work with, and the Guild's debt to him, and mine, is incalculable.

The following memorandum, taken at random from my files, is typical of dozens I have found on my desk over the years:

DEAR TERRY:

Now that we have a lull in our activities, I would like to talk to you about the following ideas for the Guild for next season:

(1) A Theatre Guild–Gilbert & Sullivan company which will make a deal with the English D'Oyly Carte Opera Company, by which they will give us their script books and business and keep out of our territory for a certain number of years.

(2) A Theatre Guild–Maurice Evans Shakespeare Company, with Maurice Evans, John Haggott and Margaret Webster. I think they are ripe for a production of this kind because we were a great help to them in getting *Macbeth* over.

(3) A Theatre Guild School of Acting. It is time you and I got our old idea on the map again. Engage an excellent teacher and give them our name and do it all on a non-profit basis — e.g., the profits made on the pupils who are not so good will pay for the training of the good pupils who have no money, and we will have some kind of call on these actors.

(4) Theatre Guild Exhibit in the Guild Lobby which is permanent. I would like to put someone on the job of going over our

past records and making up an interesting exhibit as a permanent exhibit in the Guild Lobby to take the place of the present exhibit when we are through with it.

Nothing to do until tomorrow!

LAWRENCE

There has been, for many years, a widespread and persistent impression, because of our long association and partnership, that Lawrence and I are husband and wife. Indeed, some theatrical magazines which ought to know better have sometimes published this report. Aside from the fact that we were both most happily married to other people, I am convinced that we would never have made such good partners if our business relationship had been complicated by a more personal one.

Maurice Wertheim, a former Baker 47 Workshop alumnus, was profoundly interested in the theater. A son-in-law of the Honorable Henry Morgenthau, an investment broker who, like Lawrence, had founded his own firm, Maurice was a man of insatiable interest and excitement about the arts. At one time he offered to endow a theater at Harvard for the benefit of students of playwriting, but President Conant was a scientist and the offer did not interest him.

Maurice was also a trustee of the American Wildlife Foundation, a tournament chess player, a patron of exhibitions sponsored by the Sculptors Guild, and, during World War II, he was with the War Production Board. As though all this were not enough, from 1935 to 1937 he published the *Nation,* and he made a fine collection of modern paintings which he bequeathed to Harvard University.

Maurice was not a man who wanted merely to put up money for an artistic enterprise. He wanted to be an integral part of it. For him, too, it provided a creative outlet. From the time when he stepped in to help us after our first failure with *Bonds of Interest,* he became a working part of the board — reading plays, attending rehearsals, planning policy, and carrying his full share of the load.

But he did more. He convinced us that we must learn to pay our way. He taught us how to keep accounts and to take stock of what money we had every week, so that we would not run into a big deficit before we knew it, which has been the fate of too many art theaters.

Helen Westley looked like an actress, far more so than most of them do, in private life. She had a theatrical appearance and manner, and dressed rather like a *femme fatale* — coal-black hair and black, slinky, dresses, a little like Charles Addams's young witch.

Under that dramatic façade she was a forthright person, honest, outspoken and uninhibited. As I was not only inhibited in those early years but proud of the fact — God knows why! — I was slow to appreciate Helen's sterling qualities. Being arrogantly intellectual in my reactions, I was distrustful of a person whose reactions were instinctive. It took me a long time to realize that hers were often more reliable than my own.

"Do not," Helen always declared, "try to struggle against the Life Force."

Heaven knows, the Life Force always had the last word with Helen. Each new love affair — and what an odd lot they were, from the eccentric to the extremely young — was a new revelation, the first real love. What I knew about the Life Force when I first met Helen could have been put in my eye without causing a tear; nevertheless I had the conviction that all emotions not only could be controlled, but undoubtedly should be.

Helen's Bohemianism increased rather than diminished as she grew older. Much later, in 1936, when I was in Hollywood, Helen had an apartment in the same building. I can see her now, sweeping in to welcome me that first day, wearing a huge blue silk dress that billowed to the floor and dirty tennis shoes. Her own apartment was a hodge-podge, with piles of magazines stacked everywhere and brown paper bags of vegetables dropped carelessly wherever there was room for them. At least once she was seriously ill of ptomaine poisoning from eating vegetables she had neglected to refrigerate, and when I left Hollywood the piles of magazines had crept closer and closer to her bed. In time, they or Helen would have to move. She didn't care. Someday she would have time to read them. (Though I don't know how I dare comment when I recall the stacks of *Saturday Reviews* that are encroaching on my favorite easy chair.)

After Helen's death in 1949, Lawrence Langner received a letter from Mrs. H. L. Robinson, who had nursed her during those long tragic months of her last illness. "She was a wonderful and terrible woman," she wrote.

Mrs. Robinson described graphically the drama with which Helen managed to set her own death. Like any Shakespearean character she refused to go tamely off. Her bedroom became the theater in which she acted out the last scene of her life. Even in her weakened condition and wasted with pain, one day she snatched a volume of Dickens from the hand of the attendant who was reading to her, explained how it should be read, and then read aloud, the characters coming vividly to life as she recreated them.

"What a wonderful play this would make," she cried. "What a pity to waste such good material!"

But the best curtain line, I think, was spoken by Ed Hogan, who wrote to me on her death: "She was one of the realest personalities I ever came across, and I don't think she will really be dead until everyone who knew her is."

Philip Moeller, a graduate of Columbia University, was both a playwright and a director. How good a director he was we learned rather slowly. Later, I'll have more to say about his "inspirational" method of directing and his unusual sensitivity. He, Lee Simonson and Helen Westley were the artists on the board.

Singly, Phil and Helen were both comparatively rational. Together, they were mad to the point of mania. Fast friends for many years, they kept up a constant barrage of feuds and quarrels over nothing whatsoever. The most decorous occasion or the most dignified restaurant might be disrupted by a high-pitched, infuriated argument as to whether one of them owed the other twenty-five cents. The effect on the bystander was shattering. He ducked and ran. But Philip and Helen ended their great to-do smiling and refreshed, wondering what everyone was upset about.

Lee Simonson, a graduate of Harvard, our scenic designer, expert and technical adviser, was and is a brilliant man, a superb craftsman and, unexpectedly in a genuine artist, a man with an unusually logical mind. He is widely read, and a fine writer. For all that, he was one of the most temperamental and difficult members of the board. He could perform miracles with light and he has produced some of the most interesting experimental sets seen on the American stage. But he had to be handled with gloves, or we were in for a stormy — and sometimes violent — session.

Glancing over my diary, I am amused to see how often there is a passing reference to Lee balking at director or author or both, and having to be placated before the work could proceed. Or the simple entry: "Saw Lee. Fight."

One thing about the Guild's Board of Managers, we may have been an army girded for battle, but we were, at least, an army with banners. From first to last, we marched to music, with the same excitement, the same high hope we had at the beginning.

Aside from technical knowledge, which I had to acquire little by little, the attributes most needed in the beginning by the Executive Director were thrift, tact, and ability to see all sides of the case.

Thrift, if I had it not originally, had been thrust upon me. By the end of my first year out of college I was completely self-supporting, and remained so ever afterwards; but this was hardly adequate experience for coping with the finances and stretching the pennies of an art theater.

As for tact, I gradually established quite a reputation for it, of which I was very proud. Then I lost it by my own fault. At one time, *Vanity Fair* — then, as I remember, under the competent editorship of Clare Boothe (Luce) — asked a dozen or more New York women to write their own epitaphs. HERE LIES THERESA HELBURN [I wrote], WHO BUILT UP A REPUTATION FOR TACT BECAUSE SHE WAS TOO TIRED TO TELL THE TRUTH TO FOOLS. That kind of impulsive wisecrack can prove to be a great mistake. Oddly enough, impulsiveness came as I grew older; in my first days at the Guild I established a line which was caution itself: *Do nothing for forty-eight hours.* By the end of that time, many problems had solved themselves and, even when they hadn't, there had been an interval for weighing pros and cons. This is especially necessary in the theater, where artists are apt to face a crisis emotionally. Someone has to keep his blood pressure down and try to cope with the situation in at least outward placidity. This works better if you just wait a day or two. In time, I was able to meet the stress even of an opening night with what Tennessee Williams once referred to as my "Olympian calm."

As for that third attribute: the ability to see all sides, the willingness to help bring about compromises between conflicting elements in the theater, between actor and director, between playwright and actor, between designer and business manager — that is possible only when the executive has no personal end at stake.

Occasionally, people insist that a theater can be run successfully only by a dictator. That may be all right if the dictator is a genius. But in my opinion, six good theatrical minds, working together for a common end, will prove that their varied contribution is worth more than the discipline and single-mindedness of any dictator.

One of the first things that every one of us had to learn

93

was to accept personal defeat. Lawrence Langner, Philip Moeller and I were all playwrights. Like any proud parents, we wanted to present our brain children to an admiring world. But with our dismaying rule of complete honesty and our insistence on a majority vote on plays, each of us discovered that our friends, colleagues and co-workers looked with a jaundiced eye on our plays. They didn't like them and they made no bones about saying so. Were we, they demanded, fighting the good fight to bring the best drama to the public or were we in business to produce our own efforts?

It was a bitter pill, but each of us swallowed it with a good grace. And for the nonwriters I must add this: I can recall no occasion when Helen Westley's vote for a play was influenced by whether or not it contained a good part for her; when Lee Simonson backed a play so that he could really let himself go as a designer; when Philip Moeller's opinion was swayed by the fact that he would like to direct a particular play; when Maurice Wertheim's vote was given or withheld on a question of box-office appeal. We started — all of us, I think — with personal ambitions we wanted to advance. We ended — all of us, I am sure — by finding a bigger satisfaction in a quite impersonal sort of achievement.

We met once a week, usually on Sunday evenings, because when Helen Westley was acting — and she was practically always acting — that was her only free evening. For Lawrence and Maurice, too, with their busy schedules, Sunday was the only free time.

We learned by experience that we should never skimp these meetings. The longer and more leisurely they were, the better were the results. After a few years, we began meet-

ing at each other's houses, having dinner first and then set-
tling down to talk. Just talk! There were no formal business
reports, no rules of procedure, no one to make a record of
what was said. Actually, I was supposed to keep some sort
of minutes, but as I talked as hard as anyone else, I usually
had to put them together from memory the next day.

In these meetings, we covered a multitude of subjects and
solved, after stormy debate, a vast number of problems. At
that time, the Board of Managers, working together, selected
the plays, directors, scenic artists, and approved major casting. Best of all was the moment when the business was finished: when the immediate problems had been settled and
there was still time to settle back and go on talking in the
relaxed way of tried friends and with the stimulus of a
common enthusiasm. It was in those rare hours of leisure
that the Theatre Guild attained its growth. It is from hours
like these that most creative ideas spring.

Such meetings should never be held around a polished
table with its neat pads and pencils and ash trays. A dinner
table, perhaps. Better still, around a fire on a winter night,
or in summer on a terrace looking out on lawn and still
water. This is when the talk drifts from the immediate problem to the future dream; when we ask, "What shall we do
next?"; when we look back and see our mistakes. This is the
time when each one brings out his cherished plan; a play
he'd like to see done; a project for better theater or for
training better actors or stimulating and encouraging better
playwrights. Often enough, it ends, as it begins, in talk.
Sometimes a seed is planted and begins its slow growth and
in time bears fruit. And now and then, tossed back and forth

like a ball of putty, an idea takes on new shapes and dimensions and becomes something quite different, better by the work of six minds than it could have been as the work of one.

Here are the six characters who built the Guild. Who can analyze their separate contributions? Though each had his individual task, though the executive work and the job of production fell most heavily on one or two, the end result grew out of their combined efforts, of the blending of their personalities and abilities, of their ideas and their labors and their undimmed, boundless love of the theater itself.

◇◇ SEVEN

. . . In Search of an Author

THE GREATEST FASCINATION of the theater is its eternal gamble with all the attendant dangers.

Many years ago, when I was just beginning to accumulate a small savings account, I asked a Wall Street friend if he would speculate with it for me. He refused categorically.

"Don't think," he said, "that you can beat Wall Street. If you want to gamble, at least gamble in something you know about. You are already in a gambling trade."

One thing is sure. The theater is only as good as its plays. We had set out to produce great plays. Now we had to find them. Because we were an unknown quantity, established playwrights were not sending their scripts to us. They wanted to be sure of a production that would be a commercial success. There was something about the sound of an art theater, and particularly an art theater without capital, that scared them away.

In some respects, we were in a tough spot. We had set standards and we did not intend to compromise with them, but we were at a loss to implement them. Our art theater

97

was an experiment but it was not yet an experimental theater. It could not afford to be until it had money in the bank.

Let me explain that. The usual procedure is for a producer to select a play on which he is willing to gamble; he finds investors to guarantee the production costs; he rents a theater; he hires actors, director, scenic artist, and puts the play into rehearsal. At this point, the playwright learns by actual production much of what is wrong with his play — what must be cut, what must be rewritten, which scenes must be shifted or eliminated altogether. The improved product is taken out of town for tryouts — because no play is finished until it has encountered that most potent factor, the audience. With tryout audience-reaction as a guide, the play is rewritten some more, and, whipped into shape, is ready for its final hurdle, the opening night in New York on which its future depends.

The audience is, to a far greater extent than most people realize, a collaborator of the playwright. The play that is performed in an empty theater during rehearsal is literally not the same play that is given before an audience. Whether they are pleased or displeased, amused or bored, approving or shocked, they change the play by their very participation, silent as it is, and something different emerges.

Because we had no money, we could not afford the expense of out-of-town tryouts. Every play we produced had to open cold in New York. In any case, the plays we wanted to do were, we believed at the time, best suited to sophisticated audiences, and therefore the reaction of smaller communities would be of little value to us.

There was a great pool of fine European plays which had never been tapped by American producers because they lacked wide popular appeal, and we dived into it, bringing up treasures that no one else was ready to touch. During those early years, we were constantly criticized because we did so many foreign plays, so much of the Continental drama that Brander Matthews called the "Budapestilent school" of drama. People said that we were obviously more friendly to the European than to the American dramatist. Heaven knows we wanted to produce promising young American dramatists but the successful ones were afraid to come to us and we couldn't open cold with plays from the beginners, who needed the practical workshop of the tryout in order to learn where they had succeeded and how they had failed. So a large proportion of the early productions of the Theatre Guild were foreign plays which had already been success- fully produced abroad and had ironed out their technical and artistic inadequacies.

But there was another point about presenting European plays. We felt that by showing our American playwrights the best of what was being done abroad we were performing a valuable service, providing our own writers with the stimu- lus of fresh ideas and new techniques, impressing on them the universality of theater, enabling them to weigh their own methods and achievements in the balance, to see them against the terrific excitement of the experiments coming out of Russia and Germany, out of Italy and France.

We set to work reading every printed play we could get our hands on. As we read, night and day, racing through books of plays, it seemed to me to be like the feeling one has at a secondhand book sale. I don't know anything more alluring or more fascinating than that. Though you reach the summit with empty hands, the joy of the search has been yours, the delicious trembling hope that, from moment to moment, you are going to secure the peak of your desires, marked down to thirty-nine cents.

There was only one standard we set ourselves, one criterion we applied in our choice of a play: Does it say enough to us and say it well enough to deserve the work and expense of production?

This decision, of course, had to be a joint one. Of the six members of the board, four had to agree on the merits of a play. The advantage was that, because we were such different people, we reflected a larger portion of the public than is possible when the decision devolves upon one person.

Certainly, none of the members of the board were figureheads. For each of them, the reading of plays was a constant duty. In those early years, we had no play readers to weed out the chaff from the wheat and turn over to us the most promising material. We did it all for ourselves. One of my least popular jobs was seeing to it that my five colleagues were constantly supplied with playscripts. There was practically no time when they could go to bed in peace without seeing a waiting script on a bed table, or settle back for a quiet evening of leisure without being reminded of the unread plays awaiting them.

The reading task inevitably fell more heavily on me than on the others, because I was in direct touch with the playwrights and their agents, but even so I picked up each new script with the same undimmed hope that here at last was the beautiful or memorable or off-beat play I had been seeking.

The choice of a play has always been the darkest conundrum of the stage. If you are selling shoes or toothbrushes, a new brand of cigarettes, or real estate in Florida, or lawn mowers or frozen foods, you have some idea of the potential market for these. But with a play you can't guess until the opening night whether you have a success or a flop, whether it will run for years or close within a week. And by then it's too late to do anything about it. Nor is there a technique by which you can improve very much as you go along.

I have never known a manager, no matter how long he has been in the theater, who is willing to hazard an opinion on the success of his play a moment before the curtain falls on the opening night. "Only the public can tell." And what the public decides is an unending surprise.

I can remember one play — Molnar's *The Glass Slipper* — which was thrown entirely out of kilter by the audience reaction to a single word. In accordance with our policy that "the play's the thing," we tried valiantly to keep the foreign plays we produced in their own terms. There had, as I have said, been a general tendency to have foreign imports "made American," but we held as close to the original as possible.

In *The Glass Slipper* there was a scene in which a poor little girl was cuddling a kitten. One character said that she was "suckling" it. The audience was horrified. This was a totally unforeseen reaction, which damaged the impact of the play as a whole to an incredible extent.

101

On the other hand, we did a play that was saved by just as small a detail. That was *The Brothers Karamazov,* a difficult play, whose material was not popular, but with a magnificent cast. The Lunts and Edward G. Robinson appeared in it. The audience was pretty well weighted down by the gloomy material until there was one electric moment, in which Eddie Robinson went up a staircase. He endowed that piece of business with such a terrific quality of tension, suspense, and horror that its one single thrilling moment lifted the whole play.

When I think of the excited discussion, the bitter arguments, the incredibly diverse opinions expressed by the six members of the board in regard to plays under discussion, I realize how impossible it is to arrive at a guess as to the audience reaction. In ourselves we represented a varied range of interests: a lawyer, a banker, a playwright, a producer, a scenic artist and an actress. We used to hope that meant we were a microcosm of the average Broadway audience. (Hope is one of the dominating factors in the theater.)

One thing we were sure of: if the majority of the board thought that the play was interesting, well written, and had something real to say, there was a reasonable chance the public would think so, too. And before tackling the intensive work of production and shouldering the financial risks, we needed that feeling of mutual trust and enthusiasm behind us.

When the vote was even, three to three, a play was often put aside and later brought up again for reconsideration, especially if its partisans were sufficiently excited about it. Now and then, their excitement communicated itself to others who had failed to respond to the play; or, occasionally, those in opposition surrendered out of sheer exhaustion. But I can't remember a case when it did not prove to be a mistake to produce a play which had failed to arouse majority approval on its own merits.

Later, when, after twenty years, Lawrence Langner and I took over the management of the Guild by ourselves, we found the same thing to be true. Though each of us occasionally developed a stubborn streak and overrode the other on some pet play of our own choice, we were always more successful when we were in agreement. Each of us could and did develop blind spots, and we needed the other's eyes to give us proper balance and perspective.

I'll have to admit that Lawrence was quicker to see this than I was. When I was opposed to his ideas I did all I could to persuade him to change, but there came a point when I realized that he was not to be budged, and then I would give in with as good a grace as I could.

Even so, it surprises me to realize that, in a period of twenty years, no regularity of reaction was developed, no two people came to respond alike, no individual could be counted on to follow any particular pattern of choice. We remained, as we began, separate minds working toward a common goal in terms of our own personalities.

We started by feeling our way, with some high ideals and no experience. We selected plays without considering primarily whether they had box-office draw. We were addressing ourselves to what we regarded not as a mass audience but as "the thinking few."

We discovered in the long run that much of the public was

weary of tired formulas and standardized productions, that the thinking few had become many, that there were enough of them to constitute an important theatrical audience. My experience with the Theatre Guild has led me to the startling and unpopular belief that everybody thinks, much as some may hate to admit it.

We discovered that when we believed in a play the audience was apt to believe in it, and the box-office draw, on which we had not counted, was greater than we had dared to hope.

We discovered that the more firmly you stick to your ideal the more stanchly the public will support you.

We discovered that the plays we chose have survived longer than most. Nearly every one of them has since been produced Off Broadway, while most of their competitors are as forgotten as last year's greeting cards.

By the end of our first ten years, then, we had proved that a good play can be commercial; that literary values, good writing and ideas make a play better. All over the Broadway stage, better plays were finding a welcome, producers willing to gamble on them, audiences waiting eagerly to see them. In fact, we were having to fight to get the plays we wanted! The other producers had become our competitors. We had set out to raise standards — and darned if we hadn't done it!

That is not as easy an achievement as it may sound. To keep a theater going in New York, to pay rent and living wages, not to pander to the taste of the mob but to back plays of artistic integrity and distinction, is a hard pull. What eased the burden for us was the fact that none of us lost faith in our ideal, or faith in the public.

I tried to sum up our aims when I spoke at the laying of the cornerstone for the Guild Theatre:

"The Guild knew and still knows that the function of the theater is to entertain, that its greatest sin is to be dull, that its greatest commercial asset is to leave its audience happy and contented. But the Guild knew also that the function of the theater is not only to entertain but to stimulate, not only to make you feel but to make you think, that its greatest sin is to be superficial, and that while it may leave its audience thrilled by the intensity of life, it must never cheat them by denying its underlying tragedy . . .

". . . The greatest advance in the thinking public is brought about by plays that crash the barriers, that leave their audiences quivering, uncomfortable, sometimes disgusted, but always asking: *Why?* These plays are the Guild's most precious failures, they are its realest successes, even though their success is only apparent in the seasons that come after; for the theater moves rapidly, and the dynamite of one decade is the building stone of the next."

Yes, people say, that's all very well, but how, actually, do you choose a play? The answer is easy enough. You choose it because you like it. Just personal predilection. Of course, while that was the basis of choice for each of us, every single one of us had different reasons for liking or disliking plays.

For me the chief interests were — and are — whether the play had anything to say (its theme and values), how it said it (the quality of its language), whether the characters were interesting (alive, believable, honestly characterized). I put story values last in my own private judgment. If the people were alive and interested me, I felt that they would interest other people. I was susceptible to wit, and cared comparatively little about melodramatic narrative. I shy away from bad taste.

Of course, we made a lot of mistakes while we were learning our jobs. For instance, there was *John Hawthorne,* which we produced during our third season. It read well and we were pleased — until it went into production. Then we discovered, to our dismay, that the play had an unexpected flaw. The stage directions were splendid; so good, indeed, that they were often better than the dialogue. It was as though the playwright had told his story to himself through the stage directions rather than through the words of the characters. As a result, we had a feeble and unsatisfactory play.

My own basic weakness was that I was — and am — so susceptible to French thinking and the Gallic point of view that I have always been vulnerable to French plays. One of my most exasperating qualities, and I can't seem to overcome it though I recognize it, is that I go on fighting doggedly and with grim determination for something that may not be worth all that misguided energy and belligerence. Even when we had failed several times to make American audiences savor French irony, I went right on insisting that we do French plays. Finally, I warned my colleagues not to give me any more to read. I simply was not to be trusted with them.

I couldn't seem to get into my head what my own observation kept telling me over and over: that an audience conditioned to one set of values is apt to react badly to a different set of values. In the United States everything of emotional interest is supposed to happen before marriage, in Europe after marriage. Here we have a cult, an idolatry of youth. For most dramatic and emotional purposes, there presumably are no citizens over thirty; or, if anyone totters around after that age, he lives in a state of emotional stagnation. Which is ridiculous.

In casting *The Glass Slipper,* we had used middle-aged actors to play middle-aged parts. This proved to be an error. To suit our audience, we should have cast the parts at least ten years younger. In Europe, maturity and not adolescence is the interesting period of life. But even today when I read a sparkling French play I begin to get excited, to start framing cogent reasons for producing it. Live and learn?

For a long time, when the Theatre Guild produced an unpopular play a good deal of the blame fell on me. My colleagues bolstered up every disagreement with me by unflattering references to my Bryn Mawr education and its result in intellectual aloofness and sequestration from life.

The *New Yorker* made the same point in its Profile, with no beating around the bush. The Guild, it claimed, had produced dull plays and for these "the answer lies . . . with Theresa Helburn, or fundamentally with the misbegotten intellectualism of her college years that exalted literature and excluded life."

Of course, I wasn't the only one with personal prejudices. Lawrence had a weakness for light British comedy and Helen Westley for heavy Russian drama. Helen was the best antidote for my "misbegotten intellectualism." She was, in fact, extremely good for the group as a whole. She was quick and definite in her discussion of plays. Though she had little formal education, her judgment was excellent. She could respond to the emotional qualities of a play in a way that measured the reaction of an audience far better than we.

Helen loved to call herself Cassandra. She was a prophetess who was never wrong. Whether for or against a play, her point of view was expressed with fire and wild excitement.

There was a terrible row when *Green Pastures* came up for discussion. I wanted awfully to do it. Helen stormed and shouted against it.

"I won't," she cried in tragic tones worthy of Lady Macbeth, "do a play in which God smokes a cigar!"

So we lost *Green Pastures* to another producer and I nearly broke my heart over it. What with one thing and another, I must have accumulated a lot of scar tissue over the years.

On the other hand, I was partly responsible for the fact that the Theatre Guild did not produce *Street Scene*. When I read it I saw nothing but a cheap sex murder melodrama. At that time, I thought of it only in terms of its story value, I did not think of it in terms of production. Only when I saw it later did I realize that imaginative production had made it distinguished, had added another dimension. And yet, looking back, remembering that the Guild was founded on the idea, "the play's the thing," I'm not sure I would change my original and spontaneous estimate of the play. It *was* a sex murder melodrama. The production, effective as it was, had been superimposed on an essentially sleazy structure. No, I'm not sorry we turned it down.

However, we took Sidney Howard's *They Knew What They Wanted* after it had been turned down twelve times by other managements, and with everyone assuring us that no one could produce it successfully. It became our first Pulitzer Prize winner.

We were never swayed by the prophets of gloom or the more experienced producers who turned thumbs down on off-beat material. It is heartening to recall now how often we proved to be right.

None of us were infallible in our judgment. We all made mistakes. Sometimes bad mistakes. We were all, let's face it, a little mad. Lawrence and I, I always thought, were the sanest of the lot, but he thinks it is because we bore with each other's idiocies so patiently. We all, as Helen Westley said, had Bonds of Interest, though we each expressed them from our own point of view. With the exception of Helen, we were all literary before we learned to be dramatic. Perhaps my stubborn intellectualism often held them back. It's hard to tell.

EIGHT

Behind the Scenes

FROM THE FIRST MORNING when I entered the Garrick Theater and took possession of the bare little office on the balcony, reached by way of the fire escape, I had to cope with such a host of unfamiliar activities and problems that I never had time, then or later during my strenuous life, to develop a conscious theory about the theater.

No one, I feel sure, ever learned as much about business and theatrical management as fast as I did during that first month. I had to. Not only did I have no business experience whatsoever, I had no financial adviser — because, at that crucial time, both Lawrence Langner and Maurice Wertheim were called away for extensive business trips.

Now and then I realize in some surprise how many twelve-, fourteen-, or even sixteen-hour days I have put in, and yet even now it doesn't seem like work. When the scope of your activities changes almost every hour, when there is fresh experience almost every day, when there is excitement and challenge and risk in every decision, you're so knee-deep in life you can't conceive of yourself as working.

Although I was ignorant enough, I was so full of energy and vitality that I sailed into every problem with the exuberant conviction that, one way or another, I could handle it. Fortunately, I did have sense enough to be aware of my own ignorance and this enabled me to accept group control and conform to group decisions without feeling frustrated. Such few frustrations as I did experience came much later, when I had grown thoroughly conversant with my job and was sure enough of my judgment to be prepared to fight to back it.

The fact that I was a woman in a field rarely entered by women was bound to attract a certain amount of comment, but it seemed to me then, and still seems to me, a logical place for a woman. In some ways, women are better equipped to cope with its work than are men. Like everyone who occupies a public position, I've been swamped with requests for speeches to audiences and over the radio. In one of the latter, made in 1936, I tried to explain this point:

"There are so few women producers that I am constantly being asked how I came to be one, and people frequently express surprise at finding a woman in my position.

"It is true that the Neighborhood Playhouse, a semi-philanthropic institution, was controlled by women, and Miss Le Gallienne achieved notable success with her Civic Repertory Theater, which, however, also partly endowed . . .

"As I look back now it seems to me that the qualities that made for my success in those first difficult weeks were essentially attributes that are considered feminine — tact and economy. In the theater you are dealing most of the time with artists — a group of people whose abilities are in direct ratio to their temperamental exaggerations, and women, trained as they are to adjustments in life, seem to me admirably suited to occupy a focal point.

"Women may be more personal but I do not think they have nearly as sensitive egos as men."

A considerable amount of energy and self-confidence is necessary in accomplishing almost any job. But I think I overdid it. Most of my weaknesses are due to having tried to do too much too fast. I'd work like a demon and then collapse and be driven away for solitary rest.

"Very tired," my diary read on so many days. "Very tired." Then time out for recuperation, on a "hurry up and rest" basis, and a plunge back into the maelstrom.

I also had an annoying conscience that would never rest if I delegated anything to anyone else. I'm afraid I left nothing to God, or even to my business manager, without butting in.

What is it like, behind the scenes in the executive position of an art theater? It's a little like being at the center of a web, or at a busy switchboard with flashing lights signaling calls for help from half a dozen departments.

There are six departments in a theater like ours: the production, the play reading, the technical (scenery, costumes, lighting), the publicity, the business, and the subscription departments. I read plays, interviewed playwrights and play brokers and lawyers; I haggled over contracts and I cajoled unions; I soothed temperamental actors and enraged directors; I passed on stage sets and costumes; I checked the box-office receipts and the salaries; I attended auditions and rehearsals and sweated out first nights.

But that, of course, was only in the early, simple days when we did one play at a time, before I took over the casting and directed plays on my own; before I was working with young American playwrights, helping rewrite their scripts; before we had three or four plays in production at one time, with tryouts, rehearsals, rewriting, and openings scheduled one on top of the other. Then I was really busy.

We soon acquired Warren Munsell as our business manager. He had been with the Washington Square Players until he was called into the First World War, and he was to remain with the Theatre Guild until the American government understandably required his services in the Second World War.

Warren was a staff of strength, a good businessman, and the most serene and understanding of colleagues. He was also a first-class fighter. He even won out now and then against the Shuberts in getting a theater.

He had had business experience in the theater, which I lacked; he also had a quiet assurance when it came to tackling and mastering the new business problems that were forever confronting us. When new opportunities opened, Warren grasped them at once, understood their potentialities and exploited them to the utmost. His experience, able management and serene assurance had much to do with the fact that, almost yearly, the Theatre Guild was enabled to enlarge its plans and its scope.

The job of the business department is mainly concerned

with the leasing and running of theaters, with the supervision of accounts, the control of all box offices, the making of contracts, the booking of road tours, and so forth.

One of the most invaluable qualities about Warren Munsell was that, in addition to being a sound businessman, he had an unusual degree of understanding and patience with the less practical members of the board, including the executive, though there must have been times when he found us more obstructive than reasonable and when our attitude must have been frustrating in the extreme.

I had never looked upon the theater as a business, as all my interest had been entirely from a creative and artistic angle. Though I had, willy-nilly, to learn this business, it always occupied in my mind a place of secondary importance. It was the necessary and unavoidable means to an end, that end being production; it was never the purpose for which production was carried on.

This is an attitude, I suppose, that would make most businessmen regard us as a group of mental defectives. It mirrored, however, the underlying attitude of my five associates for whom the Guild was a gesture of artistic experiment and to whom the idea of profit seemed in those early years both fantastic and beside the point. So I was tuned to the right key to voice the sentiments and execute the decisions of the board of which I was a member, even when, from a strictly business point of view, the decisions seemed impractical and extravagant.

Indeed, as I look back, I seem to have frequently found myself apologizing to my business manager for decisions that appeared to thwart the logical and successful development of his department. And it takes as much diplomacy to persuade a good business manager to sacrifice immediate profit for a vague and uncertain artistic end as to convince an impassioned director that you can't pay a star's salary to an actor who has six lines in Act I, or an inspired scenic artist that imagination must be limited by the expenses of the stage crew. Sometimes arguing on one side of the fence, sometimes on the other, the executive of an art theater must constantly be ready to shift points of view and methods of attack.

Our subscription department is an outgrowth of the business department. When I became acting executive of the Guild, the subscription department consisted of a few hundred names in a precious book kept in the cash drawer.

The day Mr. Munsell became business manager he was handed a note from his predecessor.

"Better not take any more subscriptions," it read. "We have five hundred now and we ought to keep some seats for the public."

We are constantly asked how we recruited our subscription audiences. We did it in several ways. The most effective, of course, was word-of-mouth advertising, the excitement and interest which our subscription members conveyed to others. That is not a rapid method but it is the most satisfactory I know. Of course, we used mailing lists and we always distributed literature and pledge cards in the theater. Another useful but annoying method was by making subscription speeches from the stage, a number of which I perpetrated myself.

In the long run, what built our enormous subscription

audience, not only in New York but later, from coast to coast, was that we brought people plays they wanted to see. People became subscribers because we had provided them with something they liked, so they were eager to become partners in the whole enterprise.

I am making a point of something that should seem obvious. Oddly enough, it doesn't. The growth of our subscription audience attracted a lot of attention and aroused considerable speculation. Representatives from other art theaters began to come to me, looking for information. They wanted to know what kind of formula we had, what sort of methods we employed.

Nearly all of them were attempting to put the cart before the horse. They expected to get subscription support before they had anything to subscribe to. They wanted ticket holders before they had plays or a theater or even a program of future activities to sell them.

You can't reasonably ask for support until you have earned it. An art theater is not a result of financial stability. It is an act of faith. "He either fears his fate too much" etc., applies here if anywhere.

I remember a typical case after we moved into our new theater. A pleasant gentleman from the Middle West came to call on me. A civic theater was to be sponsored in his home city by a group, especially by one wealthy citizen. He wanted to discuss their plans with me and ask my advice.

As I should like to see every town and village have its own theater, I was delighted to be of use. I showed him all over the theater, which did indeed look new and beautiful and prosperous. Then we returned to my office — and how different it was from that shabby dark hole on the balcony of the Garrick!

"Well, now," he began, "how did you do it? That's what I came to ask you."

A jumble of thoughts filled my mind. I thought of the way *John Ferguson* had been produced for a nominal sum. I thought of the long search for fine plays and promising actors and imaginative directors. I thought of Rollo and Lee creating lovely stage sets and lighting effects with worn-out equipment and meager props. I thought of the handful of faithful subscribers and how they had grown steadily, year after year. I thought of the hours and hours of work.

"Do what?" I asked.

"Do all this — get your subscribers." He made a sweep of his hand that seemed to indicate a subscriber concealed behind every chair.

"We've been producing for eight years," I explained.

"I know that. But how did you get your subscribers?" he repeated. "You say you have fifteen thousand. We want ten."

"But we have been producing for eight years."

Somehow he failed to see the connection. "We want ten thousand — and this is our plan. See what you think of it." He proceeded to unfold an elaborate system of chain tickets, reduced rates, premiums, privileges, and so far into the night.

When he had concluded, he looked at me with mingled triumph and query.

"But what plays are you planning to do?" I asked him. "Who are your actors? What directors have you? What, in short, is your production plan?" I knew by my voice that I was betraying my irritation, but he was unaware of it.

"Oh, that will all be attended to," he replied vaguely. "What we want now is subscribers. You have fifteen thousand; we want ten."

But *what*, I wanted to ask him, are they subscribing for? A subscription audience, it stands to reason, must be earned; at least, it must know what concrete plans have been made, what type of play and performance and production it is to expect. If an art theater hasn't enough faith in itself to take a chance, it certainly has no right to expect such faith in its subscribers.

One of the most heartening aspects of our subscription plan was that, in a great measure, the subscription audience became a partner in the whole enterprise. While, inevitably, a number of popular successes would be followed by a number of demands for subscriptions, by and large the variation in renewals has been slight in comparison to the solid phalanx of members who stood by, through thick and thin, accepting the bad with the good, realizing that we were bound to make mistakes but enduring these mistakes patiently for the sake of what had been and what might be to come.

Only someone who knows the hectic agony of production can realize what it means to the producer to know that, whatever happens, the play will not be stillborn, that it will be given a chance for life for at least five or six weeks. If, after that, it cannot stand on its own merits, at least it has had a decent chance from its public.

So far as the technical department was concerned, I have never mastered it as well as I should like. I have always regretted that, by starting at the top, I never acquired the knowledge I should have had. The chief advantage was that I had sense enough, as soon as we could afford to expand, to select people to work with me who knew more than I did, people who were never, in any sense, yes men; and we learned our job together.

And yet, surprising as it may seem under the circumstances, the Guild developed an extremely efficient organization. It was certainly not developed by autocracy. Perhaps the inexperience of the executive may have had something to do with it, for, with my limited theatrical background, I could not take in raw material and train it myself; neither, on the other hand, could we afford experts. It followed, therefore, that my subordinates had to learn their job along with me and sink or swim as the case might be. As, however, they had only one job to learn while I had many, it seemed fair to expect that they should not only keep pace with but surpass their superior officer.

Indeed, I soon learned that if a department head could not teach me about his department he did not belong in the Guild. This proved, of course, not only an acid test but a strong spur to the newcomers in the organization, and it is surprising how quickly and efficiently even comparatively untrained people developed under the stimulus of real responsibility and new adventure.

None the less, I still wish I had taken the time to go back stage and learn to light a show with an electrician so that I would know what I was talking about and not be completely dependent on the technicians. It was many years before I felt any confidence in myself along these lines. I can remember once, in the early days, hearing the electrician call out to his assistant, "Bring out the baby and put it on the stove." It took me some moments to realize that he was talking about a baby spotlight.

So far as the scenic design was concerned, and this is usually where there are the loudest outcries for money and more money, we discovered, from the very beginning, that our acute lack of funds provided no real hardship. An ounce of imagination is worth a carload of scenery. Lee Simonson did the entire production of *From Morn to Midnight*, an expressionistic play in seven scenes, for two thousand dollars! This was a triumph of the designer's art and all the credit belongs to Lee. He saved the cost of scenery by throwing the scenes on the backdrop through lanterns. This was a German technique and used for the first time in America. He accomplished more through suggestion than could ever have been achieved by literal staging. Give an audience half a chance and it will supply all the scenery it needs.

One wonderful scene represented a bicycle race. All the audience actually saw was a box high up, and a man with binoculars looking at the race, but that race was as real as though it were actually taking place. There was only one difficulty, as I recall. That was the fact that the actors had frayed nerves, with resultant outbreaks of temperament and near hysteria, from having to play against a translucent curtain instead of a substantial backdrop.

Actually, limitations of means has served as a stimulus

rather than a handicap to scenic artists, as the limitations of
verse forms is a help to the poet. We found that when we
allowed our scenic artists their head, instead of extravagance
helping a play, it succeeded only in dimming more important
values and was a contributing factor to failure.

Our press department has always had to struggle along
with less help from me than any other department. Often
enough they complained, and justly, that they heard news of
Theatre Guild activities from actors in the company or even
from rank outsiders.

Perhaps this is why some of our press representatives were
driven, in sheer exasperation, to move on and up to other
things. One of them was Russel Crouse, who wrote *Hold
Your Horses, Red, Hot and Blue,* and *Anything Goes* while
in the press department of the Guild, and left us to write and
produce on his own and with Howard Lindsay.

Crouse was far from meeting the general idea of a press
agent. He was the least showy of men, quiet, intelligent and
indefatigable. I cannot conceive of his putting himself forward or doing anything in bad taste. In those days, we did
not have promotion men, as all managements do today.
Russel's job, of course, was to get stories about Theatre
Guild activities into the newspapers and to plan publicity
campaigns for new projects as they came up. I can recall no
work he ever did for us that was blatant or undignified.

He knew his job well. From the beginning he realized that
a woman as head of a theater (unusual in itself) and without
experience (even more unusual) was a good focal point for

the Guild's publicity. That is why my ego was not inflated by my growing reputation in the theater. One of the strangest of all phenomena, yet one of the commonest, is that so many people come in time to be impressed by their own publicity.

For several years, that bleak little office in the Garrick Theater was the center of frenzied activities. Looking back, I can see that what made the days pass with such whirling speed was the fact of the multiplicity of problems, the constantly changing focus of interest, the pressing demands of one situation before another had been coped with. The aspects of theatrical production were so varied that there was no time to get bored with anything. It was a changing kaleidoscope, bright and glittering. One minute, contracts to be wrangled over; the next, a playwright to praise and encourage; then a union official to try to cajole into reasonable co-operation. Nothing was ever twice the same.

And always, of course, there were people; usually people who were at odds with each other and had to be soothed and flattered and talked into getting on with the job. For the theater throbs with temperament. An actor marches out, furious because he claims he is being edged downstage by an unscrupulous colleague. There is a yelp of fury during rehearsals because playwright and director disagree on the reading of a line or the interpretation of a character. The scenic artist falls into a rage because his sets are not approved. Always there is someone whose nose is out of joint and it's up to the executive to get it straight without bloodshed.

As I look back I see myself moving at a fast trot down the fire escape and into the theater. No matter how early I arrived, the telephone was already ringing. (But I can't complain about that. For years my colleagues have lamented that I am prone to telephone them at five in the morning if I get an idea at that time and feel it can't possibly wait to be communicated.) There was nearly always someone waiting to see me: a playwright with a script, young actors and actresses looking for jobs, press agents waiting hopefully for crumbs of information. On my desk would be Warren Munsell's report on box-office receipts.

I'd grab the telephone, nod to the playwright, look over the papers on my desk, setting aside a promising play to be read that night after I'd caught a new opening in my constant search for talent, and cock an eyebrow at my long-suffering secretary who was opening her notebook and waiting for the sentences flung at her haphazardly between telephone calls and interviews. And such interviews: stormy actors, designers with lovely sketches for stage sets, people whose names had been legends before I met them face to face.

Lunch at the Algonquin to discuss revision with an author. Back, at a trot, to look over reports on new plays and to audition actors. An hour at rehearsal, making a quick note for the harassed director that the performance was jerky and restless. Home for an hour of rest and telephoning. Always telephoning. Dinner at Sardi's with a new playwright. An opening night. A party at 21. Home to crawl into bed and read a play.

But no matter when I left the office, no matter how exhausted I was — and sometimes I felt as though I had been tossed all day in a blanket — I came out to Broadway and the flashing lights of theaters, with all the excitement and hope they represent. Oh, it's been a good life!

NINE

Cast and Miscast

THE SECOND SEASON of the Theatre Guild, and my first as executive, opened with John Masefield's poetic play, *The Faithful,* under Augustin Duncan's sturdy direction. As I remember it now, it was beautiful but dull. It ran for forty-eight performances, not bad for a play in verse.

John Masefield was tall, dark, slender, a quiet and charming Englishman, innately gentle. Come to think of it, all the playwrights with whom I have worked for four decades have been gentle people, with the possible exception of Saroyan. Though I'm not sure he's ungentle. Just highly individual. In all those years, and in spite of the theater's reputation for violent scenes, I can recall no one but Lee Simonson who ever raised his voice with anger in speaking to me.

In talking to the English poet, I said, "Mr. Masefield, the Theatre Guild expects you to write the next great labor play."

"No," he answered, "I will never do that."

"But why not?"

"Because," he explained shrewdly, "labor is no longer a lost cause."

We did three box-office failures in a row and we were sitting around gloomily, wondering what we would do next, when Emmanuel Reicher, the German director, reached up on the shelves of printed plays and knocked down a copy of St. John Ervine's *Jane Clegg*. Idly he picked it up. He leafed through it.

"Why don't you do this?" he asked.

Ervine had saved us from disaster by the skin of our teeth the year before; why couldn't he do it again? After all, lightning does strike twice in the same place. So we produced *Jane Clegg*, which had a popular success and ran for months. Once again we were solvent, we had enough money to carry us over another season, and the ground felt secure under our feet.

There was a gentleman who came to the box office during the triumphant run of *Jane Clegg*. He, like the stag at eve, had drunk his fill. He leaned against the ticket window.

"Say, what's this show, *Jane's Leg*, anyhow?"

He bought a ticket, sat through the play, and came out sufficiently impressed to become a subscribing member of the Guild.

To me, one of the most satisfying features of *Jane Clegg* was that every single part had been perfectly cast. This is the rarest of phenomena in the theater. There are few plays in which at least one character is not wrongly cast, often two or more. I have always found this emotionally disturbing. Frequently, I have had to leave the theater while these miscast characters were on the stage, because, for me, they destroyed the dramatic illusion and the mood of the play as long as they were before me.

We opened the next season with David Pinski's Yiddish comedy, *The Treasure*, which Ludwig Lewisohn had translated. Again, Lee provided the sets and Emmanuel Reicher directed. At once, he ran into a real casting problem and, at the last minute, called me in to help. I arrived on the scene too late in the day to be of much assistance, and I still remember with chagrin Dudley Digges and Henry Travers trying unconvincingly to act as though they belonged in a Russian ghetto, and Helen Westley before a wailing wall, keening instead of wailing.

Reicher was a wonderful director but he tried to cast from the foreign point of view and failed. That is what catapulted me into becoming casting director. I had lost a whole summer waiting for him to get a cast. Because he did not understand the American theater, he cast people whom he thought he could make over into the parts. What he did not realize was that you cannot make people over in the four weeks' rehearsal period allowed by Equity.

Nevertheless, there was much to be learned from Reicher, who came to America steeped in Continental tradition. The chief thing he taught me was the importance of putting good actors in bad parts. It is true, often, that the better the part, the lesser actor it requires. An outstanding example of this is the rôle of General Burgoyne in *The Devil's Disciple*. As Shaw has written the part, it is practically actor-proof.

In that 1921 season my duties as executive director included attending to the preliminary casting for the board which, under the Guild system, was responsible for each play.

I had the conviction that I was no good, and the curious

thing is that, in spite of this — for I believe in the value of
self-confidence — I worried through. It was an absolute surprise when I found some instinct in myself for picking actors
for parts. Casting is a seeking, unsure thing. One lies awake
nights trying to think of the man or woman inevitable for
a particular part, or sad because of the hurt that must be
inflicted on an actor who hasn't proved right for the part
and must be told. One strains for a purely impersonal view-
point; executive work must be so. But I don't think I ever
reached the impersonal absolute where disappointing a fellow worker was all in the day's work.

How much bearing the right cast has on a play was revealed here a few years ago when an English comedy was
imported. It had played in London and Paris with terrific
success. The London lead had been Ralph Richardson. But
the Broadway cast played the sophisticated comedy (a variation on the *Design for Living* theme), which should have
been handled as lightly as a feather, with a dreadful hearty
coyness, and the production was deservedly an awful failure.

Of course, the unforeseen elements make both the gamble
and the fascination of the theater. You cast Mary Boland in
a great classic play like *The Rivals* and she seems ideal. It's
as if no one else could have been a better choice. You keep
patting yourself on the back until the play opens, and then
you find that the actress is not able to combine the eight-
eenth-century language with her fine comedy method, and
so cannot be understood by the audience.

In the same play, Bobby Clark was cast as the comedy
lead. We were dubious. Bobby seemed to be completely out
of control. Then we were terrified. We never knew what he

would do next. And yet he was far from impulsive. He calculated every move. I can still remember the meticulous care with which he measured everything in the duel scene. And then, on the first run-through, he was so funny we were rolling in the aisles. His hilarious performance made the play.

One of the most interesting features about casting was the exciting results that came from trying actors out in rôles that were totally new to them. Often the results were amazing and we learned — and the actor learned, too — that he had talents none of us even suspected.

Once I took a little comedienne who had been playing in sex farces for years and put her in an emotional rôle. She proved that she could reduce her audience to tears more effectively than she ever had to laughter. Again, in desperation, I picked an unknown girl out of the acting course of a new teacher, for the road tour of a Behrman play with Ina Claire. This was Anne Meacham, who turned out to be excellent and to have an extraordinarily promising acting career ahead of her.

That's the fun and that's the joy of the profession. I can't imagine any other that has so much. I don't think an unexpectedly big order in a commercial business could give you one fragment of the satisfaction that you can get when you feel you have made a human discovery.

I am usually cautious about taking credit for giving actors their start, for the matter of credits in the theater is one of the most interesting, subtle and dangerous of all its pitfalls. There is never a successful choice that isn't claimed by somebody other than the director or producer, and time is too short to track down rumors and evidence to an authentic conclusion.

One of the most unexpected requests that ever came my way in casting was from an agent named Baldwin. At my office at the Guild one day, he asked:

"Do you have a good part for Mae West?"

"In the Theatre Guild?" I exclaimed, startled.

"Well, no, but she is looking around for a play with a good part for her."

"I'll think about it," I promised him. "Oh, I know of a play in which she could make a sensational entrance, but I don't know how she'd go on from there."

"What's that?"

"*Mrs. Warren's Profession,*" I told him.

He did not know the play; neither, it appeared, did Mae West, so I gave him a copy. After an interval he came back.

"Will you talk to her about it yourself?"

My memory of that meeting with a typical American phenomenon is bolstered by a copy of my letter to George Bernard Shaw in which I described it.

I went to her dressing room, where I found her resplendent in a white satin negligee and unsubdued by the jail term she had just served. The huge vaudeville house in which she was playing was packed. Every few minutes during our interview she had to go to the window and throw pictures of herself to the mob of admirers who were blocking traffic below. Her public, she told me, expected a certain line of work from her and she indicated the line most graphically by one of her characteristic gestures.

"What did you think of the play, Miss West?" I asked her.

"Well, I'll tell you, dear," she replied. "I feel I owe it to my boys not to play the part of a mother."

In *Too True to Be Good*, which Shaw had originally written as a one-act play, and which he himself did not think could be produced, I did one of those casting jobs which always delight me. I took Beatrice Lillie out of musical comedy and gave her her first rôle in a dramatic production.

She was splendid to work with. I have never known an actress who took direction so well or was actually so eager to have it. She came grinning to me one day and waved a letter triumphantly.

"My stock has gone up," she told me exultantly. She had just received a letter from her son. Now that she was playing Shaw with the Theatre Guild she had become an intellectual!

The secret of Beatrice Lillie's comedy method is her perfect timing. There was an unforgettable and hilarious scene in *Too True to Be Good* where Beatrice Lillie and Hope Williams rolled on the floor. She could put anything over, though she had never worked in legitimate before. Her diction was so good that you could hear every word, which would have pleased Shaw. He had only one piece of advice for actors: "Speak up so the audience can hear every word."

But we discovered that it was dangerous to use a woman famous for her comedy in a straight play. Because she was the dominant personality in the cast, the audience watched her constantly. There was one point in the play where it was essential for the audience to be attentive to the other speakers.

"Don't move a finger," I warned Bea. "Make the slightest gesture and the audience will watch you instead of the speakers. Wiggle a toe and they will know you are going to be funny and start to laugh."

So for three solid minutes during every performance she remained as motionless as a statue, one of the hardest tricks to pull off on the stage. That's the time, invariably, when you get something in your eye, or you have to sneeze, or your foot falls asleep.

Another time we were not so successful casting comedians in serious parts. Clifton Webb and Claudia Morgan played minor characters in *And Stars Remain*. Every time they opened their mouths the audience laughed. They knew they were going to be funny. It wasn't their fault. Just a serious casting mistake.

One of my favorite casting jobs was putting George M. Cohan in *Ah, Wilderness!* People were amused at the idea of Cohan appearing in a Eugene O'Neill play but it proved to be, without doubt, his greatest rôle. He was very much a star in his own right and he had to be handled carefully during the rehearsal period. Once the play was launched, of course, he was on his own and, imperceptibly, the play began to change.

I have never known any other actor who understood an audience as well as Cohan. Before he went on the stage he watched them, sensed their mood. He played them for laughs like a fisherman. He could stretch out a laugh as long as he wanted. By the time I caught up with the play on tour it was running a half-hour long. I was frantic.

Oliver, who was with me, said, "Don't worry. The audience is having a marvelous time." They were, too.

There's another problem that crops up periodically. You may cast an actor or actress who can do the part but who, too late to be remedied, develops unexpected idiosyncrasies. There was *The Lucky One,* for example, in which I cast Violet Heming in the leading rôle. The play was set in an English country house and in one scene she was to make an early morning drive in a pony cart to the station to meet her fiancé.

At the first dress rehearsals we saw that she had chosen a flowered gown with pink ostrich feathers on one hip. We took them off. She put them back on again. We took them off.

Opening night came and Violet Heming set off triumphantly for the station, complete with pink ostrich feathers. What the English in the audience must have thought makes me blush even now.

We had another embarrassing contretemps over costumes when we did *Roar China.* I think this must have been the play which, to our surprise, got us a reputation for being Communist. There was a wonderful set with a gunboat in a lake. The cast had to leap into the water and they were always complaining that they were getting pneumonia. So we had a group of men keep the water warm. Then the cast complained of being too hot. The theater is like that.

One member of the cast had to dive into the lake and make his re-entry almost immediately. In the excitement he walked on the stage without any costume at all. Being Chinese he was not in the least embarrassed. But everyone else was.

People have asked me about my method. I do my casting from the pit of my stomach. If it feels hollow, I know that the actor is not convincing in the part. If there is a more rational approach to casting, some infallible rule of thumb, I don't know it. Rather, it is a kind of empathy, an awareness of the actor's potentialities that grows while you watch him and listen to him. After interviewing in excess of ten thousand applicants for rôles in the theater, I still can't say more than that about my own method.

After I took over the job of casting, I had to spend countless hours at auditions. As a rule, a number of people apply for the same rôle. They are given the script, asked to study it, and then to read a scene or two, usually with some more experienced actor. Reading a few lines of a part is a nerve-racking experience for the actor or actress. They are desperately anxious to appear at their best and they are uncertain as to what the part requires of them. Of course, they are nervous. We always discount nervousness and, anyhow, it tends, for some reason, to heighten rather than to blur personality.

But the real problem is that inexperienced actors almost always make the same serious mistake. You ask them to read a bit of the script and they try to give a complete, well-rounded performance instead of merely indicating the character. I don't want a finished performance at an audition. The actor who gives a detailed performance at the outset is more than likely to be incapable of growth.

During my year in Hollywood, a good-looking boy from the camera department came to tell me that he wanted to act, and he asked me to give him an audition. On my desk at the time were fifteen pages of a man's part, which I turned over to him. The next morning he appeared in my office, rather pale and wan but triumphant. He had spent the whole night cramming and had learned all fifteen pages by heart. I was staggered until I realized that, in the movie studios, that is what he would have been required to do.

I explained to the young man that this was the last thing in the world that would give me any idea of how good an actor can be. I told him how parts are studied in the legitimate theater. For a week or more after rehearsals start, the company reads and talks over the parts with their director, analyzing the meaning, learning to know and understand the character, to be able to explain why he does what he does and what makes him that way. No good actor, I told the chagrined young man, attempts to learn his lines until he is so familiar with the character that the lines really come out of the character instead of being superimposed on top of it.

I, for one, listen to the audition, instantly alert if the actor appears to be reading too well, giving too finished a performance. A good actor gropes around, he feels his way, his mind meanwhile working at the meaning of the character. So, paradoxically, the strongest audition may mean the weakest performance; it may mean the actor has not the strength we need for the part, that he is soft at the core.

What I look for are general qualities. Of course, since speech is the actor's major tool, slovenly or artificial diction ruins his chances immediately. If he cannot articulate clearly or his voice is bad, there is no earthly point in his trying to become an actor. He is attempting to live beyond his artistic means.

Overacting is another serious mistake for an actor to make during the audition. The more quiet, relaxed, and simple he is, the better one is able to judge his potentialities without his own personality intruding too much. Experience is not always essential. After all, it may be bad experience.

Appearance also has its effect. When Celeste Holm came to try out for a part in one of our plays, she found out from the other actors who were waiting for an audition what the play was like. She promptly went to the washroom, where she changed her hair-do and make-up to fit her better for the part. It helped land the job for her.

On the other hand, the first time Katharine Hepburn came to my office to discuss an acting career she was carelessly groomed and she had taken no pains at all with her appearance. Still an undergraduate at Bryn Mawr, she was an odd-looking child. But when she opened the office door it was as though someone had turned on a dynamo. The air vibrated with the electric force of her personality.

Certainly, she lacked any vestige of humility. When the young people who later founded the Group Theatre first began to hold meetings, Katie attended. She listened to their plans and then she stalked out.

"That's all right for you," she told them, "but I intend to be a star."

One day, a girl came to me for an audition. She looked so sloppy and unprepossessing that I would have got rid of her instantly if she had not been sent by Helen Hayes. Helen has an old pro's point of view, and I could not imagine her wasting my time merely to accommodate an acquaintance or pass on a nuisance. So I had the girl read. After the first few speeches something came through, something alive and vivid. No doubt about it: the girl had that intangible quality that gets across the footlights.

Getting across the footlights — an intangible quality — but it is the difference between life and death on the stage. How often two girls have come in to try out for the same part. One is pretty, she looks like the type we need, she reads adequately. Then the other, with a fraction of her looks and not a type I would have imagined suitable, begins to read. Something electric comes through, something I call "released vitality." That is the thing I mean by personality.

I suppose the actress who possessed it to the greatest degree of anyone I ever knew was Laurette Taylor. Laurette, helpless and loving. Her inner radiance fell like moonlight on an audience without the use of any stage tricks that I could detect. In my day there has been no other such radiant personality as hers. She had a quality — oh, call it an ability to love, for I can't think of anything closer to it — which got across the footlights and aroused an immediate response.

And without it there is nothing. Years ago, a friend of mine who had a very handsome husband and was ambitious for him urged me to give him an audition. In a moment of weakness, I agreed. He was wonderful to look at, he read correctly and spoke clearly. And it didn't matter a damn. Absolutely nothing came through. He lacked that one extra ingredient which makes all the difference.

What you look for in the audition is that electric quality,

though you don't always — perhaps not often — find it. But you do get a general feeling of the way an actor attacks the part, of the intelligence with which he searches out its meaning. If the man is handsome and the woman is beautiful, there is an extra dividend, but not so large a one as might be expected. The stage is the place for transformation, for illusion. Of the truly great actors and actresses of the theater today few are exceptionally good-looking, but all of them can create an illusion of irresistible charm. That is what counts.

Actually, what I looked for in auditions was potentialities, appearance and diction, humility of approach to the rôle and the power of projecting personality. Not necessarily a ready-made personality for a particular part. I don't believe in casting to type, particularly if the rôle is a strong one. In such a case, the character is apt to be overstressed so that it throws the whole play off balance.

I learned this during the production of the first play of Shaw's that we produced, *Heartbreak House*. Hector Hosketh was a strongly marked character and I felt that the man I had cast in the part was perfect for it: handsome, dynamic, with a strong personality. Subconsciously, during rehearsals I was aware that something was wrong but I could not figure out what it was.

One day Gilbert Miller, who had been watching the performance, turned to me, shaking his head.

"What's wrong?" I asked.

"Hosketh. He's too much in type. The character is so strong that you should have cast it against type."

It was a lesson I have never forgotten.

The most fascinating part of casting is fitting a man or

woman into a totally new kind of part, which widens his acting potentialities and deepens the scope of his technique.

When Ralph Bellamy was suggested for the part of Franklin D. Roosevelt in Dore Schary's *Sunrise at Campobello* the choice was a deliberate attempt to cast against type. Ralph does not resemble the late president but we did not want type casting. The result would have been imitation, close to caricature, a kind of vaudeville trick.

Dore Schary knew that he would get a sound performance from an able actor. What he actually got, of course, was a *tour de force,* an inspired performance. Ralph, too, did not want to do an imitation: what he aspired to was the evocation of the spirit of the man.

Ralph approached his part as he does each one. As he had sat for weeks at police headquarters studying the plain-clothes men for his part in *Detective Story,* so he set to work painstakingly to study every detail, going to the source for each one. He studied paralytics and learned the techniques by which they walk. He practiced the heavy, dangerous falls. He acquired the mannerisms of voice and gesture. But he was never a mimic; he lived the part. Curiously, without really looking like Roosevelt or trying to look like him, Ralph Bellamy ended each performance by convincing you that he did.

There was one casting difficulty which rarely faced us. Because we did not appeal to investors for support in producing plays in those early years, we had the freedom of action that comes of using one's own money, however little it may be. One of the bugbears attached to money that is advanced is

139

the strings that often go with it. The theatrical world is riddled with these intrigues — with the fact, for instance, that money is often forthcoming if a man's mistress can be cast in the leading rôle. Fortunately for us, we were independent enough never to have to compromise by taking an inadequate actor for the sake of financing. And only once has a playwright brought similar pressure on us in offering a play.

Oddly enough, our worst problem came from a distin- guished drama critic who became permanently embittered because we would not give his temporary mistress a part for which she was clearly unsuited. His anger long outlasted the love affair. He waged verbal warfare against us for years. Human, perhaps, but not any better for maintaining the stand- ards of criticism than for maintaining production and artistic standards.

My complaint on this score is not a moral one. It is an artistic one. There is no possibility of maintaining acting standards as long as players are featured not for their abilities but for their extracurricular activities.

My duties as casting director did not end with auditions. When we brought over Jacques Copeau's company, the Rus- sian director, Komisarjevsky, was to produce Paul Claudel's *The Tidings Brought to Mary*. He was accompanied by the actress who had long been his mistress and who was to play, of all things, the Virgin.

Now it happened that on an earlier visit to the United States, as a member of the *Chauve Souris* troupe, Komisarjev- sky had made enemies. One of these, finding that the Russian and his mistress had taken an apartment together, went to Lawrence Langner to warn him that, unless this horrifying situation was rectified, Komisarjevsky would be deported on charges of moral turpitude.

"Let Terry do it" was a slogan around the Theatre Guild, so, to my consternation and dismay, I was sent to confront the gigantic Russian and explain the situation to him. Looking up at his great height, I felt like an impertinent Pekinese barking at a bewildered Great Dane.

Sinking with embarrassment, I told him what had happened. Komisarjevsky looked down at me, not so much angered as baffled. "You mean to tell me," he thundered, "that no one can live together in America if they are not married?"

I bowed my head. "Only Americans," I said.

Looking back over these pages, I am uneasily aware how vague they sound, as though the thing we seek in an actor is so intangible we can't pin it down. Well, it is, in a way. It's the fluid thing that makes one person stand out in a room, even when he may be the least impressive physically. Call it personality or what you will.

TEN

G. B. Shaw, Man of Letters

ALTHOUGH I was a child at the time, I can still remember the excitement caused by the publication of George Bernard Shaw's *Plays Pleasant and Unpleasant* in America, an excitement which persisted through my adolescence and girlhood.

Everyone was reading, discussing, and arguing the plays. *Plays Unpleasant* were, of course, too shocking for American production. It is a proof of my theory that censorship is unnecessary that I could read the *Plays Unpleasant* at that age without any shock and *Plays Pleasant* with the greatest joy. It wasn't until 1907 that any of the unpleasant plays were produced, but the younger intelligentsia were all acting the pleasant plays as hard as they could.

With the first play of Shaw's that we produced, *Heartbreak House,* St. John Ervine, for the third and last time, assisted the Theatre Guild on its way. He did so by suggesting to Shaw that we might produce the play. This was in 1920 when Shaw's popularity was at its lowest ebb. His political stand during the First World War had embittered the English people, and no American producer was willing to take a chance on presenting his plays while wartime emotions were still so passionate.

Apparently Shaw inquired of Drinkwater about this unknown theatrical organization, because Drinkwater wired him:

HAVE SEEN TWO THEATRE GUILD PERFORMANCES "JOHN FERGUSON" AND "FAITHFUL" VERY MUCH WORTHWHILE AND THEY ARE NOT RICH SOME LUNATIC HAS FRIGHTENED THEM ABOUT YOUR TERMS THEY ASK MY INTERCESSION WHICH I KNOW IS NOT NECESSARY.

The Guild, needless to say, agreed to Shaw's terms without cavil. Since that time the Theatre Guild has presented more of Shaw's plays than any other management, a record of which we are exceedingly proud. And not only the Board of Managers was delighted. The actors, too, were tremendously excited at having the opportunity to play Shaw.

"You don't know what it means to have a part that you can get your teeth into," Lucille Watson said after her first rehearsal in *Heartbreak House*. And Effie Shannon, who played Hessione, said, "This is the realest part I have ever done. It is so real that I find myself talking and feeling like Hessione at home as well as in the theater. In fact, I'm not quite sure who I am."

With the production of *Heartbreak House* we entered a totally new situation. Up to that time we had drawn largely on printed plays for production. Now we were dealing with fresh material — five of our Shaw productions were world *premières*. We were also dealing with an author who was not only very much alive but who constituted himself the directing genius — by remote control. And so began a series of letters, cablegrams and, sometimes, postcards, by which Shaw made clear to us exactly what he demanded of production. Even from thousands of miles away, he was aware of every single detail and never relinquished his firm grasp on the strings.

He was decisive and definite about what he wanted. As a playwright he knew clearly what he was trying to achieve. Out of his long experience he was sure of the methods by which it could be accomplished. With his masterly control of stagecraft and technique, Shaw is almost director-proof. Follow his detailed directions in production and you get fine results. But if you try to improvise, you usually land in a mess.

On the subject of cutting, he was adamant. While he listened to all suggestions, he almost never changed his mind. As his plays grew longer and longer, and we were faced with the problem of trying to attract and hold audiences who had trains to catch, we became more persistent in our requests for cuts. We didn't get them.

When I remember now how I insisted on the cutting of *Saint Joan,* I think perhaps I was rash to presume to criticize. In many ways I have become humbler and wiser as I have grown older. But as to who was right, only time can tell. Certainly *Saint Joan* is a masterpiece and probably Shaw's best play. People came to see it, regardless of its inordinate length. It still seems to me likely, however, that future revivals of his plays — and the majority of them will be revived as long as there is a theater — may be cut to some extent, perhaps even drastically. And I am inclined to believe that they will play better.

Our first problem arose almost immediately. We cast *Heartbreak House* and went into rehearsal. Then, like a bolt from a clear sky, Mr. Shaw told us that we could not open until after the presidential election. I protested. Lawrence Langner protested. We wrote to St. John Ervine, urging him to use his influence and expostulate with Shaw. For the first time we discovered that, once he had made up his mind, he was not to be budged.

Dear Madam [he wrote me from Ireland]:

It is useless to trouble Mr. Ervine or to expostulate with me. I have been through it all before. The theater is so out of touch with politics that it never even knows a Presidential election is on until it finds that the public is not paying the slightest attention to it and *won't* until the Monday following the first Tuesday in November relieves its mind as to who will be President next year. My lawyer (Mr. B. H. Stern of 149 B'way) has the strictest instructions to pay not the smallest heed to your entreaties to be ruined by throwing away your trump. You will find him inexorable. You must carry on as best you can until the third week in November. Then you can go ahead; and very thankful you will be to me for having saved you from a disastrous blunder. You will be wiser four years hence.

Then, with a flash of his characteristic mocking humor, he added, "This is your first election. I forgive you for not being aware of the danger."

Another letter, pointing out the dilemma in which we found ourselves, having engaged a cast and hired a theater, was answered by a long postal card.

It would be far better to produce H. H. with the first cast you could pick out of the gutter on the 15th Nov. than to produce it on the 15th October with Sarah Bernhardt, the two Guitrys, Edwin Drew, Maud Adams, Charlie Chaplin and Mary Pickford.

A running play may do very well, because people already know about it, and it needs no press. But a new production has no chance. The presidential candidates play the author and the cast off the stage; and the election crowds out the theater. If you doubt me, try — but with somebody else's play. You will never try again.

I am sorry to upset the arrangements; but a new management has to buy its experience; and it mustn't do so at the cost of an old — too old — author.

The following year we did *Back to Methuselah,* which had started with the unpromising title of *Gospel of Creative Evolution.* Shaw said to Lawrence: "You don't need a contract for *Back to Methuselah.* It isn't likely any other lunatic will want to produce it." So again we had a world *première* of a Shaw play and I've never been sorry we put it on, though we lost money on it. (According to Shaw we actually made $10,000 on his name alone as we had expected to lose $30,000 and lost only $20,000.)

One night William, the doorman, said, "Miss Helburn, it's getting better and better. Fewer people leave every night."

Being a realistic theater, we had considerable discussion as to how Adam and Eve were to be dressed before the Fall, and I can recall how Martha Bryan Allen wowed the audience when she came out of the egg at the end of the play.

Shaw said ironically that he wrote *Saint Joan* to save her from Drinkwater. As soon as we went into production we began to receive instructions from the watchful playwright.

I wrote to him: "We do not feel it wise to change the pronunciation of Rah'ce to Rheims, as the American public is not up to the level of the English. It is for the most part unfamiliar with the famous Jackdaw, and takes much more readily to the French than the English pronunciation of the word. The same is true of the word 'dauphin.' "

G. B. S. scrawled an answer on my letter:

Terry dear, you know but little of the world.

The population of New York City is 5,620,048. The odd 48 know that the French call Rheims Rah'ce and themselves call it variously Rance, Ranks, Rangs, Wrongs, Ross or Rams. The other 5,620,000 wonder what the 48 are trying to say, and call it Reems.

The 48 also call the Dauphin the Dough-fang or the Doo-fang.

The public laughs, and writes to me about it.

The 48 call Agincourt (an English word unknown in France) Adj Ann Coor.

You had better do what I tell you every time, because I am older than you — at least my fancy pictures you younger, and very beautiful.

Saint Joan was a beautiful and exciting play. But it was terribly long. We cabled Shaw that people were missing their trains. Please, please, couldn't we cut. Shaw cabled back, "The old old story." He suggested that the train schedules be changed.

But the public came and came, and the play ran on and on. The length didn't seem to have any effect in keeping them away. And Shaw scolded us like an irate parent for our insistence.

MY DEAR THEATRE GUILD [he began in a letter marked *Personal*]:

I have had your cables including the one you dictated to poor

147

Winifred. You ought to be ashamed of yourselves for getting a young actress into trouble with an author like that. Anyhow *I* am ashamed of you — thoroughly. Your nerves seem to have reached the Los Angeles level. You get such a magnificent press (considering) that it is extensively reproduced in London; and yet you run screaming to me to say that Messrs. Broun, Corbin & Co. want the play cut, and that you will be ruined if you don't obey. When I urged you to have some consideration for the public in *Methuselah* you insisted on the horror of two plays in a night, sending around buckets of coffee and finishing at two in the morning. Now that you can play in 3½ hours and begin at 7:30 if you like, you want to cut the play and to tell the public that I have cut it, and that you are beaten and that it is now quite like the *Garden of Allah* and *Chu Chin Chow*. And then you ask me to trust your judgment on the ground that you don't trust mine! If Shubert treated me like this I would never speak to him again.

I enclose an article which you can send to the press if business *looks bad* — not otherwise, mind. DON'T edit it and don't rush it to the press with this letter, unless you want a testimonial to your incapacity very badly.

You have wasted a whole morning for me with your panic-stricken nonsense, confound you! What did you do it with — morphia? There must be some dope or other at work.

Out of all patience,

G. BERNARD SHAW

When we sent him pictures of the production he wrote: "On the whole there is nothing to complain of, which is a pity, as I complain so well. However, lots of things are wrong, so here goes . . ."

This is the article, which Mr. Shaw sent us for the newspapers, and which we found, after all, unnecessary to use. It is not only amusing in itself but it reveals, as clearly as any statement Shaw made on the theater, his attitude toward his work and toward his audiences. Certainly, it is a part of the theatrical record.

As there seems to be some misunderstanding in the New York press of my intention in writing *Saint Joan*, I had better make myself quite clear. I am supposed to have set myself the task of providing the playgoing public with a pleasant theatrical entertainment whilst keeping the working hours of the professional critics within their customary limits; and it is accordingly suggested that I can improve the play vastly by cutting off a sufficient length from it to enable the curtain to rise by half-past eight and descend finally at ten minutes to eleven. Certainly nothing could be easier. In the popular entertainment business, if your cradle is too short for your baby, you can always cut down your baby to fit the cradle.

But I am not in the popular entertainment business. The sort of entertainment provided by the fate of Joan of Arc seems to be quite sufficiently looked after in the United States by the Ku Klux Klan, and is all the more entertaining for being the real thing instead of a stage show.

As to the grievances of the professional critics, I, as an ex-critic, understand it only too well. It is a hideous experience for a critic, when at half-past ten he has all the material for a good long notice, and is longing to get back to his newspaper office and write it at comparative leisure, to be forced to sit for another hour by that rival artist the author, until all the leisure is gone and nothing but a hurried scramble to feed the clamoring compositors is possible. But the remedy for that is, not to demand that the play shall be mutilated for the convenience of a score or two of gentlemen who see it as their breadwinning job on the first night only, but to combine as other professional men do, and establish the custom of beginning plays of full classical length an hour earlier on the first night.

So much for the negative side of the situation. As to the positive side, I am, like all educated persons, intensely interested, and to some extent conscience stricken, by the great historical case of Joan of Arc. I know that many others share that interest and that compunction, and that they would eagerly take some trouble to have it made clear to them how it all happened. I conceive such a demonstration to be an act of justice for which the spirit of Joan, yet incarnate among us, is still calling. Every step in such a demonstration is intensely interesting to me; and the real protagonists of the drama, the Catholic Church, the Holy Roman Empire, and the nascent Reformation, appeal to my imagination and my intellect with a grip and fascination far beyond those of Dick Dudgeon and General Burgoyne. When in the face of that claim of a great spirit for justice, and of a world situation in which we see whole peoples perishing and dragging us toward the abyss which has swallowed them all for want of any grasp of the political forces that move civilizations, I am met with peevish complaints that three hours or so is too long, and with petitions to cut the cackle and come to the burning, and promises that if I adapt the play to the outlook and tastes and capacities of the purblind people who have made the word suburban a derisive epithet, it will run for eighteen months and make a fortune for me and the Theatre Guild, the effect is to make me seem ten feet high and these poor people ten inches, which is bad for my soul, and not particularly healthy for theirs.

In theatres as elsewhere, people must learn to know their places. When a man goes to church and does not like the service nor understand the doctrine, he does not ask to have it changed to suit him: he goes elsewhere until he is suited. When he goes to a classical concert and is bored by Beethoven, he does not scream to the conductor for a fox trot, and suggest that Beethoven should introduce a saxophone solo into the Ninth Symphony; he goes to the nearest hall where a jazz band is at work. I plead for equally reasonable behavior in the theatre. *Saint Joan* is not for connoisseurs of the police and divorce drama, or of the languors and lilies and roses and raptures of the cinema, and it is not going to be altered to suit them. It is right over their heads; and they must either grow up to it or let it alone. Fortunately for me, it interests and even enthralls serious people who would not enter an ordinary theatre if they were paid to, and draws novices who have never crossed the threshold of a theatre in their lives, and were taught by their parents that it is the threshold of hell. And the class of intelligent and cultivated playgoers whose neglected needs have brought the Theatre Guild into existence, naturally jump at it.

However, even at the risk of a comprehensive insult to the general public of New York, I must add that the limitation of the audience to serious, intelligent, and cultivated Americans means that *Saint Joan* must be regarded for the present as an Exceptional Play for Exceptional People. It has cost a good deal to produce it for them, and is costing a good deal to keep the opportunity open. This will not matter if they seize the opportunity promptly with a sense that if they do not, they will miss it, and discourage the Guild from future public-spirited enterprises of this class. The solvency of a play depends not only on the number of persons who pay to witness it, but on the length of time over which their attendances are spread. Even a million enthusiasts will not help if they arrive at the rate of ten per week. A thousand can do a great deal if they do it in two days. *Saint Joan's* present prosperity cannot in the nature of things last many months. Those who come early and come often are the pillars of the sort of play that gives you something to take home with you.

After the production of *Saint Joan,* I met George Bernard Shaw for the first time. That season, my husband and I went to London together. We were told that Shaw was in Scotland, but Oliver went around to 10 Adelphi Terrace where Shaw lived over a publisher's office. There was an iron grille to prevent anyone from going up, but you could see up the stairs. Oliver sent word that he was my husband.

The maid did not seem to catch his name but she went up to speak to Shaw.

Shaw came out promptly. "How many husbands has she?" he demanded. "I thought she was married to Langner."

He asked us to lunch the following day and we met Mrs. Shaw, Sybil Thorndike and her husband and manager, Russell Thorndike. Sybil Thorndike was playing *Saint Joan* in London and I was afraid I was going to like her performance better than Winifred's, but I didn't, for the simple reason that she wasn't young enough for the part.

Since then I have been accused of coming back from what was termed my "pilgrimage" to 10 Adelphi Terrace in "an awed and reverential" mood. Perhaps I did.

Shaw looked at me in surprise. "I expected you to be tall, blond, very Teutonic, dogmatic and rather mannered. I am surprised to find you the opposite."

"Why tall and Teutonic?" I asked.

"I thought anyone who was Executive Director of the Guild would have to have a German efficiency."

cutive Director Theatre Guild:
Theresa Helburn (1928)

Producer:
Theresa Helburn
(1935)

Lawrence Langner and Theresa Helburn

Directors of the Theatre Guild: Theresa Helburn, Maurice Wertheim,
Lee Simonson, Lawrence Langner; Philip Moeller, Helen Westley

Photo by Vandamm, New York

In Shaw I felt that elusive shyness, that almost fear he has spoken of: the fear of a sensitive, creative mind that cannot be itself with strangers. Mrs. Shaw was a delightful person, real and profound, and a perfect companion for the playwright. Indeed, Mrs. Shaw was the perfect wife. She never interrupted that torrent of speech. But also she never failed to watch, not only to make sure that he had whatever he needed but in case he made tactical errors and hurt feelings. Shaw was not an unkind man, but he was not particularly aware of or sensitive to feelings, and often his quick spontaneous speech and reactions inflicted pain or inserted barbs without his knowing he had done so. Mrs. Shaw, alert and tactful, was prompt to ease the hurt.

In the early Thirties I again saw Shaw, this time spending many more hours with him. I used to drive out from London for the afternoon, talking with him until the time came for him to have his tea and nuts or whatever he was having then, when I would leave.

When he had a lot of company he was apt, as he grew older, to be a little pontifical. He would sit on a fire bench in the center of the group and do all the talking. No one else said a word. This, of course, wasn't his fault. It was what they had come for. He was always satirical and amusing.

Once, when I had an appointment, it was postponed at the last moment. Nehru, he wrote, was planning to visit him so he had to put me off until the following day.

When I saw Shaw I told him I could not have yielded my place with so good a grace to anyone else, as I had a terrific admiration for Nehru. He was, I thought, one of the greatest living men.

Shaw nodded. He said his candidates for the Nobel Peace Prize were Nehru and Stalin. I was staggered.

"Stalin?" I echoed, not sure I had heard right.

Shaw nodded. "If anything happens to Stalin," he said, "there will be chaos in the world."

A few years later, when I was in London, I arranged to lunch with the Shaws. The day before, I had lunched with Mary Anderson Navarro, still with traces of her great beauty and still much concerned with her looks.

"Have I too much powder on?" she whispered before we went in to lunch.

She told me she once asked Shaw how he kept his skin so soft and white.

"I won't tell you," he declared. Later, he whispered to her, "I never wash."

In thinking of Shaw, I always find it hard to associate the giant intellect with the charming old gentleman with the rather feeble walk whom I knew in later years. But frail as he appeared, there was no time in the long and fascinating years of our close association with him and our production of his plays when his hand on the reins was ever feeble or uncertain.

When we planned to open the new Guild Theatre in 1924 we wanted a new play by Shaw to give our grand opening éclat. I wrote to him about it. He replied in some amusement that he was more accustomed to closing theaters than to opening them. At the same time he wrote to Lawrence:

Terry's latest is a request for a new play to open the new theatre next January. She should have saved up *Joan* for it. I have no more *Joans* in me.

A month later he again wrote to Lawrence:

I received Terry's demands for articles and so forth with the composure of a man swimming the Niagara rapids and being asked casually for a light. Terry thinks I have nothing else to do but job about as her press agent, and throw in a play occasionally. She should thank God for having done so well.

Press agent . . . The very term was a red flag to G.B.S. He called them "the silly young folk who become press agents because they are congenital unemployables."

Shaw sent a postcard saying:

Everybody wants to start a theatre on Shaw. I tell them that they who sow the seed must reap the harvest and that you have an option on all my plays. Loraine wants *Man and Superman!* But you had better reserve that. You can open the new theatre without sending to England for a crowbar. Anyhow, *I* won't.

But if Shaw had no new play with which to open the Guild Theatre, there were old plays available, and we decided to revive *Caesar and Cleopatra.* Shaw had written the comedy in 1898 for Sir Johnston Forbes-Robertson, "the only actor on the English stage," he wrote, "then capable of playing a classical part in the grand manner without losing the charm (and lightness) of an accomplished comedian."

The care for detail that was so typical of Shaw appeared in a letter that Blanche Patch — for many years his faithful and often disgruntled secretary — wrote me, enclosing the words for the crowds, which "are not to be spoken consecutively as dialogue but uttered simultaneously, as these stage noises never sound natural unless the people have real and different things to say."

Every year until 1932 we produced a Shaw play. Lawrence had coined the slogan, "When in doubt play Shaw." There was an interval when Shaw devoted all his energies to writing his *Intelligent Woman's Guide to Socialism*. We were doing *Pygmalion* then, in which Lynn Fontanne scored a terrific success as Eliza Doolittle, and I wrote to see whether there was a new play being written.

Shaw sent a postcard with his picture on it and the words, "No, dear Terry, nothing doing in the play line; but the big book is finished, and a return to more frivolous literature is in sight."

He added mischievously, "Glad to hear that *Pygmalion* is completing the ruin of the T.G."

Those plays are a matter of historical record now but there are moments that stand out unforgettably. To me one of the most poignant of all was in *The Doctor's Dilemma*. No matter how many times I saw the play I always wept at Alfred Lunt's death scene. I had to leave rehearsals before he reached that moment because he invariably made me cry. That was a splendid cast and beautifully costumed.

But Shaw was not satisfied. He studied the photographs we sent him of the production and immediately wrote to complain. One of his directions called for a lay figure on the stage. The director, he said, had provided instead . . .

. . . a marionette with all a marionette's intensity and persistence of expression. . . . It is as if I had prescribed a turnip ghost and you had given me the ghost of Hamlet instead. A good marionette (and yours is a very good one) can play any real actor off the stage.

Sell him by auction with this letter attached for the benefit of the Guild; and make a note for reference in future productions.

Shaw wrote again after we did a double bill with *Androcles and the Lion* and *The Man of Destiny:*

They tell me that *Androcles* is first rate, and *The Man of Destiny* quite unbearable.

I have seen a photograph of Raina and Bluntschli in which he is holding her in his arms in the bedroom scene. She would have screamed the house down and had him shot like a mad dog.

Your producer has no *dull*icacy.

Yah!

I sometimes doubt that any playwright has ever followed as closely as Shaw each phase of the production of his plays, even when done at long range. No detail escaped him. Not only must all his words be used, without cutting a single one, but his stage directions must be followed exactly. He knew precisely what he wanted in the way of stage sets and costumes. He saw clearly the manner in which he wanted each part to be cast. For the sake of future producers, it is worth quoting the letter he wrote me in 1928 about our production of *Major Barbara*. Here was one playwright who knew exactly what he wanted and made sure that he got it.

MY DEAR TERRY,

I do not suppose there is much danger of Winifred Lenihan making Barbara a low-spirited person with large eyes, looking like a picture on the cover of *The Maiden's Prayer*, though that is the traditional stage view of a religious part.

Bear in mind that Lady Britomart has a most important part, and requires a first-rate robust comedian and grande dame to play it; for the clue to a great deal of Barbara is that she is her mother's daughter, and that she bullies and bustles the Salvation Army about just as Lady Britomart bullies and bustles her family at home. Barbara is full of life and vigor, and unconsciously very imperious.

Cusins is easy for any clever actor who has ever seen the original (Professor Gilbert Murray). The next best model is perhaps Harold Lloyd.

Do not let Mr. Waram make the mistake of making up like a Thug as Bill Walker. In appearance he is just an ordinary young workman excited by drink and a sense of injury, not in the least like a murderer in a nightmare or a melodrama. He should be clean and good-looking enough to make the scene in which Barbara breaks down his brutality — which is a sort of very moving love scene — look natural, which it will not if Bill is disgusting physically and sanitarily.

The most effective dress for Lady Britomart is a Queen Mary or Queen Alexandra dress, long and purposely a generation out of date.

He added, "There will probably be one more play if I live another year [this was 1928] but if you tell anyone this until I give you leave I will never tell you anything again."

While Shaw was on his world tour in 1933 he wrote:

I can do nothing in the fashionable theatre at present prices. I shall leave it quite out of account henceforth. . . . It is time for the Guild to drop me, and for me to cease costing the Guild more than I am now worth to it.

A few weeks later, on the same trip, he wrote again:

I am writing myself off the theatrical map, partly through senile decay, partly because I am no longer interested in the sort of thing that has any commercial value in the theatre. Consequently, unless I can find a fresh set of desperados, standing where the Guild did in the days of *Heartbreak House* and *Jane Clegg*, I am out of the running.

Is there such a thing? If so, dear Tessie, give it the address of your superannuated, G. B. SHAW.

From the beginning I had been "Tessie," first because he found my handwriting difficult to decipher; later, I think, out of sheer stubbornness. Whenever he wrote to me as "Terry" he would add in parenthesis, "which I still maintain should be Tessie."

When I was in Hollywood in 1935, Shaw wrote in answer to a query of mine about having his plays done for the screen. If they were done at all, he assured me, he himself would have to do the scenario.

I contemplate the popular Hollywood productions in despair. The photography is good, the acting is good, the expenditure is extravagant; but the attempt to tell a story is pitiable; the people expend tons of energy jumping in and out of automobiles, knocking at doors, running up and downstairs, opening and shutting bedroom doors, drawing automatics, being arrested and tried for inexplicable crimes, with intervals of passionate kissing; and all this is amusing in a way; but of what it is all about neither I nor anyone else in the audience has the faintest idea.

For years I had been groping my way toward a new type of play with music, not musical comedy, not operetta in the old sense, but a form in which the dramatic action, music and possibly ballet could be welded together into a compounded whole, each helping to tell the story in its own way (this was the idea which finally crystallized years later in *Oklahoma!*). Unsure as I was of what I was seeking in the way of a new kind of play with music, I kept toying with various possibilities. One was to have *The Devil's Disciple* done with music.

I wrote in great excitement to Shaw about it and got a firm rejection: "My dear Tessie, after my experience with *The Chocolate Soldier,* nothing will ever induce me to allow any other play of mine to be degraded into an operetta or set to any music except its own."

Shortly after his world tour, Shaw settled down in England and my husband wrote to him for permission to include one of his plays in a textbook for high school students.

Messrs. Dodd, Mead & Co. [Shaw wrote to Oliver] were quite mistaken in their announcement that I consented to a school edition of one of my works. Nothing could induce me to do anything of the sort. I consented to the inclusion of a play of mine along with one of Shakespeare's and one of Dryden's because they dealt with Julius Caesar and with Cleopatra. The editorial preface had no special scholastic character and could not be used as an instrument of torture in schools.

My plays are published and available for students and teachers and everybody else just as I wrote them. All scholastic Europe has for years clamored for school editions with glossaries, notes, and introductions written by schoolmasters for the purpose of setting examination papers. The students like them because they need not read the plays but have only to memorize the notes. Unfortunately, that process implants in them a lifelong hatred of the author's name and all his works. It is now almost impossible to induce an educated Englishman or Englishwoman to go to a play by Shakespeare. I have no ambition to join him in the pillory.

Your proposal has greatly grieved me; and I am surprised that Theresa has not taught you better.

After 1933, there was a gap in our correspondence for some time. It was in 1940 that I wrote to him, in response to a comment he had made in a letter to Lawrence Langner:

DEAR G. B. S.:

I was very much touched that you should allude to me in your letter to Lawrence as "the faithless Terry" when indeed I am not. I am still your devoted Tessie and it has been a very real regret to me that we haven't been working on a Shaw play for so long. . . .

Meanwhile we are at work on a new play by the erratic young genius Saroyan, which comes in the latter part of the week. He is as independent of any conventional structure as the later G.B.S., and I might as well admit that so far none of his plays have even paid their production cost. His characterization is fresh and inventive but I am afraid he is a sentimentalist and lacks intellectual clarity or drive. Nevertheless, his plays bring a fresh breeze into a stale theater so we continue to do our best with them . . .

Why don't you write us a new play about revolution or what you will — in a neat conservative sugar coating so that our audience can swallow the pill before they know what they are taking, as you used to do in the old days? Well, I suppose that's too much to ask but I can't be blamed for a little wishful thinking!

My last memory is of the comment Shaw made on his ninetieth birthday. Lawrence and I had gone to visit him. "Remember," he said, "our conduct is influenced not by our experience but by our expectations."

In that phrase is summed up the philosophy of the theater.

◇◇ ELEVEN

Growing Pains

OVER TWELVE YEARS AGO, a statement was published crediting me with having been involved in the supervision of more Broadway plays than any other woman in the entire history of the American theater. By that time I had had a hand in most of the 157 productions of the Guild, a figure that has now grown to 176!

As I look back, it seems like a miracle that any play goes well. The turmoil of rehearsals, the hectic rush and chaos of technical problems that, for some reason, raise their ugly heads only at the last moment, and the unforeseen obstacles that throw a play completely out of kilter are all an inseparable part of the great gamble.

My involvement began as one of the members of the Board of Managers who had initiated, as the very foundation stone of their production structure, what we called "managers' rehearsals," and which we ultimately learned were known, not only among the actors backstage at the Guild but up and down Broadway, as the "Death Watch."

Attendance at these managers' rehearsals was the second most important and inescapable duty of the members of the board — the first, of course, being the incessant and unremitting reading of plays. In time, this system almost led to the disruption of the Guild; but, from its inception in 1919 until 1936, it was the method we chose to follow. And, though there were occasional bitter outcries from directors and actors and frequent yelps of anguish from playwrights, I still feel that it was effective and that the ultimate performance benefited greatly by it.

These managers' rehearsals were special complete run-throughs of every play, usually held on Sunday afternoon before our regular board meetings, two weeks and one week before the opening night. Naturally, it was no easy ordeal for the cast to run through a play only half learned and partially rehearsed before an audience made up solely of critics; an audience, moreover, of six people already familiar with the material, impervious to the stimulus of suspense, sitting silent and apparently unresponsive, pencil in hand, flicking on flashlights or cigarette lighters every now and then in the darkened auditorium in order to indulge in the menace of a critical note.

Our own players soon became accustomed to our production system and appreciated its value, but to the newcomer it was something to be dreaded. Perhaps we never felt individually important enough to realize we might intimidate anyone. But I know how difficult it was for a company unsure of its lines, only halfway into its characterizations, so to speak, to give a performance to an empty theater in which sat six silent individuals, harmless enough in themselves, but collectively — the management!

Nevertheless, harrowing as they must have seemed to the company, burdensome as they often were to the managers themselves — who might otherwise have been spending a quiet Sunday at home or holding high revel with friends — these rehearsals proved of incalculable value in the development of the Guild. After all, we chose the plays collectively; why should we not follow through the production collectively? If six minds were better than one in play selection, six minds should be better in judging the quality of the performance that was being given, the nature of the direction, the pace and tempo of the play, the emotional impact it carried.

In my opinion, production should never be a one-man job, for the director himself inevitably grows so close to a play during the repetitive routine of rehearsals that he loses perspective. In the careful building up of detail and atmosphere, he may sometimes lose sight of the larger issues at stake; or, obsessed by some sweeping idea, he may neglect essential minutiae entirely. No one is proof against the danger. I have seen some of the finest directors guilty of the strangest lapses.

I can recall a managers' rehearsal at which the director's whole attack seemed to us wrong, and had to be shifted; another at which an important character was entirely misinterpreted; others at which there was no tempo and no variety; one where the action, grouping and interplay were amazing, and no attention given to the reading of the lines, and so on. There are innumerable stops to be played in the symphony of production, and any one of them may be neglected or forgotten by a director in his intense concentration on something else.

Perhaps the most magic moment in the theater is that when the house lights are first dimmed, the footlights go up, and the audience sits in hushed anticipation for a moment before the curtain actually rises. But for me, some of the most exciting moments were the ones that followed close on the heels of a managers' run-through.

The stage manager would bang his fist on his little table and cry, "Curtain!" For there is no scenery or crew or actual rise and fall of a real curtain at rehearsals to help the illusion. Gradually the six of us shifted from our cramped positions, felt in the dark aisles for lost possessions, and climbed the rickety stairs to the stage. The company was greeted and hurried off home as quickly as was politely possible.

Then the managers, the director, and the author — if he happened to be alive and in the country — would settle down around an improvised table. There was a moment's pause; then each in turn would have his say: This actor is miscast; that scene is misplayed; the beginning of the act is too long; the end is too weak; there is too much action or too little; these values are not realized; those are overstressed. It is surprising how many things can be wrong with what might seem to an outsider an exceedingly good rehearsal. Accustomed by our board meetings to this give-and-take, no holds barred among ourselves, we were liable to forget that director and playwright might not be prepared for such bluntness. The redeeming factor was that though we might criticize we never blamed; and the director would ultimately realize that we re-

garded the fault as belonging to no individual but as the responsibility of us all.

Destructive criticism is death to the morale and the spirit
of rehearsal, and so we allowed ourselves to think only in
constructive terms. And the director, having passed through
the fire, usually found he had been enormously stimulated by
it; indeed, for all its fury, warmed and heartened. He had
had the preliminary reactions of an audience, but with an
opportunity still to rectify weaknesses. For the first time, his
play had lived and often he was the quickest to recognize the
weakness of this premature birth. At the second showing, the
child would be infinitely stronger, better balanced, more
articulate; and after this second showing, a week later, a further conference took place to help the infant, if possible, to a
long life and a brilliant one.

I have worked with many — perhaps most — of the great
directors of the world, but I have never known one who
could not benefit, at one time or another, by suggestions from
someone sitting in the back row and keeping his perspective.

Often, of course, it was not the director but the author
who was at fault, especially if it was a hitherto untried play,
and then the conference turned to a discussion of revision,
sometimes agreed upon then and there; sometimes delegated
to the author or director or these two in conjunction, if necessary with one or two members of the board.

Indeed, one of the factors that brought us an increasingly
large number of young American playwrights was the fact
that there were three professional playwrights on the board
who could — and would — give all the help that was in them
in the matter of rewriting. (How often in my diary I find

mention of "Spent morning [or night] rewriting Act III with ——"!)

But the Death Watch was frequently a rugged ordeal for the author, particularly if he was young and untried in the ways of the theater. I remember one occasion with special clarity. The playwright was a young American, new to the theater. The run-through was completed, the actors were discreetly shooed out of the theater, and we assembled on the stage, notes in hand, for the serious business of the evening.

Each member of the group was called upon for his or her reactions and everyone was so keen on correcting what he or she believed to be wrong that no one thought of mentioning what was right. We criticized without restraint play, actors, production. Miss A. was stagy; Mr. B. was underplaying; Miss C. had an entirely wrong slant on the character. The production was jerky and restless; this scene was underwritten, that one cliché; the ending was bad. This must be cut, that must be cut. Everyone was talking at once, in a vain attempt to be louder and more emphatic than the others.

At length, out of this seeming chaos, results were achieved, decisions arrived at. But in the meantime, I had caught the author, white-faced, sneaking out of the room.

"Don't go. We need you," I said.

"In God's name, if you all felt this way about the play, why did you ever buy it?" he exclaimed.

"But we're all crazy about the play," I protested, surprised. "That goes without saying. If we didn't like it, we wouldn't be working so hard to get it right."

We were, in practice, "the dog" on which the author might — indeed must — try his wares and prove them palatable.

I have dealt at some length with this system of managers' rehearsals for it was the keystone of the Theatre Guild production arch for nearly half its existence, and I believe we owe to it the high percentage of our successes over our failures, a rate considerably larger than the average. Of course, dress rehearsals were important, too, but not all of these were compulsory upon the entire board as the run-throughs were.

These managers' rehearsals, by the way, were held not only for each new production, but also for every play we re-produced later to send on the road. At times this business of being a manager of the Guild became more exacting for the members of the board than their other individual and private duties, whether as banker or lawyer, as artist or actor, as husband or wife.

Spinoza made one of the most profound comments I know on human behavior: "Men believe a thing when they behave as if it were true." We believed in certain values and standards for the theater and we behaved as if they were true. If we made mistakes, and heaven knows we did, we continued, though not evenly, and certainly not steadily, to move forward toward the goal we had set ourselves.

There was one thing that always baffled me. If a play were solemn enough, no matter how dull it might be it was treated with far more respect than if it were gay. Some of our self-appointed critics told us we were not being true to ourselves and our ideals when we produced certain light comedies.

And yet, in a sense, laughter is the essence of the theater. Comedy, not tragedy, is the real vehicle for social criticism, and it merits respect and serious consideration. The class war has had its day in the theater, heaven knows; enough even to satisfy those who, in the thirties, began to cry exultantly — or warningly? — "The theater is a weapon."

We did not regard the theater as a weapon. We still don't. It is not a forum, it is an art form. Men cannot grapple with their souls and the powers of darkness interminably. And laughter can be a strong weapon. So occasionally we presented comedies that may not have been "important" in any world-shaking sense, but were, I think, distinguished both in their civilized point of view and in their polished writing.

The first such comedy that we did was A. A. Milne's *Mr. Pim Passes By*. I remember reading it in the old Sherry restaurant and finishing it at two in the morning. That night — or morning — I cabled Milne for it. At the time, Leslie Howard was appearing in a play about the Prince of Wales and I went to see it, thinking we might cast him as Mr. Pim. There I discovered both Geoffrey Kerr and Phyllis Povah, who later appeared in *Mr. Pim,* though Leslie Howard did not. But my most daring action was to offer Laura Hope Crews, who seemed to me one of the most finished comediennes of her day, the exorbitant sum of two hundred dollars a week, when no one else in the cast was getting more than thirty dollars.

Up to then, light British comedy had been avoided by American producers. There wasn't enough "punch" in this delicate sort of fare to attract an audience. So I was a little anxious when the managers attended the first run-through of the play. Maurice Wertheim was sitting beside me in the dark theater when Laura Hope Crews walked on the stage. She was not young or glamorous in appearance and she had not bothered to dress for the rehearsal. She wore no make-up and no girdle. Her hair was straggling. She had put on a loose bag of a garment that seemed to be tied haphazardly around her middle.

"Is that thing," Maurice asked, aghast, "what we are paying two hundred a week for?" But he ate his words when he saw her caliber as an actress.

Mr. Pim Passes By played successfully for many months. In April, we took it up to Sing Sing, where we gave a performance for the inmates. When I remember the delicate comedy, it amazes me to recall how well it was liked by that uncharacteristic audience.

One member of that audience made later appearances at the Theatre Guild. As we entered the gates, one of the convicts, a trusty, approached me and said easily, "How do you do, Miss Helburn?"

I searched my memory but could not recall the man with the strange, inhuman, masklike face, the mechanical voice. This, I learned later, was what years of prison had made of him, stripping away his humanity, turning him into a robot. He was serving a twenty-year term for forgery.

"How do you know who I am?" I asked.

"Oh," he told me, "I know a great deal about you. I am ——'s brother. My sister was a classmate of yours in college."

A few years later, when I was casting *R.U.R.*, I needed a number of extras to play the robots. One day, I was told that a gentleman was waiting to see me, an old acquaintance. My secretary ushered in a man with an inhuman, masklike face. At once I knew I'd found my chief robot. Only afterwards did I realize that this was my convict.

He wanted a job, he told me, and he got it. During rehearsals he spoke to me once, in that odd mechanical voice of his, in the darkened theater where I was watching the performance.

"I appreciate your giving me this chance, Miss Helburn," he said abruptly. "I want to feel that I can make some return. I am not a poor man and if the Guild should ever care to draw on outside sources, you can count on me for anything up to one hundred thousand dollars."

I thanked him vaguely; the idea of the Guild accepting money from any source outside its subscribers seemed remote at that time.

Night after night, my convict appeared as the head robot in *R.U.R.* Then one Monday we received a lengthy telegram. He had been on his way to Baltimore to catch the opening of a Shakespeare play, he informed us, and he had been involved in an automobile crash. He would not be on hand for the night's performance. He never came back again. What he had actually been involved in was anybody's guess. Undoubtedly, he had pressing reasons for being elsewhere.

When we began to plan our Guild Theatre, I was frantically trying to think of ways and means of raising money for it. One day when I was thrashing out various plans in a meeting with lawyers and bankers I remembered this man's offer.

"My convict!" I cried exultantly.

This stopped all conversation, at least until I had explained. The businessmen listened, tried to maintain their gravity in the face of my dead seriousness, and failed. They broke down and laughed.

"But he meant it," I wailed.

"A forged check, perhaps?" they suggested.

Then one day Joseph ("Peppy") Schildkraut brought us Molnar's play, *Liliom.* "It's wonderful," he said, "and I want to play the lead."

We loved it and we wanted to do it, but we regarded the whole idea as a kind of personal indulgence. This was something we were doing just for ourselves. The public wouldn't like it; they weren't going to accept Liliom's resurrection from the dead. We were going to lose all the money we were making out of *Mr. Pim Passes By.* But after all, we reminded each other, that's why we wanted to make money, wasn't it, so we could plow it back into more and better plays.

Frank Reicher directed *Liliom.* When we came to the resurrection scene, there was a violent division of opinion. Reicher wanted to leave a death mask on the bier when Liliom rises from the dead. Reicher was a good traditional director, solid and workmanlike, and he felt more comfortable when a production was handled literally.

With some difficulty we persuaded him that this would destroy the effect. People will accept anything if you are wise enough to stir their imaginations and leave the rest to them. And so it happened. The audience provided the transition from death without trouble, while, if we had done it literally, they would have been revolted.

Peppy Schildkraut was young, electric, naughty and exciting. Keeping him in line was a full-time job. He had come from Europe, claiming to have played the lead in practically every production that had been done there. Which I was inclined to doubt. Peppy spoke German to Frank Reicher and Hungarian to the orchestra leader. To all women he spoke nonsense.

Never were there two such contrasting personalities as Peppy and Eva Le Gallienne, the young actress who played opposite him. All they had in common was a love of the theater and a European tradition of acting. Peppy was attractive and suave, an incurable flirt, and generally outrageous in his comments, which, muttered below his breath as he walked down through the theater, would send me into a roar of laughter.

Like his father, Peppy was an intelligent actor who wanted to do only good plays, but he was a child. If someone he knew was in the audience he would give a fine performance. The next night he would do nothing but walk through the lines. Later, when he was playing in *Peer Gynt,* I caught him more than once changing his lines.

"Oh," he would say naïvely when I charged him with it, "I didn't know you were out there."

Eva is a restrained and highly intelligent actress. In some respects, hers is a director's rather than an actor's mind. To keep the peace between Eva and Peppy proved to be a formidable task. One night Peppy infuriated Eva. With great control she went through the moving love scene. Then, when the curtain fell she slapped Peppy's face with a ringing sound that echoed backstage. It got to the point where Eva, in a rage, decided to leave the theater altogether. I persuaded her to hang on, a decision for which all theater-lovers are profoundly grateful, for she has had much to bring to it as actress, as director, and as creator of the Civic Repertory Theatre.

At the end of the first dress rehearsal I walked out onto Broadway, my heart soaring. "It will not be a great popular success," I thought, "but Peppy is fine and it is a fine thing to have done. I am proud that the Guild has done it."

And then the public liked it, too. *Liliom,* which Belasco, Brady and Hopkins had turned down, proved to be the greatest box-office hit we produced in our first three seasons.

At the same time, I was still trying doggedly to write plays. While we were busy producing *Heartbreak House, Mr. Pim Passes By* and *Liliom,* I was preparing to have two of my own plays put on by other managements: *Denbigh,* in which Alice Brady was starred, and *Other Lives,* which Eddie Goodman and I had collaborated on several years earlier.

I sandwiched the rehearsals between Guild rehearsals, try-outs, openings, lunches with authors, ironing out contracts, dealing with scenic artists, giving speeches and lectures, and making Peppy Schildkraut behave — a full-time job in itself.

With the production of *Denbigh,* I got my usual conflicting reviews. "It kindles mental fires," one critic said. This comment was tempered by another: "Not pinions but pinfeathers."

I see by my diary that my only reaction to the opening of *Other Lives* was "Better than I expected."

So we were encouraged and began to plunge ahead, to want to accomplish more and more, not merely by producing plays but by attempting to fill some of the needs that existed, that have always existed in the theater. One is for a permanent acting company. Another is for a school for actors. A third, one of the important — perhaps the most important — is some sort of try-out theater for the playwright. You can't have a playwright creating plays if there is no way for him to

see his work in an adequate production. If he feels his only
chance of production is one which will have a quick Broadway success, he is immediately, consciously or unconsciously,
conditioned as to the kind of play he will write.

Beyond these problems churning in our heads, crying out
for solution, was the desire to widen our audience. We had
learned that in New York there was an eager public for
good plays. But why should such a public be found only in
one city? We wanted to see our plays produced in every city
in America, from coast to coast.

Sitting around a fire or beside a pool in the garden we
talked about these things endlessly, not as distant dreams
but as practical problems to be solved. We lived them, as
Spinoza said, as though we believed them. And in the long
run we brought them all into being.

During the course of the next season, 1921–1922, we really
got into our stride, producing such plays as *He Who Gets
Slapped, Back to Methuselah* and *From Morn to Midnight.*
In the course of three years the Guild had made itself the
most exciting theater in America.

It was during the run of *He Who Gets Slapped* that the
first of our pet projects — an acting school — was put into
practice. It came about quite spontaneously. A group of
young extras found that learning the principal rôles as
understudies was not enough to occupy their time, and, with
Philip Loeb directing them, they began to prepare some
scenes of their own. The idea delighted me and I plunged
into it, as I do everything, with both feet. We were not only
going to train our own young actors, we were going to do

175

as other art theaters have done and establish an acting school.

Let me hasten to preface this by saying that I have never rushed around to all and sundry, urging them to act. When young people come to me for advice I say: "Don't act. Or, if you can't live any other way, at least don't start until you have enough money to keep you for at least six months or a year."

I have seen too many young actors, and old ones, too, out of work. Seen their growing anxiety, the beginning of fear, the pinch of want. Some of them just weren't good enough. Some of them were unlucky in being cast in a succession of flops. But for all of them the ordeal is grim.

An acting career requires endless patience, stamina, an immense degree of vitality. And, as Oscar Hammerstein said in one of his lyrics, "You've got to be tough." Not tough in any derogatory sense, but tough as opposed to being soft. You have to be able to take it. In any field, job hunting requires a certain degree of persistence. In the theater it is required to a fantastic degree.

But if you can't help it, if you must act, then at least you ought to have an opportunity to learn your craft properly. My personal opinion is that a great deal of formal education is unimportant. In general, I don't believe in a college education for actresses. The straight emotional actress is not helped by having her critical faculty developed too highly; it is apt to inhibit her emotions and develop self-consciousness.

Primarily, an actress must be a medium for other people's emotions. She must provide an uninhibited flow of projected emotion. Self-consciousness, like self-pity, spells the death of pity from the audience.

The only two successful actresses I know who are college bred are Helen Gahagan and Katharine Hepburn. Helen long since abandoned the stage for politics and Katie, in this as in most other respects, is a law unto herself.

Despite my encouragement, several seasons passed before the acting group at the Guild had any formal organization. It began with the young actors spontaneously turning themselves into a producing group called "The Theatre Guild Studio," with Philip Loeb directing them in scenes from well-known plays and with myself and Lawrence as their audience and critics. The group included Sterling Holloway, Edith Meiser, Romney Brent and many others who later on formed the nucleus of the Garrick Gaieties. It also included Armina Marshall, who married Lawrence, and as actress, director, executive and partner has been of immeasurable value to the Theatre Guild for many years.

This studio was, to be sure, a hesitant step, but it was in the right direction. Every art theater values a training school for young actors and my heart was set on it. Not until 1925, however, did a Theatre Guild Acting School come into formal existence. What we had in mind was an opportunity to train promising material for the Guild. It was not intended as a profit-making proposition; its whole purpose was to better the quality of the Guild casts.

We soon found that paying pupils were not necessarily the most talented, and eventually I scouted around and raised scholarships so that we would have access to the most promising young actors, whether they had funds to support themselves or not. I suggested that the group be called the Theatre

Guild Studio, and it functioned under that name for the few years it existed.

During this time it fulfilled its purpose admirably. Among the young people who came out of that school were Sylvia Sidney; Romney Brent; Lucia Chase, who later headed the Ballet Theatre; Arlene Francis; and Cheryl Crawford, who became one of the founders of the Group Theatre and is now a producer on her own.

From a first meeting at the Guild Acting School developed my rewarding friendship with Cheryl Crawford. Cheryl came into my office — a slim boyish figure, looking extremely smart in a very attractive dress — and informed me that she needed a job. At that time we were losing a casting director, who was really just a keeper of records. It was a small, part-time job, and I offered it to her. Cheryl said she couldn't afford it. So we added to the part-time job a tiny part in the current play, which doubled her salary.

It was some time later that I learned just how terribly Cheryl had needed that job. The smart dress had been given to her. Both the electricity and gas had been turned off in her apartment and she was practically penniless.

The afternoon when she rehearsed for her part, she told me later, she was scared stiff. She could hardly speak. And then she heard my voice out of the darkness, startling her half to death, say, "Speak up, child. Don't be afraid." From that time on, Cheryl lost her nervousness over public appearances and later I often had her replace me and others in making subscription speeches to the audience between acts.

Shortly after Cheryl became my assistant in the casting

department I went abroad for my vacation. Cheryl turned up at my hotel in Paris.

"Would you like to take me for a drive in Spain?" I asked her.

Cheryl would. Could she speak Spanish? She could. (Of course she could. If I had asked for Hindustani or Malay she'd have doubtless known those, too.) Fortunately, my French and a one-inch Spanish dictionary helped to supplement Cheryl's "Spanish."

Neither of us had had the foresight to take our driving licenses with us. So when we went to hire a car in France we discovered that we would have to take driving tests. Then we ran head-on into a mass of red tape. No license without a test. No test without photographs. So we went back to have our pictures taken at a photomaton, "Six for the price of one." Then an appointment was made for us in what seemed to be the most inaccessible part of Paris. There we waited in the heat.

At length a middle-aged, very official Frenchman with a drooping mustache arrived, laden with a sheaf of documents. We asked about our applications. He shook his head.

"Not here," he said.

I turned very executive. I looked over his shoulder at the papers. There on top was my application, my picture in the very dress I was wearing.

"That's it," I said triumphantly. "That's my picture."

The official turned to look at me. "Oh, no, madame," he protested. "You are twenty years younger."

That epitomized the French in one sentence. Never have

I felt more charming, never have I been closer to the *femme fatale*. I even drove better than usual.

We started for Spain in a 13-horse-power Citroën, which Cheryl ultimately named *Doucement,* as it was a word I had occasion to use frequently during the next few weeks. We climbed mountains over beds of loose pebbles, where the Citroën developed a tendency to go backwards, and where, in one day, we had eight punctures.

At length, we reached a small hotel in the mountains behind San Sebastián, the Royal Household's summer residence. Never have I visited so prophylactic a place, with everyone washed so clean, inside and out, every day. Or so moral a place. Every day we rode down to the beach, where we found that no sun bathing was countenanced. Cheryl and I were nearly foiled in our intention to acquire a tan. At length, we were forced to sit on the beach, cautiously moving our shoulder straps a half-inch at a time, under the watchful and reproving eyes of the guards.

It was a difficult trip in some ways, but there is nothing like a little stress and strain to build a friendship. Out of that trip grew a fast friendship between us that has survived the tensions of show business and even the high emotions generated by the Group Theatre; a friendship that stands firm and sound today.

TWELVE

The Man at the Helm

THE VERY HEART of a production, of course, is the director. In the days of the old stock company, his function was a simple one. He just served as a kind of traffic manager to move the actors around the stage so they wouldn't run into each other. But today he is, in the best sense, the collaborator of the playwright; he transforms the words on the printed page into action; he gives the play motion and life, pace and meaning.

One of the most frustrating features about the theater is that you cannot achieve results directly. You must work through someone else to get the effects you are after. The director has to walk a kind of tightrope and never lose his balance. He must find the right line between giving the actor his head and exerting his own authority. He must establish complete rapport with the actor and make him feel that he has absolute confidence in him. *The most important thing a director can give is confidence.* This takes a lot out of one emotionally. And a director can't inspire confidence unless he has confidence himself.

Piscator, a brilliant director, later associated with the New School of Social Research, was handicapped when he came to America to direct *High Wind in Jamaica* for us. Because he had never produced in this country and did not know the ropes, he lacked confidence. He never managed to assume control of the production. Instead of making clear to the actors what he expected of them, he talked and talked, explaining. They talked back.

At the end of a few weeks' time there had been so many interpretations of the play bandied back and forth, so many points of view freely expressed, that no progress had been made. At length, we were forced to replace him with a director who could hold the reins with a firm hand.

The balance of a play is a delicate thing. You depend on the emotions of the actor. If he is upset, where are you? He has to be convinced that he is doing right and doing well. In many cases, an actor is more important to the audience than the play itself; thus the results that the director can get from him are as important as whatever work the director does on the play. I have known poor plays to go over and good plays to fail entirely on performance.

A director learns to build up the actor's assurance four inches before he cuts it down one inch. He must not, to reverse Hamlet's dictum, fret his actors but play upon them, as a conductor learns to draw out the proper combination of tones from the various choirs of his orchestra.

It still amuses me to recall a letter from a young director who wanted to work with the Theatre Guild: "Mr. Langner wants to know do I get along with people? Hell, I've got so much unrationed patience and kindness and love it's probably against OPA regulations. "

Of course, there are situations where even the most tactful handling will fail to gain the response you are after from the actor. Sam Behrman told me of watching rehearsals of a new play in Paris. One day, sitting beside the director, he remarked, "It seems to me the leading lady is too theatrical. She is overplaying the scene."

The director called the company together. After going over his notes, he turned to the leading lady, who also happened to be his wife.

"Darling," he said in melting and cajoling tones, "you have so much to carry. Be careful not to do too much in the second act. Save your strength for the third."

"So I was acting badly, was I?" his wife snarled.

"No, no," he said hastily. "Just hold back a little."

"Who are you?" his wife screamed. "What do you know about acting?"

As he remained discreetly silent, she poured out vituperation like lava, covering his shortcomings as a director. And she flung over her shoulder as she headed for the wings, "What's more, you've been a lousy lover for two months!"

Perhaps the second most important thing for the director is to have an over-all picture of the shape of the production and to be sure that he can build within that framework, that within the framework every scene has its own structure. Some directors come in with a completely clear picture of what they want. Others leave everything up to the actor for quite a long while to see what the actor himself has to bring to the part.

My own rule would be: Let the actor give you what he has before you give him anything. An actor may get off on the wrong tangent, but usually, if he is worth his salt, he will have a lot to contribute.

True, I have occasionally known stars who absolutely refused to take direction. In that case, you are stuck. You have hired a theater, made contracts with actors and playwrights, become heavily involved with expenses, and you are going to have a poor production.

At the Guild, we had the chance to observe and learn from some of the finest directors in the field. First of these was our own Philip Moeller. In the best sense of the term, Philip was an amateur and in this, I think, lies the secret of his success as a director as much as of his weakness. He never went through the usual apprenticeship to the craft.

His method was what he himself termed "inspirational" as opposed to what might be called a "structural" approach. It was absolutely impossible for him to sit with a script in advance of rehearsal, to review its weaknesses or plan the scheme and detail of the production. He wanted to keep himself fresh for that first impact of the play when read. Often he got some of his most brilliant ideas during rehearsals. He had a wonderful sense of overtones and undertones, the subtleties which characters can give to each other and which establish liaisons that are not in the lines.

Sometimes Phil seemed almost to hypnotize himself with the mood of the play. During rehearsals of *Dynamo,* for

Alfred Lunt and Lynn Fontanne

Cartoon by Eric Peters: Armina Marshall, Lawrence Langner, Theresa Helburn

Photo by Edward Ozern

Oklahoma!: Richard Rodgers, Oscar Hammerstein II, Theresa Helburn

Sunrise at Campobello: Theresa Helburn, Eleanor Roosevelt, Dore Schary

Photo Friedman-Abeles

example, he became possessed by the unreal, mystic values. For the time being, he allowed himself to be bewitched by them, blind to the obvious faults of the play — with the result that he was enabled to carry the cast with him on a wave of enthusiasm to a splendid performance.

Phil was a curious and temperamental person. In some ways, his theory of improvisation was a great asset. In some ways, it was not. While he could achieve marvelous results with experienced actors, he was not so effective with the inexperienced, who needed firm guidance and were baffled and confused by his methods. Some directors are primarily teachers. Phil could not teach acting. He was no actor and he did not want to become one. His timing was brilliant and in comedy he was unequaled. But he had his blind spots. We used to say rather wistfully that it would be nice if Phil would read a play before he produced it.

For instance, I have always felt that he misunderstood Shaw's intention in *Saint Joan*. Shaw had added salt to the play by making his Inquisitor sweet and gentle as a person. Phil insisted that he be cast as the typical Inquisitor, dour and grim.

As an example of a director's contribution to a play, I think especially of Philip Moeller's work on O'Neill's *Strange Interlude*. The board had fought bitterly over producing it — "The *Abie's Irish Rose* of the Intelligentsia," Alec Woollcott was to call it bitingly — and its supporters, of whom I was one of the most ardent, had won after a wild battle. We fought again over the production. It was Philip's idea which carried the day. His was the suggestion to make the thoughts and the speeches stand apart by having the characters remain motionless when they thought and move when they spoke.

The importance of Philip Moeller's contribution to the Guild is indicated by the fact that he directed more than half of the productions of the early years, a long and brilliant list, ranging from *The Guardsman* and *Fata Morgana* to *Mourning Becomes Electra* and *Ah, Wilderness!*

The first Russian director with whom I worked was Robert Milton, who certainly had imbibed some of the elements of the Stanislavsky method, though he did not call it that. One of the chief things I learned from him was his method of building up a play's characters as actual entities if the playwright had failed to do so. He gave each character a background, created for him a beginning and an end, worked out for him the sort of environment from which he had come and into which he would go, thus enabling the actor to grasp more fully the psychology of everything he had to do in the play.

My own method was not to provide the character's background but to leave it to the actor to do so.

"I do not get the feeling of this person," I would say. "Go home and think it out tonight. Get acquainted with his thoughts and his reactions. Discover what made him become the person he is and why he reacts as he does."

What can be done by a director, especially when aided and abetted by an actor, in changing the entire character of a play was revealed when we produced *He Who Gets Slapped,* with Robert Milton directing and Richard Bennett in the leading rôle. We had thought that we were putting on a sardonic, bitter play until we attended the first run-through. Between them Dick Bennett and Bob Milton had transformed it into a romantic comedy.

We had a terrific argument the afternoon of the first run-through. The last scene ended with Margalo Gillmore dying. At least, that was what she was supposed to do. But she collapsed so gently that it appeared like a faint, brought about by exhaustion from her previous emotional scene.

When we stormed up on the stage after the run-through, we demanded excitedly, "But does she die or doesn't she?"

"Well," Bob said gently, "let's just leave it open."

"But this is supposed to be a bitter, ironical Russian tragedy and we think the audience should know that she dies."

"It will go better my way."

"It is beautiful as you have done it," we admitted, "but this is a play about Faust and not about Christ."

Dick insisted on playing it like Christ. That was the way he saw it. Of course, given half a chance, any actor will leap at the chance to play Christ. And, as a rule, when he does so you are lost.

"Don't worry, children, it will run," Dick told us confidently.

The dress rehearsal began at midnight and ended at five in the morning, because Margalo Gillmore was playing in *The Straw* by O'Neill, which was closing that Saturday, and she could not come until after the performance. And that morning we were still worried. But on the opening night, we knew that we had a hit and Dick was beaming. "I told you so," he said.

His interpretation, though it had completely altered the intention of the play, making the theme one of suffering instead of bitterness — a play about the cruelty of the world transformed into a play about one unhappy human being — made it much more successful than it had any right to be.

In this case, it was the actor, more than the director, who set the mood of the play. Bob Milton, I always believed, was not sure what the play was about. Dick Bennett was both experienced and decided in his opinions.

"This is the way," he said firmly. And so it was.

On the second night, responding to enthusiastic applause, Dick Bennett came out to make a curtain speech. We were horrified. An art theater did not lend itself to such demonstrations.

"Folks," Dick said breezily to the audience, "thanks very much. Now don't let them tell you this play means anything. My daughter, age eight, was here last night and she loved it."

He withdrew, highly pleased, and we were stricken. But the audience loved it, too! And the play thrived.

Another Russian director who did some effective work for the Guild was Theodore Komisarjevsky, who came from Moscow to direct *The Lucky One, Peer Gynt,* and *The Tidings Brought to Mary.* Komisarjevsky was able to effect an amazing fusion of line and color, but his approach was the opposite of Philip Moeller's. Philip served the script. Komisarjevsky used it primarily as a vehicle for expressing his own production theories, which completely dominated the play.

In another respect, Komisarjevsky's approach was the opposite of Philip's. Phil, by his "inspirational" method,

groped his way into the meaning of a play, his ideas developing as he went along with rehearsals. Komisarjevsky saw the
complete realization of a play before he started rehearsals,
saw everything in terms of the play as a whole.

Apparently, the Russians are trained in the structural
approach, in seeing the whole play clearly before they start
production.

Each method had its advantages, each its weaknesses. I
have long since come to be impatient with adherence to any
single "school" in the theater, whether in directing, in acting, or in playwriting. Each has its values, each its shortcomings, and only — I believe this most strongly — by having
an open mind, by welcoming each style and exploring its
possibilities, can a theater attain richness and variety, can
it achieve growth. To be limited to a single style of acting,
of producing, of writing, is, eventually, to become sterile.

When any theory becomes dogma — a play must deal with
such material and no other, an actor must use this technique
and no other, the staging must be experimental or conventional or some one way and no other — it is not new life but
death that enters the theater. My personal Declaration of
Independence is: Be hospitable to all, be a slave to none.

To sum up, while plays must have variety, a single play
must not change mood in the middle; while a director may
have a single theory of production which he follows completely, the theater itself must welcome all theories, all
methods, all ideas.

The director is, he *must* be, the man at the helm. While
it is of benefit for the management to point out weaknesses

189

in the production, the underlying authority of the director must not be shaken or you are going to land in the department of utter confusion. I have also mentioned the importance of the director's concept of the production as a whole. An actor may often have brilliant insight into his own part. But he may lose sight of the balance of the play. It is up to the director to make him understand clearly what is expected of him in relation to the whole.

And to make himself clear, the director must be clear himself about what he wants to accomplish. One of our most pointless disasters occurred when we persuaded the Lunts to appear in Shakespeare's *Much Ado About Nothing*. They did a brilliant job of acting. The parts of Beatrice and Benedick were naturals for them. It seemed as though Shakespeare must have imagined the Lunts before he started writing. But Robert Edmond Jones, who directed, was not always as successful at achieving results as a director as he has been in so many of his scenic designs.

Bobby is a charming person, with an unclouded relation to his art and a gift for making beauty out of nothing. His plain set for a sordid saloon in *The Iceman Cometh* will always remain in my mind. In *Much Ado About Nothing* he had started with what he believed would be a tremendously effective and different way of presenting Shakespeare. On either side of the stage, Bobby had the respective dressing rooms of Lynn Fontanne and Alfred Lunt. As he had supposed, the audience watched in fascination while the famous couple changed costume and put on make-up. What he had overlooked was the simple fact that he was not merely exploiting the Lunts, he was producing a play, but with the

audience's attention riveted on two characters who were
"off stage," the main action might as well have been taking
place in another theater. Bobby finally realized this staging
was untenable, changed his mind, and ended with a totally
different idea. The play had to be withdrawn before it came
to New York.

Now that the psychological possibilities of Shakespeare's
characters have been almost exhausted, and often distorted
by modern Freudian interpretations, which, I suspect, would
have stunned Shakespeare with horror, about all that is left
is novelty of production. Today, what with Hamlet in love
with his mother, Iago in love with Othello, Richard the
Second turned into an effeminate, and Julius Caesar into a
brownshirt army, I'll settle for novelty as opposed to interpretation.

The director does not need to have the manner of a dictator in order to maintain control. Worthington Minor, who
directed the Lunts in *Reunion in Vienna* with so much
sparkle and tempo, believed that it was unnecessary for a
director to have temperament, which was a refreshing note
in the theater. He was aware that, without a definite personality, the director cannot impose his ideas, but he proved
that there need never be a clash between the director's ego
and that of the actor.

One of the most colorful of directors to swim into our
orbit was Orson Welles, who had all — and more — of the
traditional theatrical temperament. He produced *The Five
Kings,* his own synthesis of the Shakespearean historical plays.
His methods were unique, expressed with vast assurance —

but he could not maintain control. He liked to be surrounded by a large group of underlings. For instance, he had not one but six stage managers, one for each of the five kings and the spare for himself.

At the time when we were attempting to do Mr. Welles's version of Shakespeare, I was in Philadelphia with *The Philadelphia Story*, which was starting its tryout tour. Lawrence was in Boston, wrestling with Shakespeare and Mr. Welles.

Each night after the performance I would telephone Lawrence in Boston. "How was the dress rehearsal?"

"We haven't had one yet," Lawrence would reply. There seemed to be some confusion. By the time all the stage managers had signaled to each other they had missed the cue. It was too late. The play was out of control.

At length, when I called one night Lawrence said glumly, "There isn't going to *be* a dress rehearsal."

"But why?"

"Orson wants to have the dress rehearsal after the opening."

The play with its six stage managers never came into New York.

Rouben Mamoulian came to the Guild in 1927 to direct *Porgy*. Known before long to Broadway as "the Mad Armenian," he had been impresario of the Rochester American Opera Company. He taught me the value of rhythm. He produced not only a definite tempo in dialogue but a rhythmic movement of the body and a rhythm in the entire cast. In *Porgy, Porgy and Bess, Oklahoma!* and *Carousel,* Mamoulian brought something new and beautiful and stirring into the theater and added, I think, a new dimension to the contribution directors have made to the stage.

It is typical of the theater that Rouben Mamoulian achieved one of his greatest effects by sheer accident.

We were at a dress rehearsal of *Porgy.* Someone had left one light on in the footlights, which threw shadows on the stage.

"That's wonderful," Lawrence said.

"We'll use it," Rouben decided.

After that, no Mamoulian production was complete without that effect, which became almost a trade mark.

So far as I know, Mamoulian was one of the first to adapt the techniques of different media to each other. He adapted opera technique to the theater. Then Bing made a reverse switch and began to use theatrical technique in opera, beginning with his production of *Così Fan Tutte,* directed by Alfred Lunt. Now dancers have become theatrical directors. We are getting all our media beautifully mixed up, and the result may prove to be an enrichment of all.

Rouben, particularly in the beginning, gave you a sense of knowledge and experience that were beyond his actual experience. I've never met a director who was so marvelous in dealing with actors. I have known him to work in detail on almost every single word with an actor who lacked previous experience or training. There is rarely a cast with which he has worked that does not adore him.

He is a charming person, stimulating and delightful to work with — except where money is concerned. Rouben has no intention of becoming another "starving Armenian," a phrase, by the way, which rouses him to frenzy.

"Starving Armenians," he muttered once. "My first memory is of my mother working for starving Americans after the earthquake in San Francisco."

In fact, the attitude of the American press toward Armenians was an abiding annoyance to him. Once when he was asked where he was going he said mockingly, "Armenians never *go* anywhere. They flee."

When we were planning to produce the Gershwin musical version of *Porgy* — called *Porgy and Bess* — Mamoulian came up to Lawrence Langner's house at Westport to discuss the new musical play with us. On his return to New York he sent us a bill as a joke:

Traveling expenses to and from Westport . . . .$ 8.20
Professional advice 5000.00
P.S. In view of our previous close association, please disregard the first item.

Elia Kazan, one of the greatest directors, started his career as stage manager on a John Howard Lawson play I directed for the Theatre Guild.

It is difficult to define Kazan's method. He is quiet, sympathetic, and handles a cast like a conductor with an orchestra, or rather like a musician with a violin. He is perhaps the most fundamentally kind man I have known in the theater. He has a strong feeling for the basic idea of a play and for its architecture in building scenes. He always felt that there should be a big scene in the last act just before the curtain, that the success of a play depended on it. Actually, however, I don't remember one of his plays that had it.

Kazan's primary interest is social significance. I sometimes think he finds social significance in a play whether it is there or not. This he carries over into his personal life. "Gadge" — I've never known how he acquired this nickname — looks rather like a young laborer, slightly unkempt, an appearance which he makes some effort to maintain. He has done much for American acting and has probably been the leading exponent of the Stanislavsky acting methods on the American stage.

It is interesting to note how completely unlike these two brilliant directors are in their approach. Rouben is the more aesthetic; he has an exquisite sense of design. Gadge works hard to get at the meaning of the play. Rouben can work with a group. Gadge told me, not long ago, that he has to work completely on his own. "Just leave me alone," he said. "I know it is foolish but I can't help it. I have to make my own mistakes."

Rouben sees the play pictorially. Gadge digs constantly for the roots of meaning. Rouben has lovely embroideries of action and design. Gadge has exciting production ideas.

Rouben can get his effects by a kind of synthesis, as he worked the cleaning women into the jazz ballet of *Porgy and Bess*. Gadge gets his effects only by working through his actors. Rouben is an artist in the plastic sense. Gadge has an eye primarily for social implications.

◇◇ THIRTEEN

Coming of Age

IN THE YEAR 1923, a bare four years after the Theatre Guild had started on hope and a shoestring, we felt that the world was our oyster. The dreams of a few years before became, or were in the process of becoming, a reality. In the next six years we were to accomplish all that we had set out to do, more than we had ever guessed we could do. Those were the years, the brave bright years, in which the Guild made theatrical history. They were our golden age. Artistically and financially we built a structure unique in the annals of the American stage.

They were also, in a way, the highest peak we reached. The end of our first decade coincided with an event of somewhat graver importance to the country than the flourishing state of an art theater. That was the Depression of 1929. Inevitably, it proved to be of importance to us, too. Then came the talkies, which were even more important to us.

There followed the Thirties, with want stalking the western world and the consequent growth of economic unrest and political radicalism. And then the Second World War shook the civilized world out of its solid familiar patterns, followed by the Korean War, and the Cold War which hovers about us still, with its menace and its uncertainty.

At no time has the Guild ceased or diminished its efforts to expand its functions as producer and wide distributor of fine theater. At no discernible time in the future will it do so. But the greatest art requires a more stable world, an atmosphere from which the dust has settled, earth that has been cleared of its rubble. If we have not again reached the peak of 1929, I feel convinced in my bones — for I cannot imagine a world without great plays — that the peak will be reached again and surpassed, far beyond our present vision of what great theater can be.

Early in 1923 we decided to build a theater of our own. We talked it over at our board meetings. Everyone agreed that we needed a theater badly. The Garrick was too small for our expanding audiences; the stage too cramped for the kind of experimental productions we wanted to do; that dusty attic office was inadequate for all the purposes it was called upon to serve.

By March, we had decided that, since the Guild's whole structure was co-operative, it would be in keeping to make the new Guild Theatre a co-operative affair, too. We would sell $500,000 in 6 per cent real estate bonds to buy land and build the theater. As executive of the Guild I was in direct charge of the campaign to sell the bonds. Never before had I attempted to raise money — this antedated the minor scurrying around for scholarships for the Studio — but, of course, if you want to accomplish a thing badly enough, you can do it. And we did!

No one could swing a thing like that alone. It was done as a combined result of the faith of the public in us and the help given by the executive committee, which met in a vacant loft beside the Garrick and sat on packing cases while they drew up their campaign. Lawrence and Maurice Wertheim and I were on the committee, of course. It seemed pleasant and logical that Professor George Pierce Baker of the 47 Workshop should be there too. So were Walter Lippmann and Louis Untermeyer, refugees from the old evenings of play readings. Mrs. August Belmont and Otto Kahn, who had both done so much for art in New York, were also members of that committee. Later, Mrs. Belmont was to put our subscription system to work at the Metropolitan Opera Company.

By the following month we had raised more than the amount we had set ourselves, $542,800. When the four Marx Brothers each subscribed one hundred dollars, I announced jubilantly, "Now that our most formidable competition are bondholders, we have nothing to fear!"

This was to be a bigger theater than the Garrick, one that could take care of subscribers, who, at this time, totaled 18,000 and had to wait a month to see a play. The extra seating capacity would also bring in more money and help pay the expenses of more elaborate productions. In a way, we were all rather worried about the size of our new theater. The Garrick seated 550; the new theater would have 930 seats. Were we going to be able to project our intimate type of drama in so large a theater?

Work on the Guild Theatre went ahead. There were endless conferences on the countless details involved in building a new type of theater: design, materials, a huge stage, lighting, acoustical problems, decoration. All this was added to the regular work of play reading, casting, rehearsals, openings. The hours of the day bulged at the seams.

Governor Alfred E. Smith laid the cornerstone in December, 1924, and the following April 13 President Coolidge pressed a button in Washington that tinkled a bell in New York and raised the first curtain of the Guild Theatre on Shaw's *Caesar and Cleopatra.*

The theater was beautiful. My own office impressed me as much as it did anyone else. We went around in a proud daze.

I don't know when the first doubt, the first vague shadow of surmise began to trouble us. Somehow, the seats, which had seemed so frighteningly many, were already beginning to shrink. Within a few years we had 32,000 subscribers in New York alone, and the public was storming the ticket office. As we grew more successful and acquired bigger actors and playwrights, their agents began to demand bigger royalties. The Guild Theatre couldn't bring in the income they insisted on. They wanted the Shubert with its twelve hundred seats. In time, we found that we were putting our successes in other people's theaters and our failures in the Guild. Our beautiful Guild Theatre eventually proved to be a beautiful and costly white elephant.

When, during the Second World War, we finally moved out of the theater, we drew a long sigh of relief. Like Mayor La Guardia, when we made a mistake it was a lalapalooza.

No one can write of the Theatre Guild without writing of the Lunts. Their contribution to it was immense, as has been their contribution to the theater as a whole. They are not only two of the most highly gifted actors of the modern stage, they are two of the most indefatigable workers; tireless in their unending search for ways of improving their technique; continually growing in a part until the very last performance, no matter how long the play may run; fascinating to watch in rehearsal because of their technical finish; changing from part to part, from comedy to tragedy, from classics to moderns, from sophistication to simplicity.

It is one of my most rewarding memories to know that I cast the Lunts in their first play together and so began an association which lasted for many years, probably the longest actor-producer relationship. During this time they played as wide a range of parts as any actors on the contemporary stage, expanding their technique, widening their scope from year to year, until they became the most flexible of all actors, as well as the most popular couple in the American theater. But what a struggle it was to get that first play for them!

Early in our career we had bought Molnar's *The Guardsman*. Some years before, it had been produced in New York and had been a complete failure. None the less, we believed that, with the right cast and the right production, it could be a terrific success. The problem was to find the right cast.

The agent who handled the play turned down every possible suggestion. He wanted Lionel Atwill and Violet Heming for the leads. No one else would do.

To me, two brilliant young actors playing in New York at the time, Alfred Lunt in *Clarence,* and Lynn Fontanne in *Dulcy*, were naturals for the parts and I wanted them. The agent said no.

In despair, I called Otto Kahn, who took me to lunch and let me pour out my troubles. I am always grateful when I recall the patience and the helpfulness he showed on the many occasions when I took my doubts to him. A typical occasion was when we started to put on *Processional*. People were bombarding me with the incessant comment that it was too modern, it just wouldn't go.

Mr. Kahn nodded his head. He was then, as he had been for many years, a patron of the Metropolitan Opera Company.

"Well, at the Met," he told me, "the revolutionary work of one season is the conservative of the next. Don't worry. Just as you establish your frontier, you will find that you have to move on."

This time, when I had explained about my casting problem, I asked, "How can I reason with this man?"

Otto Kahn shook his head. "You aren't dealing with a man's reason," he pointed out. "You are dealing with a man's vanity. That is a much tougher nut to crack."

In the long run, all I could do was to give the agent an extra 10 per cent to get him to concede. But he never admitted, even after *The Guardsman* scored its great success, that he had been wrong.

There are a certain number of run-of-the-mill actors, and even a few excellent ones, who by the opening night have crystallized their concept of their part and, from that time on, never change it by so much as a gesture or an inflection. The Lunts are different. They do not repeat. They keep acting, adding, testing, getting good new ideas. They believe that no one can get the full feeling of a part in the first few months. It has to grow.

No matter how long they play a part, a year in New York, months on the road, they are always constantly working, changing, improving, developing as they go along so that each performance is a kind of new creation. This was not merely the enthusiasm of youth, which faded as they grew older; it is still an intrinsic element in their approach to any part they do.

I can remember a typical occasion, when they had been playing with us for more than twenty years. I had been in Hollywood and stopped over in Chicago to catch their performance. At that time, they had been doing the same play for nearly three years and they were nearing the end of the run.

After the performance, I had a late supper with them. While we were talking I noticed that Lynn wore a bandage on her leg. I asked what had happened.

Lynn explained that, in the last act, when she had to run across the stage in the dark, she had tripped and fallen, gashing her leg.

"You know," Alfred said abruptly, "just at that moment I had a swell idea for a new piece of business."

The Lunts are contrasting characters in every respect; they differ widely in temperament, but they so complement and supplement one another that the resulting teamwork is almost unequaled on the stage. Their timing, their capacity to listen while the other speaks, to build little nuances of characterization without words through their interrelationship, is the best lesson I know for young actors who find it difficult to absorb the fact that the most important part of the actor's job is learning how to listen.

Alfred is an example of the actor's temperament, suicidal and desperate. I can't remember a single play in which, sometime during the rehearsal period, he did not surrender his part and decide to abandon the stage forever.

"Let someone do it who is good in the part," he would say wildly. Partly, I think, this was a need for encouragement, especially from Lynn, but heaven knows part of it was genuine enough. How genuine this humility of Alfred's is can be seen in a letter he wrote to Warren Munsell one summer from Finland, when he and Lynn had long been regarded as among America's greatest actors, and certainly the most popular.

Night after night [he wrote] I keep waking up in a cold sweat, having had some horrible dream about our fall tour or the Guild's next season. Not a very happy vacation habit, I must say, but I do feel we are right in not playing a New York season in the fall. For one thing, I don't think the plays, except perhaps *Idiot's Delight*, would do business and I truly believe that that fair city is sick to death of us, let alone the subscribers. Maybe the road feels the same but that we must risk. I would still like to make a tour with *Idiot's Delight* and that's why I cabled what I did about Baker. If his production is better than ours so much more reason for not playing "return dates" and if it's not as good the same reason holds true. We worked like hell on that play and nearly killed ourselves (so did the company) "keeping it up," and that plays some part, too . . .

Just between you and me, I'd like to settle down in Sweden

and give the theater a nice rest for a year or two. That would be bliss!

All this beautiful weather and me writing instead of swimming.

For God's sake — ALFRED

Lynn, on the other hand, has never lacked confidence for a second. She may be angry, perhaps, but she is coolly angry. She is strong, sure and confident.

I remember when she first came here many years ago, a rather awkward English girl who showed her gums when she smiled. She was not beautiful but she was a good actress. By her own efforts, she has made herself one of the most beautiful women in the theater today.

This contrast shows up clearly in their differences as directors. Lynn can always show an actor just what to do and how to do it. Alfred will and can only suggest gently, hesitantly, with an actor's great sensitivity and a real humility. Lynn senses the actor's weakness and her method is a strength-giving one, while Alfred's is a stimulation to the actor to develop his own performance from within. Lynn gives the needed support directly; Alfred always directs an actress as Lynn would play the part.

But how completely they supplement and balance each other! A brilliant and beautiful tiger married to a gentle lion with a thorn in his foot. There is always something tortured in Alfred, something a little cruel in Lynn. Alfred never stops feeling, Lynn never stops observing. The perfect combination: Clarence and Dulcy. It can be no accident that these two were destined to come together.

It was like the Lunts to present Sherwood's Pulitzer Prize

Play, *There Shall Be No Night,* in London during the height of the bombing. They felt their services were needed. It was typical, too, that an American flyer inscribed their names on every bomb he dropped over Germany, as a token of their feelings.

"Hitler has no sense of theater," Alfred complained. "It's not that we particularly mind air raid warnings during performances; what makes us furious is the Fuehrer's dreadful timing. He always makes off-stage noises during the most quiet scenes of our play."

From the beginning of their careers until now, when, after their brilliant production of *The Visit,* they threaten to retire ("not bored," they say, "just surfeited"), leaving the stage impoverished by their absence, they have been prodigious workers.

Once Lynn declared rather heatedly, "The Theatre Guild isn't an art theater. It's a sweat shop." But that wasn't entirely our fault. Alfred is so steeped in theater that he cannot rest while any problem, dramatic or artistic, remains unsolved. Upset as he always is over his own "inadequacy," he is always able to cope with any situation that arises.

For instance, after the war, when they came back from their long absence in England, they took their new comedy, *O Mistress Mine,* to Washington. There was a terrific snowstorm the night of the opening and the scenery failed to arrive. Alice Longworth and Perle Mesta had met me at the station and we sat together during the performance. Just before the curtain rose, Alfred appeared, in costume and make-up. "We are sorry that the scenery was delayed," he said. "There will be none. Anyone who wants his money back can have it. It will, somewhat reluctantly but promptly, be refunded."

No one left the theater and the scenery was not missed. When I went backstage Alfred said jubilantly, "I've always wanted to play without scenery. We rigged up a few curtains and no one missed scenery at all."

Another reason for the Lunts' phenomenal success in the theater was that they knew exactly what they wanted. As plays began to be sent to them in perfect showers, they read and analyzed them carefully.

"We have both struggled," Alfred wrote about one script we sent him, "sitting up, lying down and on our hands and knees, trying to get through the ms . . . but I honestly do not think either of us is enthralled in any position. I have read and played in a lot of Greek tragedies, and I find them easygoing compared to this one, and I advise you to get some actors with horse blood to play in it, for it will take an awful lot of strength. Maybe it is a great play, and my knowledge of English is at fault, but I am dumbfounded by the whole thing."

The idea of my casting Alfred Lunt in the part of a bootlegger in *Ned McCobb's Daughter* amused many people. But he was splendid and the very change of type had a stimulating effect. From the beginning, we gave them widely different parts. Lynn, for instance, was as fine as Eliza Doolittle in *Pygmalion* as she was in *Strange Interlude*.

In the beginning, the Lunts were interested primarily in good parts, but before long they wanted more — they wanted good plays. It began to seem as though every playwright in America was writing plays for the Lunts. This was not always an easy situation, because it involved two clashing points of view: that of the actors and that of the playwright. Was it to be a good play or a good vehicle? The two are not necessarily the same thing. Frequently, the author's intention was altered completely by the Lunts' insistence on the kind of parts they wanted to play.

I can remember the harassment of Sam Behrman when he wrote a play for them in 1937, and then rewrote, rewrote, rewrote. His own ideas conflicted with the Lunts'; there was an endless struggle between Alfred's sound ideas for a vehicle and Sam's sound ideas for a play.

In 1935, Alfred became a member of the Board of Directors of the Guild where he remained until the Lunts went for a time with another management. It was an exciting period for the Guild. Now and then, there were explosions of temperament; Alfred was particularly sensitive about any criticism of Lynn, though he did not mind it for himself. Now and then, there would be a roar of complaint about conditions, particularly on the road. I can remember one outraged blast in which Alfred declared, in speaking of some California cities, "The SPCA wouldn't allow animal acts to appear in some of the places we've been put in."

Theater is the most ephemeral of the arts. A great painting remains on exhibit. A piece of sculpture or a work of architecture is a permanent memorial to the artist. A symphony may be played over and over. A book may be endlessly reprinted, if it has something to say. But a play has its little hour upon the stage and then, too often, is seen no more.

Repertory alone can keep the great plays of the world

alive. Once they have been produced they can be done over and over through the years. After the Guild Theatre had been built, Lawrence became increasingly emphatic about his dream of repertory. (An art theater always dreams of repertory.) But you can't have repertory without a resident acting company; and our acting company, as Alexander Woollcott had commented sardonically, consisted of Helen Westley.

The advantages of a permanent acting company are obvious. A group of players who act together, year after year, in a number of parts, develops a perfection of ensemble playing. Instead of breaking ground with each play, the actors who have played together are way ahead. They have mastered a number of acting styles.

The long-run play has always been bad for actors — except financially, of course. People frequently complain that certain actors have no versatility; but it is hard to tell when they remain in one part for a long time. With the repertory system, they may do three or four widely different parts in a single year and increase their scope far beyond what they or anyone else thought possible.

We had learned to our sorrow the problem involved in putting our actors into classical parts. We had to start at the very bottom, as though they were beginning, to instill in them the technique of speaking verse, of methods of acting at variance with the styles required by contemporary plays. We had discovered, too, that when we brought in foreign directors, as we frequently did, they had a terrible time coping with actors who had not worked together and who had no experience with different approaches to acting.

"You can't," Lawrence insisted, "achieve even a modified repertory without an acting company. It's absolutely impossible."

The value of a permanent acting company was brought home to us with terrific impact when the Moscow Art Theatre visited the United States in the Twenties and we saw for ourselves the wonderful performances turned out by a group of actors who had been trained together.

So the Guild created its permanent company. It started with Helen Westley, and included the Lunts, Dudley Digges, Henry Travers, Ernest Cossart, Claire Eames, Margalo Gillmore, Glenn Anders, Tom Powers, Edward G. Robinson, Claude Rains, Earle Larimore and Philip Loeb.

Repertory is always being tried out but, except where there is a state-endowed theater, it bogs down, sooner or later, because of the vast expense entailed. The financial problem is this: while you have to carry the salaries of all the members of a permanent acting company, you cannot employ all of them in every play you do. You've always got a lot of economic dead weight. Well, then, if we couldn't fit them all into one play, why not rent another theater and produce two plays at a time? Certainly with two plays going we should be able to cast the whole company.

This sounded all right, but we discovered in practically no time that it was no easy task — in fact, it was impossible — to select two plays and provide appropriate parts for all our company.

At this point, we quadrupled our original idea. All right then, we would produce four plays at a time. Our actors wouldn't mind having a poor part in one play if they could have a good part in the next.

This, in turn, entailed a prodigious amount of work because it quadrupled the tasks that fell on all of us: casting, rehearsing, etc., etc. We were producing the four plays on alternate weeks. Each actor came fresh to his part every Monday, so that he was doubling the number of parts he could play in the course of a year and thus increasing his versatility and building his technique.

This was all fine for the actors and good for theater itself. It was also good for the audience, because it provided additional theatrical fare. But the labor involved was incredible and the financial strain enormous. If you advertise four plays instead of one, for instance, you have to quadruple your advertising appropriation. If the public has to look up dates in the paper to see which play is being presented at the time, they are less likely to bother than if they know it is running steadily. And if one play goes well while another is met with apathy, you have another problem on your hands.

As a result of the stresses and strains of production I remember that I once got so thoroughly confused that I cast Edward G. Robinson in two plays that were to appear at the same time. Even Eddie couldn't do that.

When our repertory system really got into its stride, we reached out for the next logical step. Why couldn't we find good audiences outside of New York as well as inside? In 1923, we had sent out a few plays under the management of J. M. Gaites. Now we got to work in earnest. Within five years, we had subscription audiences in Baltimore, Boston, Cleveland, Pittsburgh and Philadelphia.

Ten years after we made our debut with *Bonds of Interest* and 139 subscribers, we found ourselves in an almost unparalleled situation. Beginning with *Pygmalion* in 1926 we had had eleven successes in a row. One out of five is a good record and we had something like two out of five. But in 1929, we had four hits playing in New York and seven plays on the road. We had 200 actors and 75,000 subscribers. We had presented 70 plays and given 9000 performances.

On that tenth birthday, Burns Mantle wrote: "Nothing is more exciting than the winning of an obstacle race. In ten years, from bankrupt beginnings, [the Theatre Guild] has become the dominant play-producing organization in the world."

◇◇ FOURTEEN

Chips and the Block

IN JUMPING AHEAD to our golden age in the theater, I have neglected the Studio, our acting school, which had begun so spontaneously. Through the Twenties the need for some kind of acting school had been growing all over America. Before this, young actors had learned their job in the only satisfactory way. They had learned it professionally, starting at the bottom in the old stock companies, learning first things first, and advancing step by step as they acquired technique and absorbed their craft.

Then the movies came along and the old stock companies practically went out of existence. There was no longer a professional training ground for young actors. Training was almost entirely on an amateur level. It began to reach a point, more than twenty years ago, when the sources of trained theatrical people had almost dried up and there was a growing danger that the theater would dwindle because of an acute lack of actors who knew their jobs.

That was the need which the Studio attempted to fill.

While it came to an end within a few years, it was to leave behind it two real gifts to the theater: one was the *Garrick Gaieties;* the other was the Group Theatre.

Probably the most important change in the art of acting in the twentieth century was developed by Stanislavsky at the Moscow Art Theatre. For a generation his was a name to strike an actor with awe. He taught the actor to identify himself with the rôle and help the spectator to live the part with him. It was an effective method and it has done much for theater. It was especially helpful to the "made" actor (as opposed to the instinctive actor) to learn the technique for creating emotion, the so-called conditioned reflexes of Stanislavsky. But carried to extremes, treated with reverence as a cult instead of with common sense as a technique, it becomes more pretentious than it is worth. In perspective, it is one of many ways to convey emotion on the stage — not the only way.

I suppose what bothered me most about the Stanislavsky method was its uncomfortable parallel with the training of Pavlov's dogs, a category in which I would grieve to put actors, and a concept which I find degrading and humiliating.

One point, I think, is sure. Whether the actor learns to convey emotion through conditioned reflexes or by any other technique, he must understand the emotion. This has been brought home to me in working with Christian Scientists, who, conditioned by their religious beliefs, have no grasp of the more violent emotions of sin, hatred, evil, and therefore cannot convey them convincingly on the stage.

Lawrence and I once asked Stanislavsky, "Will you direct a play for us?"

"I will be interested," he replied. "Of course, I will need two years." Art is long and time is short. Equity allows only five weeks at most for a production. That ended that.

I do not wish to downgrade Stanislavsky, who had a great impact on the theater as a whole and for whom I had a great respect.

"There are no little parts," he said, "there are only little actors." And this, I think is profoundly true.

When Komisarjevsky was in New York we discussed our acting school with him and explained what we were trying to do. The Russian director shook his head. "You can't have an acting school in the attic," he said firmly. "You must have it in the cellar."

What he meant was that we had to train our actors from the beginning, and as rapidly as possible we must absorb them into the Guild acting company.

After talking with him, I worked harder than ever to involve the students in the acting school with the work of the acting companies. The weakness of the situation was that the Guild was doing sophisticated plays in which there was no place for beginners. We could rarely fit our students into our productions, and that left an unsatisfactory gap in the structure.

But from that time on, I became deeply involved in the problems and activities of the younger generation. I did not, of course, try to teach acting in the Studio. I couldn't have

done it if my life had depended on it. My knowledge of acting was not first hand. Rather it was acquired partly from
books, partly from in front of the curtain, and mostly by
talking to directors and actors.

But I did try to find practical ways of helping them. For
some time the young group in the Studio had been working
on scenes from plays under Philip Loeb's direction, preparing an act of *You Never Can Tell* and doing *Fata Morgana,*
which the Guild later produced for its subscription audience.

The youngsters, for practice, began going about doing
songs and sketches for charity or social functions. Many of
these were at the home of Lawrence Langner who was then
engaged to marry Armina Marshall, a member of the group.
One day a lawyer friend of mine, Benjamin Kaye, brought
two young men to see Lawrence and me. Their names were
Richard Rodgers and Lorenz Hart. They had been writing
some songs and sketches which they hoped might be put on
in a special performance at the Garrick some Sunday night.

Sitting on the empty stage of the Garrick, Dick Rodgers
played the songs and Larry Hart, a slight frail youth, not
over five feet high in spite of his elevator shoes, sang them
for us. When they came to the song "Manhattan" I sat up in
delight. These lads had ability, wit, and a flair for a light
sophisticated kind of song.

Rodgers and Hart — the names fit together now, in our
memories, like a pair of gloves; but it was a strange collaboration. Dick was a responsible young man even then; Larry
was irresponsible. Dick was increasingly poised and sure;
Larry was increasingly unsure, increasingly unpoised. I can
see him, so small, so frail, so conscious of his diminutive size,

215

beating his hands together in a characteristic gesture as he walked up and down; gradually drinking more and more, gradually destroying, almost deliberately, the witty mind, the sweet nature, the fine original talent. Together, he and Dick, in so short a span of years, brought color and music and gaiety into the theater. But he should have had so much more to give.

They got to work, and we provided what help we could: the free use of the Garrick for two performances and five thousand dollars to finance them.

They put together a new kind of show, the first intimate revue, which they called the *Garrick Gaieties* and which they rehearsed in my old attic office and on the stage after evening performances of *The Guardsman* were over. Among the members of the youthful cast were Armina Marshall and Carolyn Hancock (Mrs. Lee Simonson). A minor member of the cast was Lee Strasberg and the stage manager was Harold Clurman, whom we had hired a short time before as play reader. The two latter members of the troupe were soon to branch off in a special enterprise of their own.

After a long period of rehearsal, Dick Rodgers came to me to say urgently, "Please pack up the Lunts and let the *Gaieties* open."

The Lunts finished their run, and we expected the *Gaieties* would have a few Sunday evening performances.

The dress rehearsal was to start at 11, and I sneaked out of the house by the kitchen door, as my husband did not approve of my working all night. The rehearsal went on until eight in the morning, and for once, I was almost sorry to have the rehearsal period end. It was the first time I had done any work in musicals and it seemed that, no matter how weary one got, there was always the music to keep one going.

The *Garrick Gaieties* had an engaging quality, which grew not only out of the lilting music and the witty lyrics but out of its light-hearted capacity for laughing at itself. The first night's response was so terrific that we put the *Garrick Gaieties* into a regular run for our subscribers, and so one promising group of young people was launched on its professional way.

For several years, there were annual editions of the *Gaieties*, and then Dick and Larry became involved in the writing of their highly successful musical comedies. For years, I bombarded them with my obsession: plays combined with music. I wrote Larry, urging him to work on O'Neill's *Marco Millions,* on two of Sherwood's comedies, *The Road to Rome* and *Reunion in Vienna,* and on Aristophanes's comedy *Lysistrata,* in which I wanted to cast Ethel Merman.

But Larry answered fewer letters, he was harder to find, he was drifting away from us all, physically and spiritually, seeking degradation as an escape from some inner pain that was intolerable to him. Without his sparkling wit Sardi's wasn't Sardi's for a time. By the time *Oklahoma!* had crystallized in my mind, at long last, Larry could no longer work on the book.

At the opening of the *Garrick Gaieties* the first thing that struck the audience was the youth of this new revue: young actors, young composer and lyric writer, young thinking and feeling. Even while we rejoiced in this flowering of youth, it gave us a queer feeling. The Guild had been a young group, only a few years ago; and here, in our own theater, was a younger generation, chips from the block. Why, we discovered, we were middle-aged!

But if the youngsters of the *Garrick Gaieties* made us acknowledge middle age, the next chip off the block practically made us feel the oncoming of senile decay.

Three young people associated with the Guild in different capacities — Harold Clurman as play reader, Cheryl Crawford as casting director, and Lee Strasberg who had a few small parts in Guild plays — felt that we were getting behind the times and that they could inject new blood into the theater.

A new approach is always a good idea, and I wanted to give the group a boost, although Harold Clurman's definition of theater was a trifle over my head: "Theater is philosophy in a fleshed design of action." Nor did I feel that any theater would be able to grow if it followed a single point of view, a single school of thought, a single method of acting. In the long run, one generation's radicalism is the next generation's conservatism, and the one-school man is apt to be hoist by his own petard.

At the time these three set to work, the world was unlike the one in which the Theatre Guild had started. We had begun in a period of prosperity. The young people who entered the theater after 1931 were coming into a depression world. They were thinking in terms of economics. This was no longer an abstract science, it was something that affected daily life and the amount of food in the larder.

Because people never seem to be able to do things by halves, the youngsters of the Thirties were not content to criticize the weak spots that had developed in our system; they wanted to scrap the whole thing and start fresh. Harold Clurman summed us up: "A sort of summation of the intellectual trend of the time on both their position and their negative phase was unconsciously presented by the Theatre Guild."

I was not a radical myself, but radicalism seems to be a part of youth so I felt I should be sympathetic toward the point of view and feelings of this group. In any case, I was sympathetic toward the young, particularly those making their way in the theater, and I was eager to help in any practical way I could.

At that time, the first Soviet play to reach America, *Red Rust,* had been sent to us and we had taken an option on it. I called Harold Clurman in to my office and told him that we'd like to do it as a special Sunday night performance and suggested that the three youngsters see what they could do with it. They put it on, with a fair degree of success.

The young group then decided to branch out on their own, but it was not until I saw notices in *Variety* that revolt was brewing in the Guild that I knew anything about it. I talked to Harold Clurman. It was true, he said, that they were working out some ideas of their own; something rather more far-reaching and profound than the Theatre Guild had attempted. A technique of the theater, he explained loftily, had to be founded on life values. However, when they had selected their actors and completed their plans, they would be glad to tell the Guild Board of Managers what we could do for them.

By now they called themselves the Group Theatre, and

Herbert Biberman, who had spent some time in Russia and had acquired a pseudo-Meyerholm technique, directed for them. They used the Stanislavsky method and seemed to follow Stanislavsky's theory of plenty of leisure in which to produce a play. They spent months in training their actors in the "conditioned-reflex" technique and in rehearsals. The first summer they lived in a camp at Brookfield Center, Connecticut, and the second summer at Dover Furnace, New York.

That second summer I went up to Dover Furnace to visit them. The whole place was more than casual. The company seemed to be spending most of their time sitting around in undershirts reading Karl Marx. There were no such bourgeois amenities as locks on bathroom doors.

"Are you Communists?" I asked.

"We are making up our minds," they explained.

To the best of my belief, none of the founders of the Group Theatre ever became Communists. But there was a small group on the fringes whose cry was "The theater is a weapon," and who endeavored to turn the whole organization into a Communist cell for propaganda purposes. I am happy to say they never succeeded.

It is difficult for many people to recall the emotional atmosphere of the Thirties, and to see its effects on compassionate young people. In the overwhelming number of cases, they were simply searching for ways to right wrongs, with no self-seeking of any kind, and most of them left their excesses behind as their world stabilized.

For the Group Theatre, the influence of the Moscow Art Theatre provided an additional attraction in Russian ideas.

Both Cheryl Crawford and Harold Clurman went to Russia for brief periods, to explore the stage there. Naturally they found it exciting and stimulating.

In moving away from the Guild activities, Harold and Cheryl opposed us as the older generation. "I was severe with the Guild," Harold remarked later, "because I was young and because it no longer satisfied the demands of the generation that was to burst forth in the Thirties. It was looking for something new, for something else." We were a group of old fogies who had manifestly outlived our usefulness, and our only surviving purpose, apparently, was to support them while they showed us the error of our ways. This was not an attitude that simplified things for me in trying to persuade the board to give them money for the Group Theatre.

I still remember the high blood pressure registered at the board meeting when Harold told us what they wanted to do, what they expected us to do, and made clear that we belonged artistically among the dinosaurs. The board, for once, was quiet. In fact, it was speechless.

Their actors, Harold said, were prepared to do new types of plays and ours could not. Men like John Howard Lawson, for instance, were not as interested in seeking playwriting technique as in "ideological clarity."

"We want to establish a theater," he told us, "not merely a production organization."

"What do you mean by that?" Lee Simonson asked.

"A theater," Harold explained, "is a homogeneous body of craftsmen to give voice to a certain point of view which they share with the dramatist, whose works might be described as the most clearly articulated and eloquent expression of the theater's conscience."

There was a moment's blank pause. Phil Moeller recovered first. "What is so new about that?"

Lawrence, who had been following all this in a kind of daze, listened to Harold's account of how the Group could influence dramatists.

"Do you think," Lawrence then asked almost gently, "you would have anything to tell Eugene O'Neill?"

"Certainly," Harold replied with magnificent confidence.

Things went from bad to worse, and when I tried to get money for them, the members of the board began to fight back.

"Why the hell should we do anything for them? They are kicking us in the pants."

"I know," I admitted. "But they are young. They should be helped."

The young group felt that we should give them both plays and money, that we should support and sponsor them, but we must keep our hands off. So far as the Guild Board of Managers was concerned, the Group Theatre did practically nothing to win friends and influence people. Nevertheless we released to them Franchot Tone and Morris Carnovsky, who were under contract to us; we turned over to them two plays, Paul Green's *The House of Connelly* and one called *1931;* and we provided seventy-five hundred dollars to help with production. I even tried to arouse some public interest in what they were attempting to do at a talk in Town Hall:

The Group Theatre is attempting an important experiment in maintaining a permanent company with a single production method back of it, and attempting to integrate its authors and designers with the fabric of a theater as a whole. But it is up against tremendous odds in a city like New York, where costs are so high and competition is so keen. . . . The American theater is an uncertain gamble from start to finish . . .

Should any good-sized city in America offer the capital to finance a strictly professional theater for the production of new as well as old material over two years, I would be tempted to leave home, husband and Guild, to prove to them that a vital theater could not only be created beyond New York but that the third year could even show a profit for the organization . . . But I am safe. No one in the theater ever looks three years ahead . . .

The Group Theatre, needless to say, was radically different from the Guild. According to Equity rules, we had four or five weeks in which to produce a play. The Group Theatre, for the most part unsalaried and living a kind of communal existence, took as many months. Their approach to acting always left me mildly stunned. Watching from backstage the antics of the young members as they got in the mood for their entrance — imagining the death of a friend or calling up some emotional stress of the past — I found that at times it was only a small step from being ludicrous. The aim of the Stanislavsky method, according to Harold Clurman, "is to enable the actor to use himself more consciously as an instrument for the attainment of truth on the stage." I was irresistibly reminded of Bacon's comment: " 'What is truth,' said jesting Pilate, and did not stay for an answer."

But the thing that was the sharpest change from our concept, "the play's the thing," was the Group theory of the

function of theater, of its message. If the play did not provide the proper message, they felt justified in changing it to
suit their needs. They did this with *The House of Connelly,*
changing the author's intent and the ending from tragedy to
"a helpful message."

Once the theater starts being "helpful" it runs into danger.
It can be helpful only in terms of one individual or a single
group with its own concept of what constitutes being helpful.
Therefore, with the best intentions in the world, they find
themselves not serving a play or serving art; they are dishing
out propaganda.

At the run-through of *The House of Connelly* the board
members were greatly disturbed. The Group wanted us to
put up all the financing for the production. We explained
our point of view in regard to keeping the integrity of the
author's intention and they heard us out impatiently. Their
attitude was that of the child toward its parent: "That may
have been all right in your day." We ended up giving them
half the money for production and they had to raise the rest
of it themselves. If they had been disgusted with us before,
they were bitter now. However, they managed to raise the
money and *The House of Connelly* was successful and got
them off to a good start.

Later, I suppose, we both helped and hindered them. We
helped them when we put on our subscription Saroyan's first
play, *My Heart's in the Highlands,* which they had produced.
Though everybody loved it nobody bought a ticket. I think
it did two hundred dollars a night.

On the other hand, we were wrong, I think, in our action
on an earlier venture. My recollection of this play is dim; I

must have thrust it out of my mind as fast as possible. It was a pioneer opus with a crowded cast of American Indians. I have a memory of howling Indians running around frantically. It struck me as being a cartoon rather than a play.

The Board of Managers sat through the run-through, looking more and more stricken, wide-eyed with disbelief. Then Helen Westley cried out with her usual vehemence, "This is terrible. It must stop." And we stopped the production then and there. That, I think, was a mistake and caused needless bitterness. I don't mean that our opinion on the production was wrong, but they were young and, instead of stopping the production, we should have taken the time to explain, to show them that they had gotten on the wrong track, and let them make the decision about the play.

In any case, after *The House of Connelly* the Group Theatre became a separate organization. They were on their own. Perhaps it was just as well; sooner or later the break would have had to come.

The Group Theatre existed for ten years before the perennial problems of the art theater forced it to come to an end.

In the course of this comparatively short life, it provided high standards of acting and two fine playwrights, Clifford Odets and Irwin Shaw. For this the theater as a whole must be grateful to them.

◇◇ FIFTEEN

The Battle of the Ban

IT HAS ALWAYS struck me as odd that one of the freest minds ever to write in English should have been directly responsible for the censorship law governing the stage which still shackles England. Henry Fielding, before he wrote *Tom Jones,* had been busy turning out popular plays for the stage. Then he wrote one in which he excoriated Walpole, who set in motion the machinery that drove Fielding from the theater and put a crippling ban on it which has been a source of irritation to this very day.

Just when the censorship threat began to raise its ugly head in New York I'm not sure. I imagine it was after Mae West produced *Sex* and another opus of the same kind, which the police had closed. The outraged moralists began to cry for stronger censorship laws to protect them from exhibitions of this kind. In the midst of the sound and fury, Gilbert Miller presented *The Captive,* a play as unlike *Sex* as could be imagined; as different as a great painting is from an under-the-counter "art" book.

226

Pressure groups got to work on the New York State Senate to bring in a censorship bill that would have really tied up the American theater. I leaped into the fray. The Theatre Guild called a mass meeting. At the end of the meeting I proposed a new type of self-censorship, which would, I hoped, save the theater from further inroads upon its freedom by outside groups.

But before I spoke, Joseph Wood Krutch, my old friend and neighbor, and the *Nation's* most brilliant drama critic, got up.

"I don't know what Miss Helburn's plan is," he said. "But whatever it is, I am against it."

He made the point that if we established our own code of censorship we were admitting the principle of censorship. All we were demanding was that it should be more intelligent.

He was right, of course. I was just trying to help the theater maintain jurisdiction over its own activities, operating on a basis of good taste.

What we were aiming at was a balance between plays that endanger the morals of the theater, and censorship that endangers the existence of the theater. "We are all theoretical anarchists," I said at the time, "who want absolute freedom, and would be practical anarchists except that we know it won't work out."

H. L. Mencken spoke his mind roundly on the subject:

"In general, I am against any sort of censorship. It is always stupid, and usually it is also dishonest. The public taste, I believe, is a sufficient check for all ordinary purposes. When and where that taste is so degraded that it delights in unmitigated filth, such filth will be duly provided for it, no matter

227

how many pious laws are passed. But there is no sign of anything so lamentable in New York or anywhere else in America . . . No play ever written was ever half as filthy as the mind of the average volunteer censor."

When the censorship law came up for debate, a Committee of Nine was formed to look into the situation.

Shortly afterwards, a member of the State Legislature came down to see us. He looked around and smiled benevolently. "I'm sure," he said, "that none of you ladies and gentlemen would like to see sex perversion on the stage."

Only Arthur Richman and I spoke up. Not because we had any particular fondness for the subject but simply because you can no more stop it in the theater than you can in life. What exists will get into the theater if the theater is alive at all. Nothing real can be kept off the stage.

The Committee of Nine went up to Albany to state our case. Arthur Richman, who was beside me, looked around the chamber and shook his head.

"Just look," he said in a tone of despondency. "It's no use talking to these men. The theater doesn't mean a thing to them. They're the kind who go down to New York for a pornographic fling once a month. They won't understand what we are talking about."

About all we accomplished on that trip to Albany was to postpone voting on the bill.

From that time on, I found myself called upon for speeches on censorship. One of them was at the Community Church in New York, where I pointed out that "The question of the morality of a play is the motive behind it." I tried to point up the growing tendency toward standardization in American life and the contribution of the motion pictures to this standardization as factors harmful to the theater. I pointed out that a spirit of revolution was necessary to keep dramatic art alive.

Because I had been so outspoken on the subject and was fighting tooth and nail against censorship, the *New York World* arranged for a meeting between me and John S. Sumner, Secretary and leading light of the New York Society for the Suppression of Vice. As we were two of the key figures in the battle of the ban, the *World* evidently felt that our meeting would make sparks fly. Here is a transcript of that curious dialogue as it appeared in the *New York World,* February 16, 1930.

Sumner: When you use the word censorship you are starting all wrong. Censorship is merely an unpleasant word, used against us by the enemies of our work. What we are after is simply a set of laws which shall insure the spiritual and mental health of citizens just as our Pure Food and Drugs Act or Narcotic Law protect their physical health.

Helburn: You may call it anything you wish, laws, censorship, taboos — the fundamental thing remains unchanged. Let us get down to essentials. In the first place, do you feel that these laws are at present working in a satisfactory way?

Sumner: Yes, fairly so. Except that they should be more strictly and more consistently enforced!

Helburn: I just wanted to determine that! Then, since you speak of health, why is it that in an age when physicians and psychologists have brought us complete evidence and proof that taboos on sex, that shame and sex-suppression are immensely injurious to spiritual and mental health, people who say they are fighting for humanity's welfare still insist on such taboos and such suppressions? Why do you still, against all knowledge, wish to darken and dwarf our plays, our books, all the fertile expression of our art, with the old religious fear of sex-expression?

Sumner: You mustn't think it is all sex we are concerned with. I think that certain plays that show in detail the workings of the minds of criminals should also be suppressed. We have such a law at present concerning printed matter — a law which upholds our right to bar writings which incite to "bloodshed, lust and crime." We should have similar legislation concerning the stage. I attempted to enforce this law a few months ago when a notorious tabloid newspaper made flagrant infringements. Unfortunately, the case was lost.

Helburn: Let us stick to the point. At the present time, there is no legal ban in the theater except on obscenity. And, by the way, Mr. Sumner, when was that obscenity law passed?

Sumner: The passage in reference to obscenity in the theater is No. 1140-A of the Penal Laws. It was passed in 1909.

Helburn: Yet since 1909 our conception of what I suppose you call morals has drastically changed. In some aspects, this obscenity law is now as outmoded as that still unrepealed statute left over from the Puritan days which forbids a man to kiss his wife on Sundays.

Sumner: There are some moral concepts which never change, a basic morality that will always govern human action and should govern such things as plays and books.

Helburn: Oh, you believe in a fixed and absolute moral code? How curious! What then are to be those eternal moral laws? Do you consider monogamy one of them?

Sumner: No. Murder is one of them!

Helburn: What about war? Do you think that should be censored?

Sumner: Killing in war is not a legal crime! There must be malice to make it legal murder.

Helburn: But I thought we were discussing a higher morality. I consider the waste and stupidity of war much more criminal than enraged personal murder. And that its malice is a wholesale product is not exactly mitigating. But let's find another example. Spartan mothers, when the birth rate was too high, exposed their children and let the fittest survive. This was the highest of moral principles according to their standards.

Sumner: Thieving.

Helburn: Would you not steal food if you were starving?

Sumner: I might, but there are people who wouldn't, and it seems to me that this example would benefit our children if brought to our stories and plays.

Helburn: I should find such people merely stupid, unlifelike and weak in the desire to survive. Do you really think, Mr. Sumner, that villains are punished and virtue, whatever that is, is rewarded? It seems to me to sentimentalize life, to put such fallacies before our adolescents as truth.

Sumner: But there is a basic morality, that something which appeals to your nature, that separates right from wrong. You know very well what I mean.

Helburn: No, I really do not. That something which separates right from wrong tells a different story to every generation and every individual. I think I have proved that already. Why go round and round?

Sumner: The obscenity law does not prohibit sex in our plays. Only anything which tends to arouse lustful or lecherous desires is legally obscene. The artificial stimulation of sex desire has been proven to cause ill health and is a definite social menace.

It is not in accordance with nature, and what is unnatural is invidious.

Helburn: But the whole of civilization is artificial. We do not train our bodies to be natural. We wear fur coats outdoors and turn on the steam heat indoors. We do not rise with the dawn and go to sleep with the fall of darkness. Life has become fuller than that, expanded with new sensations. All books and plays are artificial stimulants, intellectual luxuries; not to speak of radio, airplanes — all the whole widened, artificial panorama of modern existence. To be consistent in this argument, you would have to take us back to nature and the stone age. And even then, a stone-age woman, like Anatole France's penguin, would find a dress and artificially stimulate the males of the clan.

Sumner: But there are certain practices, Miss Helburn, which even you must admit are depraved and abnormal and it is these against which we have dealt most stringently, these we have made an example of.

Helburn: You are a good deal more erudite than our most famous psychologists, Mr. Sumner, if you can define abnormality for me. Science has discovered again and again that the normal and the abnormal meet and merge. And, again, what is one generation's normal is another's anathema. But I think I know what you are referring to. Such plays, perhaps, as *The Captive.* I'm glad you brought it up because it is an excellent proof of the miscarriage of censorship.

In every vaudeville show, every burlesque, every phase of bad art — and it is bad art only that seems to me cheap and vulgar — there are suggestive leers and lewd innuendoes at what I suppose you mean by "sexual abnormality." But let a play like *The Captive* come along, a play that attempts to treat this not unimportant subject seriously and movingly, and you want to close it up.

Like Prohibition, your censorship has miscarried because you cannot fit a false structure around life and cramp life in. And the saddest part of it is not that you occasionally close a good play, but that by doing so you intimidate many producers to a point where they refuse to handle plays which are works of art. That is what your "examples" have thoroughly accomplished.

Sumner: You remind me of a young newspaperman I met the other day who called himself an intellectual aristocrat. We do not make laws for intellectual aristocrats, nor do we make them for the majority. We make them for a minority, a weaker minority. And the newspapers often hurt these laws and our work by giving publicity to the plays and books which we have found unfit to be seen. I believe in a silent censorship.

Helburn: Good for the newspapers! Good for all the forces that will not let the censor function in his obscene silence, but demand light upon the censor. I want open discussion, an open press, an open theater, an education which will give people their own independent code of taste. Secret censorship would be as liberal and democratic an institution as the Spanish Inquisition.

Sumner: But what about youth? What about adolescents and persons whose moral strength is not of the greatest? Think how they may be damaged by a play like *The Captive* where perversion is made so attractive that its participants, in the end, find it preferable to normality.

Helburn: I evidently have a greater faith in humanity than you have. I certainly do not think *The Captive* could hurt anyone. Scientists tell us that such perversions have their source in early youth. It is ridiculous to think they could be originated by a play.

Moreover, I do not feel it necessary or desirable to scale the level of plays down to the least common denominator — the weak-minded and the moron. As for young people, no adolescent was ever hurt by a finely conceived, finely acted play. It is the taboos, the bans, the shames which endanger our children. Psychiatrists tell us that there is nothing which a healthy mind resists so terribly and damagingly as a taboo.

You want to perpetuate a state where the intellectual and aesthetic destiny of a nation rests in the hands of two or three people with religious, economic and personal prejudices. I want the widest, finest, completest possible world and stage, even at the cost of the overstimulation of a few unhealthy people. And I believe that our generation — the younger generation — is with me in this attitude. For it seems to me that our young people, more than any other, for all their crudeness, all their blundering, are attempting to overthrow the vagaries that we used to call high principles in favor of the simple principle of free intelligence.

Sumner: I do not agree with you.

In May 1929, Eugene O'Neill was awarded the Pulitzer Prize for *Strange Interlude,* "as the American play performed in New York best representing the educational value and power of the stage in raising the standards of good morals, good taste and good manners." In September 1929, after running for eighteen months in New York, it was banned in Boston.

According to Mayor Nichols of that city, the play was "a plea for the murder of unborn children, a breeding ground for atheism and domestic infidelity, and a disgusting spectacle of immorality."

At once the Guild went into action. Lawrence and I went up to Boston to protest to the Mayor while Walter Prichard Eaton went along to organize a citizens' protest committe. The Civil Liberties Union joined the wave of protest that swept the country. Finally, Lawrence, Walter Prichard Eaton, and I took twenty minutes on the radio to present the Guild's case to the American people.

Nichols, however, remained adamant. Then mayors of several smaller Massachusetts cities offered to let us present *Strange Interlude* in their communities. The play opened at last in Quincy. I wrote Eugene O'Neill about it:

It has had considerable reverberation, and not done the play any harm — although we could have dispensed with the publicity. You would have been amused at the opening night in Quincy — with cordons of police, quantities of reporters and photographers flashlighting everybody on their arrival; and the mayor enjoying his supreme moment to the full! I felt a bit sick about it all before the curtain went up, because the idea of people coming to the play looking for smut was rather unbearable, but immediately it began, the whole atmosphere changed.

And yet, as I look back, from the time of the censorship battle there was a change in the audiences that viewed the play. Before that time, they had accepted it as it was. Afterwards many of them came looking for dirt, and managing to find it. You can always find what you look for. They were alert for words, as previous audiences had not been, and laughed where there had been no laughter before. It is curious to recall that it was the clean-minded censors who endowed *Strange Interlude* with smut.

We ran into quite a different audience reaction at the time of the Federal Theater during the depression years. The fact that the project was paid for by taxes made people feel that everyone had a right to criticize what was done. Censorship loomed over us in a terrifying way. It began to seem as though the whole American public, men, women, and children, had turned into theatrical critics overnight.

"Are we financing a theater to do shocking plays?" one would complain.

"We can't allow them to mention such naughty things."

All the advantages of state endowment were jeopardized by this point. It's not simply that politics inevitably enters the situation, but widespread and stultifying censorship smothers you like a thick fog. You have a vast public piling down on top of you.

Years later, in 1947, we again ran into censorship trouble with another O'Neill play, *A Moon for the Misbegotten,* when we opened it in Detroit.

This time, it was not the mayor but the chief of police whose finer feelings were outraged. He threatened to close the play. Then he told us how to rewrite it. Armina Marshall, who was with me, and I fought it to a standstill. We didn't rewrite O'Neill plays, we told him, and he wasn't going to do it either. He could take it or leave it. He took it.

The battle against censorship isn't over. Today the American Civil Liberties Union is making a gallant fight against blacklisting in radio and television, which not only causes great injustice but is completely contrary to the American spirit. A condemnation, without facts or proof, which the individual cannot fight because he does not even know the evidence against him, is unspeakably ugly. An individual completely innocent of any wrongdoing can be destroyed professionally. The consequences of this sort of thing are incalculably damaging.

Throughout history there have been attempts to silence the human mind. There will always be such attempts, so we can never afford to stop fighting for freedom at any time. At this moment, books and theater are the only media in which we are free from state censorship, free from advertisers' censorship. We've got to keep them that way.

◇◇ SIXTEEN

The Care and Feeding of American Playwrights

UP TO NOW I've been neglectful of the most important commodity the Theatre Guild had in its early days — its indigenous playwrights. We had started with European plays which had gone through the mill of production. It was not until we had become fairly well established, had a little money in the bank, and were more sure of ourselves, that we began to produce the new work of young American playwrights.

In 1922, with Elmer Rice's *The Adding Machine,* we made our third venture into producing the work of a young American playwright. This was our first American expressionistic play, and our first union problem arose over it. The huge adding machine that dominated the stage was the bone of contention. The carpenters claimed it was property and the property men declared it was scenery, so neither of them would move it. We had to call in some arbiters to decide whose job it actually was.

238

While we were working on the production I lunched at Sardi's one day with Elmer Rice, who was a down-to-earth, practical playwright. A well-known director paused at the table.

"I hope the Guild is treating you right, Elmer," he commented.

"Very well indeed," Elmer assured him.

"You never can tell," the director said darkly. "They aren't used to dealing with authors who aren't three thousand miles away."

But if up till *The Adding Machine* we weren't used to dealing with American playwrights, afterwards came the deluge. Sometimes it seems to me that the late Twenties and the early Thirties proved to be the high point in the craft of playwriting in America. What a host of talent appeared at that time! Sidney Howard, John Howard Lawson, S. N. Behrman, Eugene O'Neill, Du Bose and Dorothy Heyward, Philip Barry, Lynn Riggs, Maxwell Anderson, Robert E. Sherwood, Thornton Wilder, William Saroyan. Later, there were to be Arthur Miller, Tennessee Williams, and Dore Schary, but no such wide blossoming of talent as appeared in those first few years.

They Knew What They Wanted was our first play by Sidney Howard and memorably cast with Richard Bennett, Pauline Lord and Glenn Anders. It was, I think, Pauline Lord's greatest performance. One of the unforgettable moments was that when, in her breathless voice, she announced, "Well, I might as well sit down." It got to be a slogan around the theater.

There were rumblings on the horizon over *They Knew*

239

What They Wanted. That was the great censorship year, with most of the agitation stirred up by Mae West's goings-on, and there were a few shocked outcries over the language in the Howard play. As we have done few plays in the course of our long history which have not stirred up comment and dissension of one kind and another, we were not greatly bothered.

Two years after *They Knew What They Wanted* we produced both *Ned McCobb's Daughter* and *The Silver Cord,* which firmly established Sidney Howard's reputation. It is a great pity and a great waste that he should have died so young, before he had done more than make a brilliant start.

Sidney Howard had great charm and I enjoyed working with him. So far as I can recall, he was the first American dramatist with whom I worked intensively on rewrite. Only once was I disgruntled: when, after I had struggled with him for weeks on a play, he came to tell me that Katharine Cornell liked it as it was and she was going to do it. So he took it out of my hands then and there.

One of the American playwrights with whom I worked, and for whom I had both admiration and respect, was Maxwell Anderson. Max was a lovely person, sweet and gentle. I can't recall ever hearing him lift his voice. He was very slow, not only in his work but in his speech and manner, which was sometimes a little ponderous but never pontifical. Partly because of that unhurried pace of his, he gave an impression of great maturity.

He wrote a number of plays, turning out about one a year for thirty years. I never understood how he got things done with that snail-like progress. We used to pray that it would rain; if it rained, Max would stay home and we'd have a chance of getting some work out of him.

Over the years we produced a number of his plays: *Elizabeth the Queen, Both Your Houses, Mary of Scotland, Valley Forge, The Masque of Kings.* It is one of the ironies of theatrical history that *Both Your Houses* closed because it was not drawing an audience. The next day it won the Pulitzer Prize and we had to bring it back again.

Valley Forge, I always thought, had some of Max's finest stuff in it and a beautiful performance by Philip Merivale. But it would have been better, I have always believed, with an all-male cast. Women did not belong in that play.

It was through Max that I obtained my most important directing job from the Guild. He asked the board to let me direct *Mary of Scotland,* and they agreed. I always suspected that Max wanted me because he thought I would not cross him too much; he would not brook being crossed. Like all playwrights who are worth their salt, he could get stubborn at times. If a playwright lacks the courage of his convictions you have no standard to work by. It is a delight to a director to have an author who is sure of his purpose, for there is nothing so bad for the theater as uncertainty. An author unsure of his own material or intentions is far more of a handicap than one who resists changes. (God knows I am not urging intractability in authors, merely finish of craftsmanship and integrity of line.)

Directing *Mary of Scotland* proved to be a challenge. Aside from producing *Chrysalis,* which Lawrence had tried out at his Westport theater, I had no experience at all. The play was inordinately long and, because Max wrote in verse, it was far more difficult to cut than prose drama. Anyhow, Max was a hard man to persuade on cuts. By the time we took the play out for tryouts it was still running twenty minutes overtime. I can remember staying up until three in the morning to convince Max that some cuts were necessary. I went to bed more dead than alive. Next morning he telephoned to say in his slow voice that he had changed his mind. The material was to stay in.

Theater to Max was more than a career, more than a craft. It was a religion. He was the son of a Baptist minister who would hardly, I suppose, have approved of Max's lifework, in spite of the fact that he won a Pulitzer Prize and two New York Drama Critic Awards. But Max's approach to his art was as serious, as dedicated, as his father's had been to his church. He regarded the stage as a place for a kind of symbolic struggle between good and evil. Once he declared that if you set a man on the stage you knew at once where he stood morally with the human race. Max had vast tolerance except for drama critics, whom he called tartly "the Jukes family of journalism."

I had a wonderful cast for *Mary of Scotland:* Helen Hayes as Mary, Philip Merivale as Bothwell, Helen Menken as Elizabeth, and Fritz Leiber as John Knox. Robert Edmond Jones did the settings and costumes. Helen Hayes tells me that what she remembers most vividly is the fact that I developed one peculiarity as a director. I wouldn't let them play in the center of the stage. She didn't know why. Neither did I. It just felt wrong. Not a particularly cogent reason, perhaps, but in a way it represents my approach to theater.

How pleased I was when the play was awarded ten "best" honors for the season!

Helen Hayes is the most technically skillful actress I've ever known, sensible and practical. She has been acting since she was four, and is so experienced that she has less temperament than anyone I've ever worked with. Most actresses, when interrupted in an emotional scene, get furious and blow their tops. They have to start all over again to work into the mood. But you could interrupt Helen with a suggestion at the peak of an emotional scene. She would listen and then go on with the scene, picking it up at exactly the same pitch, a technical performance of which few actresses are capable. I have often thought that this unassuming woman has an almost complete command of her medium.

As a result, the contretemps that upset most actors never disturb her in the least. She could — and can — cope with any emergency. Once during a performance of *Mary of Scotland* her wig — she is very tiny — caught on the sleeve of one of the halberdiers and was pulled off. Catastrophe? Not for Helen. She slipped behind the extras on the stage and adjusted her wig so deftly, while continuing her lines without a break, that almost no one in the audience was aware of what had happened. In an emergency, if someone fluffed his lines, she could even put in a line or two of blank verse of her own without missing a beat.

A contrast to Maxwell Anderson is John Howard Lawson. Max knew exactly where he was going. Lawson was always most amiably ready to try anything, but he was not sure of his own destination.

My most amusing memory of Lawson is of an incident that

occurred when we were preparing to do *Processional.* "I want," he said, "to use the burlesque technique."

I had never seen a burlesque show. I thought it was infra dig. So Lawson took me to Minsky's on Second Avenue. As I recall, I was the only woman in the audience. It was a pretty hot show. Actually, I was having a very good time, intensified by the fact that Lawson, during the whole performance, kept up a running commentary in extremely highbrow terms about what he meant by burlesque technique and how it should be analyzed. The men around us were tremendously impressed.

It was in the summer of 1926–1927 that we introduced another new American playwright, S. N. Behrman, with *The Second Man.* Sam had served his apprenticeship in the theater as press agent with the Shuberts and Jed Harris. He is a delightful person, a most co-operative colleague, and a highly talented playwright. Sam's forte is dialogue and character. His weakness is structure. Of all the playwrights with whom I have worked over the years, Sam, I think, was the most rewarding to deal with on the problems of rewriting. To some playwrights their work is sancrosanct. They resent criticism. They rewrite reluctantly. But Sam knew both his strength and his weakness. He was aware that his basic lack was in doing his scenario. He accepted criticism without annoyance and reworked patiently and efficiently. He's one of the people whom it's especially nice to have known.

Sam and the Theatre Guild worked happily together on a succession of plays: *The Second Man, Meteor, Biography, Rain from Heaven, Amphitryon 38, End of Summer, Jaco-*

bowsky and the Colonel. In both *End of Summer* and *Biography* — I've always thought the latter his most brilliant work — he was fortunate in having Ina Claire, one of America's best comediennes, as his star. It was a great pity that Ina limited herself to a certain kind of comedy! I suspect she had a whole untapped range of dramatic ability she never used. But in her field she was unsurpassed.

Ina has three levels of comic acting. At one and the same time, she lets you see what she feels, what she thinks, and what she does. How she conveys all this I've never known. It's a special technique of her own. She was enormously helpful to Sam in the rewriting of *End of Summer*. Ina does not pretend to be a playwright but her suggestions are always sound and useful.

I've never forgotten a moment that occurred during a performance of *Biography*. The setting was an artist's studio. There was an old-fashioned stove in which a red mica fire glowed, a necessary prop because of the burning of the manuscript, which was the climax of the play. One night during the moving love scene when Ina stood clasped in the arms of Earle Larimore, she was appalled to hear a titter from the audience. What was wrong?

Cautiously she looked down. Was her slip showing? What had happened?

The titter grew to little spurts of muffled laughter.

Ina turned in that passionate embrace and looked down again. There was Goldie, the Guild cat, tail in air, circling the lovers and staring at them in fascination.

Ina released herself, picked up Goldie with a swooping

gesture, opened the lid of the stove and dropped the cat into the mica fire. She slammed down the lid.

There was a moment's hush and then the audience broke into a shout of laughter. They roared. They whooped. They rocked in their seats. When they began to grow quiet someone would let out another shout and they were off again. It was minutes before the performance could go on.

In twenty years we produced ten Behrman plays. I remember *Wine of Choice* especially, because that was Alexander Woollcott's first appearance on any stage, so far as I know, in the guise of an actor. Alec, the petulant prophet of Wit's End — as Dorothy Parker named his place — the gadfly of the Round Table at the Algonquin, was, in my opinion, a perpetual amateur in his approach to the arts, whether as actor, drama critic, or reviewer of books and teller of tales on his Town Crier program. His enthusiasms were unpredictable, ranging from "going quietly mad" over third-rate sentimental fiction to waxing hysterical over Faulkner's *Sanctuary*.

As a drama critic he could be not only malicious but quite unbelievably cruel. He could sacrifice his best friend for the sake of a quip, and sometimes did.

As an actor he was, bluntly, a trial. He never grasped, as the professional actor does, the relationship between the actors on the stage — how they support each other, how much they give each other. He knew better. He refused peevishly to take direction. Alec was not a man to be told. He knew. He told *you* — in a spate of reckless words.

All this has taken me away from Sam Behrman as a playwright. I suggested once that he make a play of a Somerset Maugham story called *Jane*. I wonder if any play has gone

through as many permutations. In its first version, as Lawrence and Armina produced it at Westport, it was light
comedy. Later in England, and with Maugham's blessing, it
was turned into a farce.

Finally, Sam turned *Jane* into a serious comedy for its
Broadway appearance. For some reason it never quite jelled.

In 1939 we produced *The Time of Your Life* (in association with Eddie Dowling), William Saroyan's first full-length
drama. (*My Heart's in the Highlands* had been Saroyan's
first play produced professionally.) It was an exciting show,
very different from most other plays, and it was voted the
best play of the season by both the Drama Critics' Circle and
the Pulitzer Prize Committee, although Saroyan refused to
accept the Pulitzer Prize.

Saroyan is a law unto himself. I first met him when he
came to the Guild to see me. He was an attractive young
man, hearty-looking, strong and sturdy, outspoken and direct — not a smoothie, as theater people sometimes tend to
be. In fact, there's no category for Bill. He's a natural, with
no pose in him. He means what he says and he is not hampered by conventional ideas.

That first day I had to keep him waiting five minutes.
After we had talked for a while I asked him to lunch with
me, but he refused. Bill was not a man to waste time. He
had spent that five minutes dating the telephone operator.

Because the major part of my energies during the past
twenty years have been devoted to working with authors on
the revision of their scripts to prepare them for production, I

247

have given a lot of thought — I've had to — to the problem of rewriting.

With the exception of Eugene O'Neill, whom I shall discuss at length in a separate chapter, I have never known an American playwright whose plays were practically ready for production except for the inevitable cutting (I might point out that cutting can make the difference between a good scene and one that lags, between an effective speech and a poor one).

Authors simply do not do enough groundwork of their own. Some feel that what they have left undone will be taken care of, in some magic way, by the director and the cast. An increasing number of them feel that they must see their play in rehearsal or tryout before they can tell what is wrong with it and what rewriting is required.

Rewriting done before a play goes into production may be accomplished with a collaborator or a "play doctor." We never used play doctors, as Lawrence and I could handle this work ourselves.

Rewriting done during rehearsal and tryouts is strictly up to the author himself. The cast is called on stage after the evening performance when they are at their best, alert and excited. The cuts and the new material are read. That is when the experienced actor is often invaluable to a playwright.

"I can't say that," he or she may protest. Or, "I need a line here to help me across." Or, "Somehow this doesn't feel right."

Occasionally, you find an author who resents the actor's making suggestions — a number of playwrights have denounced the Lunts for wanting to change the play to make it a vehicle — but the ideal, of course, is a collaboration between the two.

Ben Hecht is more fertile in ideas than any playwright I know. When we did *To Quito and Back* he rewrote so fast that sometimes we could not keep up with him. He would come back every day with what amounted almost to a new play. The trouble with that method is that you are bound to lose perspective after a while and not know what kind of play you have.

Time and again, the Guild has had to go into rehearsal in order to show an author specifically what was wrong. Even then you can't be sure that they are convinced. For instance, when we did Saroyan's *Love's Old Sweet Song* we knew the act divisions were wrong. The weakest point of the play came at the end of the second act.

"Unless there is suspense," I told Bill, "people won't come back after the second act."

Saroyan does not believe in structure; he has no use for technique. I feel that, between them, he and Tennessee Williams have just about thrown structure out of the window, substituting mood instead. If we talked structure, if we became technical, Bill Saroyan dug his heels in.

Bill, as I have said, does not believe in technique. He is impatient at the idea of building climaxes. He held out over *Love's Old Sweet Song* until it got a bad press in Philadelphia.

Thank God for bad presses out of town! There is no producer who does not rejoice in a really unfavorable press when he knows that the play needs more work on it. Given a good press the author will say, "You see? I told you so. There's nothing wrong with it. We'll bring it in as is." But when the press is bad, the author is apt to prove far more amenable.

After the Philadelphia opening, Bill capitulated. We re-built the second act curtain.

Then George Jean Nathan told him indignantly that an artist must follow his own bent. He should listen to no one but himself. Bill listened to this advice and found it good.

"We'll go back to the old order," he told us.

We did.

The play opened in New York. After that opening Bill knew he had made a bad mistake. He took a plane out of town and from a safe distance wired us, DO WHAT YOU WANT.

That was just one day too late.

Playwriting is about the most hazardous pursuit known to civilized man. The odds against a play's succeeding are forty to one. When people stick to the theater as a way of life, come hell and high water, it's not just because of the excitement of the gamble — after all, there's always Russian roulette and it's not much more dangerous — it's simply because they can't imagine any other kind of life.

At the risk of appearing didactic I'd like to set down a few of my own convictions about playwriting.

The technique of playwriting is probably the most diffi-cult of all writing techniques, except perhaps verse; and the apprenticeship should probably be much longer than for any other literary work. The most important asset a young play-wright can have is something to say, something fresh and genuine and worth the effort and expense of production. The second most important thing is to know how to say it in terms of the theater.

Playwriting is the shorthand of narrative, and a knowledge of structure is essential. I recommend Aristotle's *Poetics*. He says:

The plot, which is an imitation of an action, must represent an action that is organically unified, the structural order of the incidents being such that transposing or removing any of them will dislocate and disorganize the whole. Every part must be necessary and in its place; for a thing whose presence or absence makes no perceptible difference is not an organic part of the whole.

The essence of good playwriting is not only what you say, but how much you say in how short a time, and how much you imply without having to state it. There is no better schooling for theatrical writing than an intelligent study of Shakespeare and the great classical writers.

And working in a theater, in any capacity, is invaluable training. It is the only way the young writer can observe and understand the relation between the actor and the dialogue, indeed the actor's whole contribution to the play.

During the years, I have thought a lot about the problems of the young playwright and how he is to acquire the techniques of his art. A writer in other fields can, if he has the guts, hold down a job and work out his apprenticeship in his spare time. But to practice playwriting by writing novels and short stories is like practicing the trombone to become more proficient on the violin.

Someone once said that playwriting consists of getting your characters up a tree in the first act, throwing stones at them in Act Two, and getting them down in Act Three.

With my predilection for architecture I'd like to make my own architectural formula: the first act is in the living room where the characters are introduced; the second in the bedroom where emotional conflict takes place; and the third on the attic stairs, with the hero uncertain whether to escape by the roof on the sleeping porch or to go down and face the occupants of the living room like an honest man.

Fledgling practitioners in this difficult craft need time, and, above all, experience, access to the theater itself. For no play is alive until it meets an audience. But if it is difficult for a young writer to find a publisher willing to take a chance on a first novel, where the investment is comparatively small, it is infinitely more difficult to find a manager who is willing to take a risk on an inexperienced playwright, where the investment is a great deal larger and the odds against success astronomically higher.

Then how are we to keep the supply of plays coming? There have always been art patrons, there are scholarships and contests for young musicians, but what was there for the budding writer for the stage? I wanted to find a way of affording promising writers enough money for a breathing space in which they could continue, for a while at least, to learn the craft that most interested them.

It used to be that the most essential part of training for playwriting was two years in the theater, whether as actor, stage manager, or whatever. In recent years, this two-year apprenticeship has been replaced to some extent by courses

252

in the drama in various universities which focus attention on practical as well as literary aspects of playwriting.

So it was to the universities I turned when I established the Bureau of New Plays. And later it was largely from the universities that we drew the young writers for the annual play-writing seminars and our later work in the Dramatic Workshop of the New School for Social Research.

The Bureau of New Plays started as a playwriting contest for undergraduates or young people who had recently left college. Any play submitted was first to meet with the approval of the drama department of the college — if any — or to be sponsored by a member of the English department. The project was financed in the beginning by the six leading motion picture companies, all of whom were as aware as I of the danger of the source of writing talent drying up.

The chief thing I learned by that first annual contest of the Bureau of New Plays was that the caliber of the plays submitted seemed to be in direct ratio to the college drama department in which the youngsters had studied. As it was too much of a coincidence that most of the promising young playwrights had picked certain universities, I came to the conclusion that the results were due for the most part to the quality of the instruction they were receiving.

The young contestants who had worked with Kenneth Rowe at the University of Michigan in Ann Arbor were outstanding. The next year we were fortunate enough to persuade Mr. Rowe to spend a season in New York, where he conducted a seminar in play writing for the most promising young people discovered through that first annual contest. Later, we gave scholarships to a few young aspiring playwrights to work at Ann Arbor with Mr. Rowe. Among them was Arthur Miller, a tall, earnest, brooding young man, burning with all the injustice of the world.

Working with the Bureau of New Plays and the New School for Social Research, I came straight up against the basic problem. Much can be done in teaching the fledgling playwright technique. But without the practical workshop of a tryout — of seeing the play in actual production and the shortcomings of the work, whether dramatic or structural, whether in development of convincing characters or of dialogue, whether in faulty timing or in lack of tension — the playwright simply cannot learn the basic principles of his craft.

The commercial theater cannot afford to provide these tryouts. The producer is not supposed to be a teacher, he is a dealer in the finished product. And yet — and yet — where is the preparation to come from?

So far as I can see, the filling of this need must continue to rest, as it does today, with the universities. Where the teaching is good, much is achieved. Where it is primarily "literary" or theoretical and aloof from the practices of the living stage, little can be accomplished. It seems to me of pressing importance that the colleges themselves provide facilities for local tryouts of prize-winning plays. The experience of putting a new play into actual production, and testing its value before a live and critical audience, is of inestimable value to the playwright, and such local productions of new plays cannot help but enrich the American theater as a whole.

On the other hand, I do not feel any particular pang at the vanishing of the great "patron" of the Renaissance world for whom many young aspirants long. There's such a thing as too much cushioning. If a young man or woman is good enough and has enough driving interest in the theater, he can find a job, because radio and television have increased the opportunities so greatly. I think with sufficient drive a playwright can take a paying job and still find time to write. In fact, I know he can. Many have. But I'm afraid that too many of the playwrights expect too much in a competitive world. It's the truly plucky and talented few who ultimately find their way to Broadway.

And there are groups of established playwrights — men like Lindsay and Crouse, Rodgers and Hammerstein, Moss Hart and Elmer Rice and others — who have worked unselfishly, trying to find ways of helping promising playwrights to reach their goal. One of these organizations is the New Dramatists Committee, and there are others for the young writer who wants to find out about them and profit by the seasoned help of experienced playwrights, directors, producers, actors, stage designers, all the countless people who help to create the ultimate illusion on the stage.

One of the things that pleased me most was the establishment, in 1948, of a Theresa Helburn Chair of Drama at Bryn Mawr College. Looking back to the time when I had to do research on Pinero at the Philadelphia public library because there were no modern plays at Bryn Mawr, I felt we had all come a long way.

255

◇◇ SEVENTEEN

Eugene O'Neill,
Playwright Extraordinary

EUGENE O'NEILL made his first appearance at the Theatre Guild in 1929, thanks to the continuous efforts of Lawrence Langner, who made a special trip to Bermuda in 1927 and coaxed Gene into the Guild fold. That season we produced both *Marco Millions* and *Strange Interlude*.

Without question, Gene was the giant among American playwrights. Never was there any question of casual or unfinished craftsmanship on his part. Never any doubt as to what he wanted. Like Shaw, he knew his craft from the ground up, he knew the effects he wanted to achieve, and he knew the techniques by which to attain them.

I can see him now, sitting quiet and impassive in the front row, watching rehearsals hour after hour. He had spent so much time on the preparation of his script that he was ready to answer promptly and without any hesitation every question thrown at him by director and actor.

256

By the time it went into rehearsal, indeed, O'Neill had devoted more work to it than many playwrights do to half a dozen plays. He wrote longhand, such tiny writing that I can decipher it only with the help of a magnifying glass. He worked slowly, laboriously, painfully. He spent more time in preparation than in the actual writing of the dialogue. His original notes for a play would have filled a book; they served only as a background for his characters, giving them depth, so that Gene knew them thoroughly.

After writing a first draft he would put it away for three months so that he could regain his perspective, and then rewrite it from the beginning. This draft was put away for a year. Then he wrote his third draft. If necessary, he would do even a fourth.

We found Gene almost as difficult as Shaw on the subject of cutting. He believed in saying he was going to say something, then saying it, then saying he had said it. He seemed to fear that without this painstaking reiteration of ideas he could not make his meaning clear to his audience. I have always believed that he could have saved a couple of plays that proved to be failures in his later days if he had been willing to cut. As the years went on and the scope of his plan for plays became bigger and bigger, more and more complex, he became more prolix.

Later on I learned that I could not argue with Gene. He was very self-confident. I would suggest cuts here and here and here. He would shake his head. He needed it all. He had to be complete.

"Well, Gene, go home and think it over," I would say.

Occasionally he would come back and make a few insignificant cuts. Then he would smile, that sweet, gentle, lovely smile of his, and I would know I was beaten. None the less, for us the play was the thing and we gave him, as far as we could conceivably do it, what he wanted. This was particularly true of *The Iceman Cometh,* at which time he was feeling ill and insecure about cutting a play written while in better health several years before its production. That this way may not always have been the most successful is indicated by Eric Bentley's comment: "I had seen what came of author-worshiping directing in the Theatre Guild production [*The Iceman Cometh*] where all O'Neill's faults were presented to the public with careful reverence." Well, Gene respected his craft; I saw no reason why we should not respect his point of view.

Strange Interlude was a daring experiment for us. In some ways, I think it was one of the most daring experiments in the theater. There were, as everyone knows now, nine acts; the play ran from five in the afternoon until eleven at night with an hour for dinner. It played through one of the hottest seasons on record and in an uncooled theater. But for a year and a half every seat was filled.

I had to go to Europe that summer and left just after rehearsals started. The afternoon I returned to New York, I went from the boat straight to the theater and sat through the performance enthralled, before I went home to unpack.

I remember writing, more than a year after *Strange Interlude* opened, to tell Gene that the play was still attracting standees. He replied: "This treads on fanaticism, it seems to me. Myself I wouldn't stand up 4½ hours to see the original production of the Crucifixion!"

I feel strongly that the two greatest plays the Guild ever produced were Shaw's *Saint Joan* and O'Neill's *Strange Interlude*. Certainly the latter was the finest serious production that Philip Moeller ever staged. He was at the peak of his brilliance as a director at that time, with *Volpone* probably his greatest work in comedy.

When we followed *Strange Interlude* with *Dynamo*, Eugene O'Neill was traveling from China to the Basque country and did not supervise the rehearsals. At that time, his marital difficulties had become almost too much for him. He loathed the newspaper stories, which he regarded as an outrageous invasion of his privacy; he hated the emotional turmoil and uncertainty, which made it difficult for him to do creative work; and each letter or cable warned us solemnly not to divulge his whereabouts to anyone. None the less, he was happier than he had ever been in his life. His great love for Carlotta Monterey, who later became his wife, was to dominate all the rest of his days.

My marital affairs [he wrote from the Basque country, when we were working on the production of *Dynamo*] had something to do with my resolve to travel — the only thing I'm grateful to the mess for. Things are at a deadlock. I cannot, out of pure self-preservation and in justice to my need for some kind of financial security to work in, agree to the exorbitant price for my freedom now being demanded. Both the other party concerned in this and I have agreed that, under the circumstances, the only thing to do is to stick it out as is. It means staying out of the States until reason returns to the demander but, after all, I am happier in my present state over here than ever before — so why not?

Later, during that hectic year of his divorce, he wrote from France: "Keep address strictly under your hat." Speaking of demands on him for money he added: "Of course, I'm not wholly objective in this. Can't be. I have one wife, three children and one stepchild dependent on me already — and it's the mere shank of the evening! . . . Remember I'm living quite alone in another part of Europe."

When we opened *Dynamo* he cabled: "Wish I could be with you but domestic deadlock unchanged and will never return States until Carlotta and I are married."

Some eight months later, Carlotta, then Mrs. Eugene O'Neill, wrote fervently, "We feel we have earned our happiness!"

But if Gene was not on hand to supervise the production of *Dynamo* in person, he, like Shaw, bombarded us with suggestions by mail. I have before me eight sheets marked "Suggestions, instructions, advice, along with sundry snooty remarks and animadversions as to the modern theater for *Dynamo*." Some of the "suggestions, instructions," etc., are particularly interesting for the light they cast on O'Neill's theories and what he was trying to achieve in the theater. Especially on *how*.

I may seem to be a bug on the subject of sound in the theatre [he wrote], but I have reason. Bobby Jones once said that the difference between my plays and other contemporary work was that I always write primarily by ear for the ear, that most of my plays, even down to the rhythm of the dialogue, have the definite structural quality of a musical composition . . . although it is the principal reason why I have been blamed for useless repetitions, which to me were significant recurrences of theme . . .

This is a machine age which one would like to express as a background for lives in plays in overtones of characteristic . . . sound and rhythm — but how can one unless a corresponding mechanical perfection in the theatre is a reliable string of the instrument. . . . The only answer is, it cannot be done. Looking back on my plays in which significant mechanical sound and not music is called for (nearly all of the best ones) I can say that none of them has ever really been thoroughly done in the modern theatre although they were written for it.

In regard to casting he said of one feminine character:

I have no suggestions — only a warning that if whoever plays it is ever conscious of being funny for even a moment or rides her lines for laughs, I will swim back all the way from China with a kriss between my murderously gritted teeth and slay that actorine.

Dynamo was a good play but not, I think, one of Gene's great ones. Gene wrote me from China that the play was about a mother complex, but that was never clear to me, and I'm sure it wasn't to the audience. I remember it chiefly for the wonderful stage set, and for Claudette Colbert in a tight-fitting red dress running up and down stairs.

Gene began writing to us about *Mourning Becomes Electra* nearly a year before we saw the script. I wish all young playwrights would read and re-read his letter about it. It might send them back to their scripts for more work. If the masters find rewrite so rewarding, certainly the apprentices should, too.

261

I got to Paris today [Gene wrote in 1930] after finishing getting over my second draft. I did so much on this job it practically amounts to a third draft. We are off for a month's motoring in Spain now. When I come back I will type a fourth and (I hope) final draft . . .

This fourth draft will probably take two or three months. Then I will send you a copy and you can all see what you think. After that, I will have six to seven months leeway before next fall to lay it aside for a lengthy period and then go over it a fifth time if I feel that is necessary. This looks like a good scheme to me and I ought to get a first draft of a new one done in that interval, too, if the gods are good.

It seems in pretty damn good shape now to me but I am so close to it I can't see the whole for the parts. It's bad enough to try to see one play whole when you're close to it, but with a trilogy! —

Tell Phil I have thrown out my scheme for soliloquy and most of the soliloquies. They were all right enough in themselves but I found they held up the play instead of helping it and I could well do without them. This was especially true in the first play. Soliloquies are more in the picture in the second and third plays — they are called out of the mood there instead of being thrust upon it.

In April 1931 Gene wrote from Paris:

I am sending you the script of *Mourning Becomes Electra* by this same mail — two scripts — so that the Committee can get quick action on it.

As you will see, no departures in technique are involved. *Interlude* soliloquies and asides only got in my way in these plays of intense passions and little cerebration. The masque idea has also gone by the board. It simply refused to justify itself in the final accounting. It confused and obscured instead of intensifying. All that is left of it is the masklike quality of the Mannon faces in repose, an effect that can be gained by acting and makeup. The dialogue is colloquial of today. The house, the period costumes, the Civil War surface stuff, these are the masks for what is really a modern psychological drama with no true connection with that period at all. I think I have caught enough Greek sense of fate — a modern approximation of it, I mean — out of the Mannons themselves to do without any Greek theatrical effects.

Mourning Becomes Electra, O'Neill's trilogy, was produced during the depression. One night after the performance, I was standing in the lobby as the audience streamed past me. I heard one man say to another, "Gosh, isn't it good to get back out into the depression again!"

Two years after we did *Mourning Becomes Electra* we produced *Ah, Wilderness!* — O'Neill's delightful comedy. Gene, unlike many playwrights, who expect to do half the work on the play after it opens out of town, usually saw absolutely no point in tryouts. He wanted no part of them. *Ah, Wilderness!* was the only time when he agreed to an out-of-town tryout.

Unlike his other plays, *Ah, Wilderness!* was full of comedy. We knew that it was only fair to try it on the road so that the laughs could be timed and the actors could get a sense of the pace of the play. At length, Gene agreed, though reluctantly. We opened in Philadelphia, and it was some time before he would even come down for a performance. He saw it through and returned to New York. "You see," his attitude suggested; "I knew all the time it was unnecessary."

After *Ah, Wilderness!* there was silence. Gene had em-
barked on the great project of his life, a *comédie humaine,* a
cycle of eight — later nine — plays into which he planned to
put everything he knew. And then time passed. Gene, at his
Sea Island beach home in Georgia, which he called Casa
Genotta, had withdrawn into the private world in which he
immured himself for the great project.

I knew of it first in a letter from Carlotta, who wrote:
"Gene has started on plays that give him some scope for his
ideas — his next will be a history of the human race."

Of course, both Lawrence and I were tremendously excited and we began to question him about the project.

It is only fair [Gene wrote me in March of 1936] to warn you
on this point, too. As I am writing [Lawrence] I'm not going to
discuss this series of plays with anyone, nor release any of them
for production until I have at least three of them completed —
and up to date only three-fourths of one of them is done.

A few weeks later I went to Georgia to visit the O'Neills.
At Casa Genotta, a lovely house which Carlotta described as
"bastard Spanish peasant style," Carlotta and I talked and
drank coffee all morning. After lunch I talked with Gene in
his study, which was built like the master cabin of an old sail-
ing vessel. There he spoke to me about his prodigious plan
for the great cycle, discussing particularly *A Touch of the
Poet,* showing me the endless notes and the detailed scenarios.

Later we walked along the endless beach outside his house.
At least, it seemed endless to me, for I have never been a
good walker. Like most shy people, Gene was at his best
when with only one other person, and that day, though the

walk was rugged and the wind blew sand in my eyes, I made my first discovery of the real man himself. After my return to New York I wrote:

I don't know whether in spite of my gray hair[1] I am shy with you or whether it's just that old-fashioned quality called reverence which I feel for your work and your relation to it. But I do know that after I leave you I always feel I have been inarticulate and perhaps gauche in expressing my feelings and ideas. The scope and the depth of the eight plays — even from those brief glimpses into their content that you gave me — moved me more than I can say, and the thought of them stays constantly with me. When I think of the way the average script, even from our so-called best playwrights, is presented to us, in half-baked versions requiring revision up to the very last minute, I realize what a privilege it will be to work for and toward the achievement of your *comédie humaine*. But I realize, too, that the special problems and size of the task before us probably precludes any thought of a company not definitely focused on these productions, because working on your cycle will absorb all our surplus energy and more for the next two or three years. But we must continue this summer and next fall to organize our acting material so that we will have sifted through and tested out both its caliber and its spirit before our O'Neill season begins. You are quite right in feeling that work, conceived and carried out as yours is, demands from all concerned an approach rare in the theater today.

Of course, the sooner we can read a draft of any of the scripts, the sooner we will be able to judge whether the people we have in mind for association with us will fit practically into the scheme of things.

[1] Actually at that time I dyed it a bright defiant blue as my challenge to encroaching age.

The idea of any pressure being applied, even such mild pressure as I had used, appalled Gene; although, considering the immense scope of his project and the vast amount of work and financing it would require, I had felt, in the interests of the Guild, that the point should be made.

This is a word of warning [he wrote] in regard to planning ahead that I feel bound to repeat now, in justice both to the Guild and me. Don't begin to plan for the production of the cycle, except in a very general way, until you receive finished plays from me to plan on. Don't expect first drafts. I hate letting anyone see first drafts. Mine are intolerably long and wordy — intentionally so, because I put everything in them, so as not to lose anything, and rely on a subsequent revision and rewriting, after a lapse of time with better perspective on them, to concentrate on the essentials and eliminate the overweight. But to a person reading a first draft, that draft is the first impact of the play on them, and it is apt to be a very misleading impact indeed. My first drafts always bore me for long stretches, so I can hardly expect them to do less for other people. And being bored by a first draft would be a disheartening approach to this Cycle for the prospective producer.

And don't rely on receiving the first plays at any definite future date, for though I may do some speculating about the matter, I cannot honestly even tell myself just when it will be. It depends on so many things which cannot be foretold. For example, the old subconscious might get on the job in great shape, and I might find myself in a surge of creative energy when I could keep going on, in first draft, from one to another until five or six or even all eight were written. In which case, as you will appreciate, I would be insane to pause for any interruption — especially such an exhausting interruption as production is for me, followed always by a long period of blank uncreativeness. It would be better in the long run, from both our standpoints, for me to go on without a break, even if it meant a delay of one or two years. It would be much better, from your angle, if, from the start, you had all eight to base a company on.

All of which sounds like handing you a large package of uncertainty to go on with. But the ill of uncertainty is inherent in authorship — at least, my kind of authorship. You're always dependent on factors in yourself you cannot control but which control you. And your prophecies, optimistic or pessimistic, have an ironic habit of changing sides on you before the game is finished.

Please [I wrote Gene hastily] don't let the thought of dates worry you. I realize how you feel and that your spirit will be cribbed, cabined and confined by the threat of a deadline. If there are no scripts next fall, I will simply hold you to your next to last paragraph and go down to Sea Island again, in the hope that by that time you will feel like reading me enough here and there to give me some sense of the characters involved. That will probably be enough to hold me for some time. . . . All love to you and Carlotta.

Our "permanent" acting company had, little by little, become impermanent, and we were once again seeking players whom we could use continually instead of starting all over again with each new production. Only a few years before, we had had our pick of actors and actresses. Now soaring salaries in Hollywood were tempting more and more of the best players away from the legitimate theater. It became increasingly hard — and increasingly expensive — to cast a play. The only bright spot was that the stage itself, with the immediate audience response and the opportunity to build a part, never loses its allure for the born actor. And there are, fortunately, many of them.

In October, I wrote to Gene:

Since I saw you and Carlotta I have traveled twelve thousand miles in the interests of the Guild . . .

The very fact that I have had to go both to Hollywood and to London in an effort to cast our plays confirms me more and more in the necessity for collecting permanent acting talent, although the economic problems continue to be very difficult. Once we get this season under way it must become my major task.

Later, after the O'Neills gave up their Georgia house and moved to California, I did a piece on Gene for the *Saturday Review of Literature*. To my chagrin, the magazine, in the same issue, published a sharp attack on him written by Bernard De Voto. I wrote to tell Gene how sorry I was and in reply he wrote cheerfully that he never subscribed to a clipping bureau, he hadn't read the article and he had never heard of De Voto. Anyhow, "a too unanimous chorus of approval would make me feel a tombstone was planted over my head! The only writers that all writers agree are good writers are dead!"

That year Gene won the Nobel Prize but he was too ill to go to Stockholm. He was in a hospital. "I am beginning to feel as old as the Nile myself," he wrote in reference to a book I had sent him, "waiting for Carlotta to return, so very long does this first real separation of ours seem, each day the reign of an Egyptian dynasty, so to speak. Such are the pangs of love and how lucky I feel to be panged! . . .

"Lucky I didn't go to Sweden! My appendix would probably have burst as I was making my speech at the Nobel banquet, and ruined the occasion."

I continued to sound out O'Neill on the great Cycle. He had been working on it for some six years or more. What was happening? Where were the plays? When was the Guild going to launch the great project? I didn't ask *how* we were going to do it. We'd find a way, all right. But unhappily, it wasn't necessary to look around for ways and means. The plays were still a great secret.

No [Gene wrote me firmly] absolutely no hope for any play next season. I don't even want to think of production until I have four or five of the nine finished, and (if I can do it without winding up in the Poorhouse or the Home for the Aged and Infirm), I'd like to wait until all nine are completed. This last is the ideal, of course. Then we really could engage a repertory company for the whole Cycle — show the actors and actresses we have parts that would make it worthwhile, out of pure self-interest, to tie up for several seasons under our conditions. No stars, of course, but show the young and ambitious their chance to become stars through this Cycle . . . I'm very obdurate on this point. In fact, to be blunt, I won't allow it to be done any other way.

But when will I be ready with even the minimum of four or five plays — let alone the full nine? . . . I did manage to finish the first draft of another play — the new No. One of the nine — last summer and fall and early winter. This makes three I now have in first draft. But two of them are still far from what I want them to be and have to be rewritten. The other — No. Three — is in pretty good shape for a first draft and won't need much work . . .

Another thing, writing one of the units in this Cycle is a much more complicated business than doing a single play, or half of *Strange Interlude* or one of the *Electra* trilogy. Often I start a work day writing dialogue for the play I'm on and wind up writing suggested notes on a scene in the eighth or ninth play! Of course, this will all be very valuable in the later stages but it does eat up time and energy and slow up progress on the immediate job.

Another year passed and Gene was still laboring at his great project, none of which we at the Guild had as yet seen. I wrote to him:

I have been thinking a lot about you and the plays and trying to find some way that you could experiment on them with us, without getting tied up in the atmosphere of "show business," which I know you hate, and which God knows we would be only too happy to escape . . .

You know you may feel free to choose any way you want to work, any director or stage designer, in and out of the Guild. Lawrence and I have functioned together as the production administration for the last couple of years, finding it easier and more satisfactory not to burden an author with more collaboration than he needs or wants . . .

Oliver [I added with some asperity, for my husband was working tremendously hard at the time] got involved in three books simultaneously.

Gene wired that there was to be no finished play for us that season. I wrote back promptly, still ridden by that dream of mine for some new kind of musical play.

I am sorry we cannot look forward to doing some new O'Neill this season or next season but there is another idea that has been on my mind for a long time — and that is, to make a musical version of *Marco Millions*.

Today, I had lunch with Kurt Weill, who is extremely intrigued with the idea and who, I think, might do a very good job. Do you know Weill's work and does the idea appeal to you? We also thought of Dick Rodgers and Larry Hart but they are involved in a musical with George Abbott for next season.

Carlotta answered me.

Terry dear, Gene thinks the *Marco Millions* musical idea *a very good one* and would like to hear more about it. He also thinks *The Fountain* lends itself to music!

Dear God, could you but see the West Coast dressed for what they term "Fiesta"! Bewhiskered, becostumed. Guns — God knows what. Looking like a lot of unwashed bums — no matter what size — what age — the Spirit of Fun is rampant! Thank God we live in the hills with the animals.

I learned, to my chagrin, that Oscar Hammerstein was at work with Jerome Kern on the Byron *Marco,* so that project was brought to an end. Gene, however, was genuinely interested in the whole idea of making musicals of his plays. He wrote:

Another play to think of in musical connection is *The Hairy Ape.* Coates, the conductor, was once going to make an opera of it. He didn't. I mention this to show you that the idea had occurred to a famous musician. But I'm not thinking of grand opera now but of something more like *Porgy and Bess.* Give this idea a little pondering, will you? With the right composer, it could work out into a most striking and out of the ordinary rut affair. And very timely. Because I think we are all a bit sick of answers that don't answer. *The Hairy Ape,* at least, faces the simple truth that, being what we are, and with any significant spiritual change for the better in us probably ten thousand years away, there just is no answer . . .

That season Lawrence and Armina's Westport Country Playhouse presented a revival of *Anna Christie.* Bennett Cerf, who was staying with the Langners, sat beside me during the performance and told me he thought Gene was working on a new play which was not to be part of the Cycle. I wrote Gene about the success of the *Anna Christie* revival and hinted that we'd like to hear about the new play Bennett had mentioned.

There wasn't, Gene replied, going to be a new play.

It's good to learn the production of *Anna Christie* at Lawrence's theatre was so well done. As for it being a grand play, it isn't for me. It's dead as hell. But there does seem to be a lot of theatrical life left in the old trollop . . . I had thought it had been movied and radioed until nothing remained to interest anyone.

Periodically reports appeared, from one source or another, that Eugene O'Neill had broken with the Theatre Guild. One report, published by *Variety,* declared that he had joined the Playwrights Company.

I'm about as fed up with these rumors [Gene wrote me] as I imagine you all are. They're as unfair to the Guild as they are to me. I bitterly resent that as soon as the Guild has a run of bad breaks these rumors started. Seemingly it is assumed that I am the kind of heel who would naturally try to get away from you the moment you had tough luck! I don't like it. And it's all so damned idiotic, too, when you consider that I am not in a position yet to talk production of plays with anyone!

Another report was that Gene was leasing the Broadhurst Theatre to put on the Cycle himself. "Of all the bloody nonsense I ever heard that is the worst," Gene wrote furiously to Lawrence. "Can you picture me leasing the Broadhurst to embark on a producing career? Two preliminary steps would be necessary before that could happen. No. 1, I would have to be adjudged insane and committed to an asylum. No. 2, I would have to escape."

Gene's absorption in his plays was broken inexorably by the growing chaos and havoc in Europe. In May, I wrote to him:

Knowing how depressed you were about things some months ago, I can imagine how you must feel about the state of the world just now. There isn't anything one can say in the face of the present events. It certainly makes the theater — and everything else — seem futile. And yet, I know that that is the worst point of view that anyone could indulge in.

As a matter of fact, I feel that the theater next season will probably have more real importance than it has had for some time. Apart from the escape comedies and musicals, and the release of laughter, I believe that people will need greatness and beauty and emotional lift intensely.

I wish to goodness we could be at work on one of your plays but, as we can't we can't, and that's that. This is just to hope that you're not going to let the world get you down, and to express my sincere belief that we need the contribution of your genius more profoundly than ever. However, it looks now as if that need would persist in the world for many years to come, so there's no hurry.

It was Carlotta who answered me, answered me with ominous news. The war had silenced Gene. He couldn't work any more.

Here [she wrote] we are completely demoralized with the war news and keep our ears to the radio day and night. Gene has been so upset that he has given up all idea of working. He says the theatre seems very futile to him at this moment . . .

Terry, this is a crazy letter. But I am crazier. I feel so disintegrated. I can't separate reality from nightmare. Life is so mad these days. Gene has, for years, said what we needed was a second flood. I am beginning to think so, too. Greed has killed all spirituality and no people can exist without spirituality. I read history day and night and, it appears to me, that all this is a mere repetition of what has gone before. Man always destroys himself . . .

Come to see us if you can. We would love seeing you at our table — love to talk with you — and perchance, we may even laugh a bit!

Later that year, Gene sent *The Iceman Cometh* to Lawrence, who read it at once and wrote to express his enthusiasm.

I'm damned pleased you liked it so well [Gene wrote him on August 11, 1940]. Personally, I love it! And I'm sure my affection is not wholly inspired by nostalgia for the dear dead days "on the bottom of the sea" either. I have a confident hunch that this play, as drama, is one of the best things I've ever done. In some ways, perhaps *the* best. What I mean is, there are moments in it that suddenly strip the secret soul of a man stark naked, not

274

in cruelty or mock superiority, but with an understanding compassion which sees him as a victim of the ironies of life and of himself. Those moments are for me the depth of tragedy, with nothing more that can possibly be said.

But O'Neill did not want any part of his Cycle to be produced during the war:

Later on, after the victory in the war which must be won is won, and the reaction to the realities behind the surface of the peace sinks in, there will again be an audience able to feel the inner meaning of plays dealing with the everlasting mystery and irony and tragedy of men's lives and dreams; plays which are propaganda only for life as the artist attempts to illuminate it and transmute it into Art. People are too damned preoccupied with the tragedy of war now — as they should be — to want to face such plays. And I don't blame them. I'd rather spend an escapist evening with legs and music myself — or with pipe dreams that were treated as truth . . .

My health has been bad — Parkinson's* disease much worse, for one thing. Some days I can't write — I mean physically can't write longhand — and couldn't type even if the old dog could change tricks and compose on a typewriter. However, I've done some work in '42, despite these annoyances and a generally futile feeling of "What's the use?" But I've had to give up the physical work around the grounds — I used to take care of quite a lot — because it brings on spells of complete exhaustion when I feel like a wet anaemic fly crawling up a cold windowpane.

As the war years crept along, O'Neill's health deteriorated and his discomforts increased. Carlotta wrote:

* Extended medical research demonstrated that Mr. O'Neill did not have Parkinson's disease but suffered from a hereditary tremor which afflicted him only occasionally.

Terry dear, Gene asks me to tell you he is "enjoying" a bout of Parkinson — and has asked me to thank you for your letter.

Gene's and my problem is becoming more difficult every day. There is nothing to do for Parkinson, it just gets worse and worse. And now that I have fallen apart I am not so brave in facing it! There are days when my heart aches so I can hardly face him — which, of course, is the worst possible thing for him. But on the whole, I manage to keep on and *try* to make things as pleasant as possible. With war, and all it does and *will* mean, I am really stuck, for the first time in my life, as to what is the best thing to do regarding a future home for Gene. He should have warmth, ocean and sand (!), doctors and good nourishment. . . .

I wrote Gene about the possibility of selling *Mourning Becomes Electra* to the movies:

As you know, ever since I was in Hollywood in 1935, I have been trying to interest various picture companies in *Mourning Becomes Electra*. Even at that time I had the idea of Garbo and Hepburn in it. The answer was always frustration, frustration, frustration. Then, as you know, we got Hepburn excited and she did her best to sell it to Metro-Goldwyn-Mayer. She says the scene was fantastic and finally Louis B. said only over his dead body. Surprisingly, Kate didn't shoot him on the spot.

Gene sent me a long typed reply, with insertions in his microscopic handwriting. It reveals much of his attitude toward his work, his fine sense of responsibility for the way his ideas were to be presented to the public, and a touch of exacerbation that was rare in him but which his worsening physical condition explains.

I've never liked having distorted pictures made of my plays, and the picture medium has never interested me. I thought long

276

ago when I saw *Caligari* that there could be a genuine, original art form developed along that line. Talking pictures seem to me a bastard which has inherited the lowest traits of both parents. It was the talkless part of *The Long Voyage Home* — the best picture ever made from my stuff — that impressed me the most . . .

So you may understand what my feeling is about a film sale of a favorite play I know Hollywood will distort. Let's consider *The Hairy Ape*. It remains one of my favorites. I have an enduring affection for it as drama, the more so because so few people have ever seen what it was all about. But let that go. I sold it because, with Tao House and ranch overhead on my neck, I had to sell it or sell some of my securities whose income pays the alimony! . . . I didn't really want to sell because I knew no one in Hollywood had the guts to film *my play,* do it as symbolic expressionism as it should be done, and not censor it into imbecility, or make it a common realistic stoker story. I remember that its first stage production was one of my most satisfying times in the theater. I remember Wolheim was practically perfect as "Yank" and was also a pal of mine. I don't want to have that memory spoiled. So when I tell you I am not going to see the film — nor read one word written about it — nor even admit that it exists, I sure mean it! But all the same, I will always feel guilty. The memory of what *The Hairy Ape* is, was, and should be, will, in a sense, be spoiled for me. The picture, even if financially a hit, will be soon forgotten, and the play will remain as if no picture had ever touched it. But still, I will always regret.

About *Mourning Becomes Electra,* I am sure Hepburn would be splendid as Lavinia. The rest I'm afraid would be a dreadful hash of attempted condensation and idiotic censorship, as the *Strange Interlude* film was.

How about General Mannon's speeches about war, death, etc.,

and what Orin has to say of war when he returns? Would these be ruled out as morbid pacifism or something? Yet to me these contain an implication, at least, of deep spiritual truth. Do you remember when Orin says to Lavinia in Act III of *The Hunted:* "I had to kill another in the same way. It was like murdering the same man twice. I had a queer feeling that war meant murdering the same man over and over, and that in the end I would discover the man was myself!"

But I'm getting away from the point — and also, getting to the point where I wonder if we ought to sell *Mourning Becomes Electra* at any price. After all, it was a splendid Guild production — your high spot, as a theatre, I think — a great Guild achievement against great odds — an event that was a high example of the combined acting, producing, and writing art of the American theatre — so compelling that in the depth of the depression this tragic trilogy brought packed houses to the theater in late afternoon for weeks at a six-dollar top! [*Strange Interlude* was produced in boom days.] And to me, it is also a high spot. It did more than any other single play to win the Nobel Prize. In every capital of Europe where it was done before the war it was an event. And it still goes on, despite the war, thirteen years after your production, and will go on. Only a year ago, it was produced in Lisbon and later revived there — a great success. People came to the theater in the early evening, something they'd never done before except for Wagnerian opera. It has been done in Switzerland since then. Now they want to do it in Madrid. It is no boasting but plain fact that, no matter what exceptions are taken here and there by this or that, for this or that reason, it is generally regarded in Europe as the high point of American dramatic writing. Well, all that belongs to the Guild, too. And whether people of this country give a damn about it or not — and they don't — it belongs to them. Furthermore, you of the

Guild and I are — well, being you're a lady, I won't say growing old but at least entering the period when one begins to select, if one can, some memories of one's work in life worth cherishing and keeping untarnished.

Do we want to let Hollywood debase it (as it must, being at heart, even with the best intentions, merely a commercial mob-amusement racket), the *Mourning Becomes Electra* of our memories, the achievement that had great significance, whereas the picture will have none?

Am I being sentimental? The Guild will probably think so, since I notice that *Mourning Becomes Electra* is not even included in the list at the bottom of your letter paper — presumably a list of your greatest achievements, box office or no box office. You omit *Mourning Becomes Electra,* although any international jury composed of critics of dramatic art would tell you it is the most significant modern play you have ever produced since the Guild began. Why, Christ, compared to it, a lot of the plays on your list are, as far as fine drama is concerned, merely things to hang on a hook in a backwoods privy! The jury I speak of would, I know, agree to that judgment with enthusiasm.

Well, the above has rankled for a long time. Now you have it. It doesn't matter a damn, I admit, except that I can hardly be expected to see it as an expression of loyalty to my finest work — or, what is worse, loyalty to yourselves for the important work you have done for American drama and an American theater (as distinct from the Showshop Business).

In 1946, the Guild brought out two O'Neill plays: *The Iceman Cometh* and *A Moon for the Misbegotten,* neither of which fared well commercially.

The last time I saw him, Gene said, "These audiences don't want my plays."

But they *do* want them. Today, he is being revived as only two other English playwrights have been revived — Shakespeare and Shaw. For all his modesty he would not, I think, be surprised. His knowledge of human beings was deep, and he wrote, as he said wartime playwrights should write, "of timely things in a timeless way."

EIGHTEEN

Oklahoma! and *Carousel*

WHEN I WAS very young and opinionated I regarded musical comedy as a kind of intellectual slumming. It
is ironical now to know that what reputation I leave behind
me will rest chiefly on my contribution to a field I so long
looked upon without respect.

The war years found the Guild staggering back from its
second financial and managerial collapse. At the beginning of
1942, we had about thirty thousand dollars in the bank.
Lawrence was dividing his time between Washington and
New York, immersed in work at the National Inventors
Council which he initiated. I not only had the detailed
weight of the Guild on my shoulders but I was deeply involved in the Stage Door Canteen, bond selling, and a dozen
more activities to which most theatrical folk gave as much of
their time and energy as they possibly could.

At that historic and uncertain period, serious interest in
the theater seemed like fiddling while Rome burned, and,
because of the tremendous demands on capital, it was almost

impossible to wheedle or beg any money for the stage from investors. Yet this was when I decided the moment had come for the fulfillment of my dream, the production of a totally new kind of play with music, not a musical comedy in the familiar sense but a play in which music and dancing would be aids to and adjuncts of the plot itself in telling the story. As we had only about thirty thousand dollars ourselves, I was also in the new position of finding investors who would put up the estimated ninety to one hundred thousand dollars, but I went ahead anyway. It was at this time, when I explained the financial situation to Lawrence who had agreed to the production being made, that he coined the expression "Helburn's Folly" for the enterprise. Since he was often away in Washington, the greater part of the task of raising the money fell on my shoulders. However, in order to help on the situation, Lawrence took a six weeks' vacation from his work in Washington, returned to New York and gave his full time to helping by attending the auditions and rehearsals and securing part of the financing. He also spent a full three weeks out of town helping in the production with Armina, a native-born Oklahoman. He never mentioned the words "Helburn's Folly" again.

For years, as I have said, I had been looking for the right vehicle, ranging from *Lysistrata* to *Marco Millions*. Long before, we had produced, though not with any outstanding financial success, a folk drama by Lynn Riggs called *Green Grow the Lilacs*. I don't remember when I became convinced that this was what I had been looking for. What I do remember is trying to make other people share my conviction. When you're trying to raise a lot of money, people reminded me, you ought to offer them a sure-fire success, not a play that hadn't done so well in the past. Musicals, they said in disgust, don't have murders in the second act.

I ignored the prophets of gloom and looked around for someone to do the book and the score. I thought at once of Larry Hart and Dick Rodgers. Larry, by that time, what with increasingly heavy drinking and poor health, declined to work on the book, and I have always believed that it was seeing the play on opening night that broke his heart and hastened his death. Poor Larry, so warm and exuberant and sweet in spite of his underlying sadness. Larry, who was never quite in tune with life.

Dick Rodgers, however, was interested but he needed a collaborator to replace Larry Hart with whom he had worked so long and so successfully. Dick said he liked the work that Oscar Hammerstein had been doing and suggested that they see what they could accomplish together. So the great partnership was founded.

It didn't seem great at the time, however, at least to the people whom I bombarded with pleas to invest. Hammerstein, they told me sourly, had had ten successive flops since his big hit with *Show Boat.*

Dick Rodgers and Oscar Hammerstein, knowing the financial situation of the Guild, set to work without even asking for an advance and finished the book late in the summer of 1942.

Then began the work of production — and the nightmare of raising money. Day by day, I grew more frantic. Rouben Mamoulian, who had successfully staged for us one of America's most important musicals, *Porgy and Bess,* came to town,

283

and we engaged him as stage director. We also engaged Lem Ayers for the scenery and Miles White for the costumes, both of whom were used in the earlier production of *The Pirate*. In spite of this, it seemed to others that the Guild was building up for the worst flop in theatrical history.

On the opening night of the Ballet Russe de Monte Carlo, Agnes de Mille was to dance in her own ballet *Rodeo*. She had written Lawrence suggesting herself as choreographer for the musical, and Lawrence passed the letter on to Richard Rodgers. I persuaded Dick and Oscar to go with me. After the performance I wired Agnes: "We think your work is enchanting. Come talk to us Monday."

Well, she came and she did the choreography that was to make her famous, but at that time she was a girl who had been unable to obtain a hearing anywhere.

We started the prodigious job of auditioning. We needed actors and singers and dancers and musicians. We needed just about everything but sword swallowers. One thing we discovered right at the start. We weren't going to get a cast of stars with big names. Nobody had any faith in the new musical that was being cooked up by the Guild. For the part of Laurey I remember we asked Mary Martin, who said no and then cried when she finally saw the show, and Shirley Temple, whose parents thought the part too mature for her.

So, perforce, we had a show without stars: Alfred Drake, Joan Robarts, Celeste Holm. They were not well known then — but they are now.

Auditioning was no bed of roses. Oscar wanted people who could speak his lines, Dick wanted people who could sing, Agnes wanted people who could dance. Why, I kept asking, can't we have girls who can dance and also have pretty legs? It seemed reasonable to me. It seemed unreasonable to Agnes.

Looking back, the chances are that at about that time I was highly unreasonable. I don't think I have ever worked harder than I did in trying to wrest and beguile that hundred thousand dollars from reluctant and frankly skeptical investors. At first I thought I had it licked: Metro-Goldwyn-Mayer had originally owned *Green Grow the Lilacs;* maybe they would finance the whole production. But Metro-Goldwyn-Mayer turned thumbs down. "Another Western," they said with contempt.

Then I turned to rival producers, who usually buy a slice of each other's productions. They looked over the book. "Too clean," they declared. "It hasn't a chance."

Next came the regular Broadway angels — or investors. The response was universal. "No gags, no girls, no chance." Helburn's Folly began to be known on Broadway as "the Guild's 'no' play."

One of these investors, Howard Cullman, later hung on the wall over his desk a framed copy of the letter in which I had asked for money. He estimated that his "no" cost him $970,000 in profits.

Then we started arranging cocktail parties at which the songs were played and sung by the principals. I remember the flat, empty feeling I had when one woman for whom we put on this performance said in a chilly voice, "I don't like plays about farm hands."

I became almost demented in my attempts to get investors. For the first time since the Guild had really got into its stride, we had no business manager. Warren Munsell, staff of strength, had been called into the army. For one black period Dick Rodgers expected to get a commission in the Air Force and Oscar wondered if perhaps he'd be wiser to call it quits and go out to Hollywood.

I began luring prospective backers into the theater to watch rehearsals, hoping that some of the fresh enchantment that so delighted me would meet with a response. Once, by parading some of my prospects through the room where Agnes de Mille was creating her ballets, I broke up the rehearsal. Agnes was driven, as we all were, to the point of exhaustion. As she describes the scene in her charming *Dance to the Piper:*

> I blew every fuse I had. Hurling my pocketbook at her head, I shouted and denounced and was dragged off screaming by Max Platt one day and held under a faucet of cold water until I quieted down.

With those ballets, created out of so much travail and turmoil, nerve strain and confusion, Agnes came into her own as one of America's leading choreographers. She not only has a highly distinguished and original talent but she is a distinguished and original person, honest, colorful, dominant and forthright. If she was sometimes annoyed past endurance with me during the exhausting weeks while the show went into production, she had some justification for it.

At that time, the salaries for dancers were low; so were the salaries of musicians, so were the salaries of the crew. Agnes herself was paid a fairly low salary. Since then, all the basic wages have risen greatly and chiefly because the

286

success of *Oklahoma!* opened up a new market for their services. And while Agnes was paid less than she felt was fair, her work with us gave her the first chance to show what she could do and opened the way for the future. If there was temporary injustice, and I hope there was not, the results have more than restored the balance.

Dick Rodgers was one person associated with the production who maintained his calm when all around him were going mad, though one day he said with good-humored exasperation, "Your name should not be Terry but terrier."

In all the years I have known and worked with Dick Rodgers, I don't remember his ever losing his temper. And that doesn't mean he doesn't have a temper. He could be boiling inside but he never boiled over. Oscar, too, never lost his temper or flared up but he has a greater inner serenity than Dick, who is a controlled dynamo rather than a steady flame like Oscar.

Another interesting aspect of Dick is his fine business sense. Once when we were going over a production report, I said, "Dick, how can such a great creative artist be such a good businessman?"

"You forget," he replied, "that music is largely numbers."

These two men, I think, have proved to be the most astounding partners in their field, not merely financially, not even because of the magnificent work that has grown out of their collaboration. What has impressed me most is the way in which two totally different personalities can supplement one another so perfectly. Perhaps the only other comparable team was Gilbert and Sullivan, but that partnership was marred by personal hostility and bitterness.

Nothing could be more unlike the collaboration of Dick and Oscar. They plan the main pattern of what they want to achieve, agree on mood and pace and their objective. Then Oscar, working slowly and laboriously, rewriting, polishing, but always with deep emotional conviction and sincerity, produces the book and lyrics, bit by bit, and turns them over to Dick.

Dick reads the lyrics and turns out his delightful songs with almost lightning speed. Some of his most successful songs have been composed in twenty, ten, even five minutes! He seems to read the lyrics, reach into the air and get from it effortlessly the musical phrases that best express them.

The weeks of rehearsal were frenzied. There wasn't an inch of the theater that wasn't being used by chorus, principals, dancers. Mamoulian, who integrated drama and song and dance, sweated at his task. Agnes drilled her dancers relentlessly. Dick sat at his keyboard, watching, listening. I bit my nails and scurried around and wondered if I had made the most fatal mistake of my life. Everyone else thought so.

Then Rouben decided he must do something to get a farm atmosphere. He thought of cows and horses and chickens. They didn't, for a number of obvious reasons, seem practicable. He settled on homing pigeons. Later, they made their solo flight on the tryout in New Haven. They never came back home so they may still be nesting in the rafters of a New Haven theater.

One of our minor — or major — worries was a title. Oscar originally called the play *Oklahoma,* but this was turned down, as people might confuse it with "Oakies." I suggested the title "Away We Go" but this was not approved, either, and was dropped after Boston. Armina, who was born on the Cherokee Strip, suggested the name "Cherokee Strip" for the title, but there were objections to this too. People might think of "strip tease." Finally someone suggested putting the exclamation point after "Oklahoma," and this was agreed upon.

When we opened, one blustery November night in New Haven, there was no special excitement. People said we would have to rewrite the second act; you can't kill people in a musical. Who ever heard of a murder in a comedy?

From New Haven we went on to Boston. In a drawing room on the train we practically rewrote the play. Boston was a nightmare. By the time of the opening almost all of us were sick. I caught a germ which kept me in bed for a week, though I did sneak to the theater twice with a trained nurse in attendance. Conferences with Dick, Oscar, Rouben, Armina, *et al.* were held beside the bed where I lay with ice packs to lower my temperature. Agnes de Mille had German measles and spread them to the ballet. The spots had to be covered with grease paint so the dancers could go on. Mrs. Hammerstein had a raging fever. The chorus kept getting bad throats and croaking through the performance. Lawrence, who was not sick, was at the theater in Boston every day organizing the work and consulting on the rearrangement of Act 2. A good time was had by all.

We brought *Oklahoma!* to New York. After the opening we gave a big party. At midnight we turned on the radio to get the first report of the critics.

"The show," we heard the news commentator say, "won't last a week."

Next morning we knew, for the first time, that we had a smash hit. Every newspaper carried a rave review. New York took *Oklahoma!* to its heart and a new kind of play with music had been created. It is my great pride that critics have claimed that in this type of musical America has made its greatest and most original contribution to the theater of the world.

The statistics in regard to *Oklahoma!* are part of theatrical history now. It ran for five years and nine weeks in New York, a total of 22,248 performances. It was on the road for years, celebrating its tenth birthday in Washington in 1953. People who had — and how reluctantly! — invested $1500 made $50,000 on their investment. One of these reluctant investors was Sam Behrman. I had appealed shamelessly to his gratitude to us for having produced so many of his plays, and he had invested, feeling that he was making a donation rather than putting up money with any idea of a return.

Oklahoma! played in Germany, England, South Africa, Sweden, Denmark, Australia, France, Italy. It toured the Pacific bases of the United States forces.

By the end of its first year it had won a special Pulitzer award. It started the recording of Broadway musicals with the original cast, which has grown into a sizable industry.

In April of 1944 I was able to write exultantly to Philip and Ellen Barry:

I found the shows all in good shape and going strong. It is pleasant to have successes but tiring to have to stand up in all one's own theaters. Friday night the mayor pulled up the curtain for the beginning of the second year of *Oklahoma!* He told the audience that if Ado Annie arrived on stage late and a little weary it would simply mean that he had been in her dressing room working on the city budget. That pleased them mightily . . .

The *Oklahoma!* party Saturday night was voted a great success by everyone and I must say I enjoyed myself, even though I had to take both coffee and benzedrine to withstand any party that started at one o'clock in the morning. Lawrence and I did a radio dialogue which Lawrence wrote in the morning, in which we figured as an old gaffer and crone celebrating the 20th anniversary of *Oklahoma!* I don't know how good our performances were but we were ham enough to get our laughs. Dick and Oscar did Ado Annie's "I Can't Say No" song, Oscar apparently singing but the soprano voice coming from a record of Celeste Holm's behind him.

And H. I. Phillips in "The Sun Dial" had the following ditty called "The Guild and the Gold":

> Eugene O'Neill was no playwrighting heel;
> For the Theatre Guild oft he made money.
> And that fellow G. Shaw made its life less than raw
> With a play that was often a honey;
> But the records all fell to a sweet fare-thee-well,
> And prosperity followed (and how! boys),
> When the Guild so sedate pulled a big thirty-eight
> And went in for the musical cowboys! . . .
>
> With the big problem plays it had plentiful days,
> Then "significant" stuff was its baby;
> Any genius who had little notes on a pad
> Got production at once, and not maybe.

But the bankroll grew fat when the Guild went to bat —
(And the fates did it one of their best turns) —
With those cowboys galore and a musical score,
As the dignified group fell for "westerns" . . .

But *Pygmalion's* through, for she won't spit or chew
And *Electra* cannot get a hearing,
For the Guild's gone all out with a rodeo shout
As the cow ponies tear through the clearing.
Broadway's all in a daze over what type show pays,
As the Guild goes to town with its furs on;
It once razzed the old girl and her old-fashioned curl
BUT SHE AIN'T THE SAME GAL WITH THOSE SPURS ON!

All this was good clean fun. It had also been a prodigious amount of work and a fantastic gamble that paid off, over the jeers and jests of Broadway. The excitement of *Oklahoma!* kept up for a long time.

Late in 1946, there was a prodigiously colorful opening in Oklahoma City. Our arrival at the station was heralded by loud-speakers booming "Oh, what a beautiful mornin'." We were met by what seemed to be all the town fathers, complete with a stagecoach drawn by six horses, cowboys, Indians, assorted livestock, all of it bedecked with bunting. There was supposed to be a great parade, but the streets were so icy that November day the horses couldn't keep their footing and it had to be abandoned.

Next day, Lawrence Langner, his wife Armina Marshall, and I were adopted into the Kiowa Indian tribe where I, wearing a great feather headdress to my stunned surprise, was given the name of "Little Woman Who Sees Far."

During most of the long run of *Oklahoma!* Dick, Oscar,

Lawrence and I had lunch once a week at Sardi's in order to discuss the various business and casting problems which would constantly arise. We called ourselves, as a private joke, The Gloat Club, as we happily enjoyed our unpredicted success. Others who had given us loyal assistance, such as Jerome Whyte, often joined with us.

After the success of *Oklahoma!* Lawrence and I made lists of other plays which might benefit by similar musical treatment. Among these were Ferenc Molnar's *Liliom,* and Robert Sherwood's *Reunion in Vienna.* We settled on *Liliom* as the most desirable, and began a patient propaganda to get Dick and Oscar to do for the play what they had done for Lynn Riggs's *Green Grow the Lilacs.* Molnar was reluctant to consider it. Many people had asked permission to use his play as a libretto. Even the great Puccini himself.

"Liliom," Molnar said, "is my best play; it is my masterpiece. I want it to be remembered as a Molnar play and not simply as the libretto of a Puccini opera."

At length we persuaded him to go see our production of *Oklahoma!* When we saw him again he nodded his head. He was willing to trust his *Liliom* to the hands of Dick and Oscar.

As I remember, it took about nine months to persuade them to undertake the job. Oscar Hammerstein didn't like the Budapest setting. He didn't feel at home in it.

"Well," I suggested, "why don't you set it in New Orleans?" That, I pointed out, had an exotic sort of color and yet was primarily an American background.

Oscar mulled it over. The Southern vernacular wasn't one he felt he could handle convincingly.

Dick Rodgers, who had been listening to all this, said, "If you're not at home with the Southern vernacular, what's wrong with New England?"

Without quite realizing it, without having definitely made up their minds, the two partners had unwittingly set to work, tossing ideas back and forth, beginning to build a structure.

I'll never forget the moment when Oscar read his soliloquy song aloud to Dick Rodgers. Dick's face lit up. From then on he was in love with *Carousel*. Today, even after *Allegro, The King and I, South Pacific* and others, this remains his favorite among all his works.

Carousel was, technically, I think, an advance over *Oklahoma!* In fact, in my opinion it is the finest musical produced in my time. For all the great popularity of the much later *South Pacific,* I think it remains unequaled.

There was another person who was delighted, too. I still remember Ferenc Molnar, white-haired, sitting in the back of the theater, his monocle removed from his eye while he wiped away his tears. This was his *Liliom,* not distorted but transfigured!

In *Carousel* there seemed to be no division at all between speech and song; they blended together. The play won the New York Drama Critics' Award as the best musical of the season and the Donaldson awards in eight different categories. It ran in New York for over two years.

Allegro, the third musical of Rodgers and Hammerstein, was a good job but it lacked the appeal of the others and it never won the same degree of popularity. It ran only forty-one weeks on Broadway. Here, I think, the problem was, at least in part, a production that was top-heavy. It was too elaborate for the comparative simplicity of the story itself; the framework sagged under the experimental stage tricks.

In 1950, on the 25th anniversary of the *Garrick Gaieties*, which had first brought Richard Rodgers to the Theatre Guild, we held a reception for him. Some of the performers from that first intimate revue were there: Libby Holman, Betty Starbuck, Sterling Holloway. Rouben Mamoulian, who had done so much to integrate the various factors in *Oklahoma!*, came too, and Mary Martin, Helen Hayes, Charles MacArthur, Deems Taylor. That was a good party and a warm tribute to a great musician and a fine man.

And in between, and ever since, I have tried to work out the right kind of musical setting for Sherwood's *Reunion in Vienna* and for Molnar's *The Guardsman*. How many lunches at Sardi's have been spent outlining my ideas to Gian Carlo Menotti, to Irving Berlin, to Leonard Bernstein, to Kurt Weill, to Sigmund Romberg, to Cole Porter!

The play with music and ballet and its eternal mutations has not exhausted its possibilities. As yet we have barely glimpsed them.

Hits and Misses

BY THE END of its first decade the Theatre Guild was at its peak. By the end of its second it was in debt to its directors. It came as close as it ever will come to being abandoned in despair. What had happened? A combination of things: the long and devastating effect on the economy of the nation caused by the depression; the enormous and rapidly increasing costs; the fact that Hollywood had claimed not only many of the finest actors but a number of the most promising playwrights. Other theaters were now offering real competition by presenting fine plays. And last, but not least, a whole series of financially disastrous plays.

As part of the theatrical record, however, I must point out that the Guild was not alone in having difficulties. In 1937 there were only 28 theaters in New York as against 80 in 1929.

The drama critics have since accounted for our near debacle by the quality of the scripts we accepted for production. Well, what was the record? Between 1929 and 1936, the Theatre Guild presented the following plays:

Elizabeth the Queen, Green Grow the Lilacs, Getting Married, Mourning Becomes Electra, Reunion in Vienna, Too True to Be Good, The Good Earth, Biography, Both Your Houses, Ah, Wilderness!, The School for Husbands, Mary of Scotland, They Shall Not Die, Jig Saw, Valley Forge, Rain from Heaven, Escape Me Never (co-produced by Charles B. Cochran with Elizabeth Bergner), *The Simpleton of the Unexpected Isle, Parade, The Taming of the Shrew, Porgy and Bess, Call It a Day, End of Summer, Idiot's Delight, The Masque of Kings, Amphitryon 38, Wine of Choice,* and *The Sea Gull.*

Brooks Atkinson wrote: "In the choice and variety of its plays, in the quality of its productions, and the general excellence of the acting, the Guild is still the best that the American theater has to offer."

Then where was the flaw in the structure that nearly bankrupted the Guild while it was offering such a list of plays by distinguished playwrights, well produced and, for the most part, brilliantly acted?

In our first ten years, the Guild had been a pacesetter on the American stage. Its number of successes balanced its number of failures. Our average was about two successes out of five, whereas an average of one out of five was considered good for any producer. In the course of the next ten years our failures increased by 50 per cent. And from the opening of *Pygmalion* in 1926, we had eleven hits in a row.

From the early Thirties on, changes began to come quickly. Our board system of production was beginning to meet with widespread protest. What had worked splendidly in the beginning was working painfully now that we were dealing

297

with living playwrights who balked at having six pairs of hands in the broth. A group of the best playwrights, most of whose work we had been producing for years, turned away from the Guild in a body and formed the Playwrights Company. Now they were producing on their own.

Then, too, the Guild's subscription system proved that it could boomerang. When all went well we were in clover. We could start a season with more money in the bank than most producers ever saw. If our plays succeeded, the money could remain as a nice and comforting nest egg. But when the plays flopped we were in trouble because we had to continue to run them until all the subscription audience had seen them. In that case, we were taking a real beating.

Another problem began to loom more and more on the horizon. In the early days, it was possible for a management to build with an author. You gambled on his first play and perhaps on his second, and when he was successful you both gained by it. But the situation began to change. If the young playwright had a success, there was no assurance at all that he would even submit his second play to you. There was no longer a feeling that writing and production formed a kind of partnership. So whereas in the past we could assume that the next script would be submitted to us automatically as a courtesy, we now learned that we had to pay a high option on it, sight unseen.

And, nightmare of the producer, we came increasingly to face the problem of financing plays. The Theatre Guild held out much longer than most managements against using outside capital. We were able to carry our own load for years. But, with mounting costs, this was no longer possible if we wanted to survive. In the early years, even if we had a flop on our hands, our losses were relatively small, about one-sixth, perhaps even less, of what they are today.

So today the Theatre Guild plays, like those of other managements, are put on with borrowed capital. This necessarily alters the picture. This money is invested in a gamble, true, and the investors are often willing to take chances — but the odds must be at least partially in their favor. You cannot urge people to invest in something that, from forty years of producing, you know perfectly well will be a financial loss.

As a result of these problems, the Guild, for the first time in its financial history, became the target of the critics for being less of an art theater. Where, they wondered acidly, were those experimental plays we had put on as a special bonus for our subscribers? The answer to that was easy. The play we could put on for a couple of evenings in the past as a theatrical experiment had cost us perhaps $5000. Now it cost $80,000 or more.

One of the finest New York drama critics, perhaps one of the finest drama critics anywhere today, is Brooks Atkinson of the *New York Times*. Over the years I frequently thrashed out this idea with him, particularly when he took the commercial theater to task for its shortcomings.

Doesn't it come down to this [I wrote him on one such occasion]: Should the theater pay for itself or should it be endowed like music, where apparently costs have risen above the demand? Is the standard of theatrical entertainment to be that people want it enough to pay for it? Or isn't it? This is something that should be settled between the critics and the producers. It would make for better understanding and less bitterness . . .

I imagine all the producers of standing reacted somewhat similarly when you said at the end of your deservedly enthusiastic review of *Candida*, "Let this department add a slightly bitter postscript. Why is it that we have to wait for labors of love to see the commercial theatre at its best?"

Is it possible you don't know the answer? And if so, may I be pardoned a slight bitterness that you don't. . . . The answer to your question is simple. When things have to be measured by money they *can't* compete with things that can be measured with love.

It was largely as a result of intolerable conditions in New York that, early in 1935, I went to Hollywood to fulfill a contract I had signed with Columbia Pictures Corporation. I went to find out what, if anything, the movies had to teach the stage, to learn new techniques, to see what each of us had to give the other.

I had been in Hollywood only a few weeks when I discovered that I was literally a spy in the enemy camp. The Theatre Guild had done Maxwell Anderson's *Valley Forge* and Frank Capra was, unknown to me, bidding for it. Columbia was so anxious to keep me from finding this out that I was prevented, by machinations worthy of a spy film, from meeting Capra until the sale had been closed.

My first job for Columbia was work on a script for Grace Moore, with all the Hollywood paraphernalia of conferences, story meetings, and viewing daily rushes. I settled down as much as I ever settle down — in a lovely little pine-paneled office — and began to learn something about the business.

My initial reaction was one of excitement over a new medium, over the incredible fact that there were unlimited production funds, over the kind of mass excitement engendered by the fact that I was in a community where everyone shared the same interests. It was all new and it was all exhilarating.

Before long, I had come to see that Hollywood was a mere personality market which ruins both actors and dramatists. Most of the material I handled was far worse than the run-of-the-mill scripts that came to me at the Guild. When I found a halfway decent script I lost my perspective, thought it was fine and produced it, independently and disastrously, when I returned to New York.

I began to understand for the first time the reason for the problems that had arisen in the past when we hired movie actors for the stage. Screen acting is largely synthetic. The legitimate actor must build his character from beginning to end; the movie actor, working in brief scenes which are not shot chronologically, creates a character in isolated fragments. The legitimate actor has to create the whole illusion; the movie actor has the camera to do nine tenths of his work for him. The legitimate actor must have a trained voice; the movie actor can rely on the amplifier for volume. The legitimate actor, by relating to his stage partners, can build his emotions on their responses and deepen his characterization; the movie actor, using the fragmentary method, is deprived of this interplay.

My year in Hollywood convinced me that the real artist in the theater would never find full creative satisfaction in the movies. More money — of course. A more widespread fame — naturally. But more satisfaction — far from it. I realized that for all its uncertainty, for all the stress and strain, for all the grinding unceasing hard work, it was the theater to which I belonged, and I returned to Broadway and the Guild.

The accumulated pressure of years had led to the complete collapse of the board system. We had more and more irreconcilable differences of opinion. For years, in fact from the beginning, Lawrence and I had been the producers. The others were primarily artists and they wanted the privileges of artists without the responsibilities of management. They had no grasp of our financial difficulties. At one point we were so low we could not pay ourselves any salaries. "But why not," one of them asked, "if we can still pay the stenographers?"

So, after so many years of operating as a group of six, Lawrence and I took over the Guild; and for the last half of our existence we have run it together, with Armina participating later on, first as associate director and later as executive producer of the radio and television departments, and in the last five years as a full partner.

The beginning of that new system of management was such a deciding point in our careers, in fact in our existence as a theater, that I'll have to give some space to it, for it is as typical as any story I know of the unpredictable quality of all theater.

This is the story of Philip Barry's play, *The Philadelphia Story,* and of Katharine Hepburn. Kate and Mary Martin, incidentally, are the two finest women I have known in forty years in the theater.

Philip Barry, very Irish, temperamental and delightful, had been having a bad time as a playwright. In fact, he had been looking at his list of failures with something like despair. Kate had had some disastrous Broadway experience during which Brooks Atkinson had been tough on her and Dorothy Parker had written the celebrated review in which she said Kate had "run the gamut of emotion from A to B." A succession of poor pictures had done little for her reputation as an actress. She was, according to Hollywood, "box-office poison."

Philip and Kate were two of the partners in the enterprise. The third was the Guild, disrupted in management and tottering on its feet.

Kate was in Hollywood doing the film version of Philip Barry's *Holiday*. Philip began to discuss a play with Kate and before long he had started to write *The Philadelphia Story* as a starring vehicle for her. He talked to me about it. He wanted the Guild to do it.

I had worked with Kate in the past. She had come to me long before, looking for a job, and got one as an understudy for the road tour of *A Month in the Country* with Nazimova, though it had not worked out.

Then I cast her as the lead in *Jane Eyre*. I might say here that the play was not good. Something is wrong with that story for the stage. I don't know of any successful attempt to stage the novel.

Working with Kate was a delight; she is a wonderful person to do a play with, honest and forthright, and unusually generous. Fred Stone, who had co-operated with her in the movie version of *Alice Adams,* remembered how, when the film had to be cut, Kate went to the director to say, "Fred has done a marvelous job with his big scene. If you have to cut, cut out some of my stuff." I don't know of any other incident quite like that in Hollywood.

Kate has a rock-bound sort of character. Her loyalties are unswerving. Her friends last. She lives simply, never flamboyantly. Her family, made up of distinguished scientists, never took her career seriously until she made her smash hit in *The Philadelphia Story.* I still grin to myself when I think of the party Kate gave after a performance. As long as her family was there she served beer; when they had gone she brought out the champagne.

Working with Kate on that first play, *Jane Eyre,* had been an interesting experience, because, with a movie background, Kate had to learn from the beginning how to create and build character. She was a hard worker and highly intelligent. She knew how to do the little pieces of the mosaic by which a film is built up, but she had no conception of building a character through three acts. It was wonderful to watch how she did it, groping her way from a stale performance that had a certain brilliance and charm, but no solid characterization, to the full realization of the woman whom she was portraying.

Jane Eyre paid back its production expenses on the road, doing terrific business, particularly in Chicago, but we never brought it in to New York.

Two weeks after *Jane Eyre* closed, I went out to lecture in New Jersey to help out an agent. I was to substitute for a speaker who was too ill to go. The president of the club told me I was the first new speaker they had had in seventeen years. Then he asked me when *Jane Eyre* had closed.

"Two weeks ago," I said.

"I missed seeing it," he said regretfully, "but I did see you in *Little Women*."

Incidentally, on one occasion I really did substitute for Kate Hepburn. Bryn Mawr was having a fête and asked Kate to appear as Queen Elizabeth. When she refused, they asked me to do it. Kate sent me a make-up man and for most of an afternoon I worked at a long counter with two telephones and an enormous mirror in front of me while he wiped out my eyebrows, remodeled my face and perched a red wig on my head.

"Now," he said, "you can do it."

Well, I couldn't, of course. I'd been too busy telephoning to watch how he did it. So I settled for the red wig. There was a production of *Gammer Gurton's Needle* that day at Bryn Mawr and a Robin Hood procession, and I was carried on a palanquin high on the shoulders of our professors, poor dears. Aside from the fact that the throne proved to be too narrow for my farthingale, all went well on this my only appearance as Queen Elizabeth.

We opened *The Philadelphia Story* in Philadelphia where it made a great hit. There was no doubt about it, Phil and Kate and the Guild had struck a bonanza.

Let me point out, however, that this was not the end of the job. It might be interesting to those who aren't familiar with theatrical procedure, to see Lawrence's notes made during our first conference after the Philadelphia opening:

Main Jobs

1. Set theme and mood in Act I before the Uncle William—father situation.

2. End of Act Three.

3. Middle of Act III.

Minor Jobs

1. Dexter — point up character throughout and build his position in relation to Tracy and clarify situation in Act III. (Not telephone call to George.)

2. Cut Sandy scene, Act I, by making exposition clearer and cutting down exposition of publishers' papers, etc.

3. Improve Stacy scene beginning Scene 2, Act 2.

Act III, make clear that Dexter motivates Dina telling the dream.

Deepen Dexter–Tracy scene.

Develop idea of Tracy having become a better person — do this in situation if possible.

Cut letter reading scene and George denouement. Avoid dragged in effect of the Destiny speech. Can this be handled more deftly?

Final denouement of play too long.

Cut last part of Act III.

During the tryout period we went on to Washington. Of course, we had a theater booked in New York but the big question was: to bring the play in or not to bring it in. On that decision rested the future of all of us.

At that time Lawrence was wrestling with the peculiar activities of Orson Welles and his *Five Kings* in Boston and he left the whole thing to its fate while he came down to Washington to discuss the momentous question.

We sat around the hotel most of the night, drinking milk and orange juice — typical of theatrical people in spite of their reputation — balancing the pros and cons. Should we? Shouldn't we?

"For God's sake," Kate exclaimed, "don't throw away your money. Let's be practical about this. We've got a fortune if we stay out of New York."

On the other hand, I pointed out, if we kept the play on the road for a long time we would take the bloom off it by the time we brought it in. The performances would have lost their freshness. It pulls a performance out of proportion to be long on the road because of the large theaters in which it is played.

Phil thought we were taking a big risk if we brought it in. On the other hand, he was prepared to take the risk.

Lawrence and I weighed pros and cons. We made a list of them and we thrashed them out one at a time.

We looked at each other. We nodded. We were going to bring it in. We were shaking in our boots.

Kate threw up her hands. "Do anything you want, dear," she said in a tone of foreboding. "Throw your money away."

Well, we brought it in and we had a smash hit. It re-established Philip Barry's reputation as a playwright; it made Katharine Hepburn famous; and it paid off the Guild debts. That's the theater for you in a nutshell.

Later, and after long persuasion, Lawrence talked Kate into doing *As You Like It*. She had been terrified of attempting Shakespeare and finally came to love doing it.

I was in London when I received a letter from Lawrence:

307

"Kate definitely wants to do *As You Like It* . . . Kate and I both feel that there can be some good casting done in England . . . As this may be the beginning of a very important series of things for us, Kate says 'Don't be cheap — we only live once,' and Lawrence says, 'Don't be extravagant either.'"

I returned to England to get a director for Kate in *As You Like It*. I found Michael Benthall at the Shakespeare Memorial Theatre. Kate insisted on seeing him before she made up her mind, and as she was in California at the time I had to persuade him to leave England and make the trip to Hollywood. They liked each other at once and worked together splendidly.

Later, during her season at the American Shakespeare Festival Theater in Stratford, Connecticut, Kate was an inspiration to the whole company, with a quality of vitality, understanding and kindness that made them all adore her. Though she is as vital as a dynamo she does not have the rampant ego of most actresses. She knows clearly what she wants but she says so directly, instead of using the devious methods of most women. She argues out her points and tries to see your point of view as well.

She took a scholarly approach to her Shakespeare parts, did a lot of work and research, planned her own costumes, and so forth. It was also her idea to produce *Measure for Measure* as a Western.

While Kate went on from triumph to triumph, Phil Barry, too, continued to write successful plays. An interesting situation came up in *Foolish Notion* in which we starred Tallulah Bankhead. Because Phil was ill and unable to do the necessary rewrite on his play, it opened in New York in an unfinished condition and was later revised for a road tour on which it played to record audiences.

Tula is a law unto herself and unlike any actress I have ever known. How beautiful she was in those early days! One of the loveliest women on the stage. She was also the most difficult. A director had his hands full with Tula. Because she had difficulty sleeping, she was generally at her most alert in the small hours of the morning, at which time she expected to be entertained. More than one hotel has raised complaints over the storm and stress issuing from the Bankhead suite while other people were trying to sleep. So a director had to talk to her, entertain her, keep her quiet generally, so the show could go on.

Two moments stand out in my recollections of Tallulah Bankhead. One was when a pet lion cub of hers tried to climb on my lap in a hotel room, considerably to my alarm, though Tula assured me he was "only playful." And once when she turned on Lawrence and me and exclaimed, "The trouble with you two is that you are too damned normal!"

TWENTY

In Search of Theater

ONE OF THE most revolutionary events in the theater occurred during my Hollywood sojourn. That was the acceptance of the new contract of the Dramatists Guild, which took authority out of the hands of the producer and gave it to the author, where it remains today. I say "revolutionary" advisedly, for the contract completely altered and emasculated the functions of the producer.

In the theatrical world in which I had been trained, the producer was the boss. Today, he is almost the puppet of the author. Now this will, I suppose, arouse frenzied outcries from the authors, but I'd like to make my point, anyhow. The writer's job is writing. Period. A man may be a brilliant playwright but that does not mean that he is also an expert or even an effectual producer. The two rôles require different qualities; they require different experience; they require different training.

The contract as it stands today allows the author to have the final say on casting. There is no field, I suppose, in which writers make more frequent or more serious mistakes. Even Eugene O'Neill, sure and experienced in his craft, was almost always poor in casting.

The producer accepts the play, finds the money to put it on and then, too often, has to watch, impotent and helpless, while the writer destroys his own work by his interference in matters about which he is not well informed. The producer, seeing ruin stare him in the face, cannot put his foot down. He must persuade, he must cajole, he must convince. Small wonder that production more and more lands in a mess.

I could name a dozen plays, in as many seconds, in which the writer's interference with casting or direction either made his play a flop or would have done so if a silver-tongued producer had not managed to talk him out of his ideas.

And speaking of talking, sometimes I wish authors would be content to be read and not heard. I remember one play we did which had a terrific third-act curtain. But the author, a tall, thin, rawboned man, was hell-bent on making a speech on the opening night. The director was warned, the producer was warned, the cast was warned. And a lot of good it did. Short of chloroform nothing would have stopped him. He went out, with practically no public demand at all, and talked and talked, a long rambling speech so dull and point-less that it took the edge off the final curtain and spoiled his play.

With the producer reduced now to a money-raising office boy, a lot of producers say, in a disgruntled tone, that from a commercial angle it would be wiser if they all became agents, taking 10 per cent instead of going in on 50 per cent of the play.

Why then do we continue producing? Because we've got to. Because, with all its drawbacks, there isn't any other kind of life we can even contemplate.

We at the Guild started, young and ardent and full of ideals, to create an art theater that would permit a hearing of theatrical ware that could not obtain a hearing elsewhere in the commercial theater. Without vanity, I think we achieved what we set out to do.

With the passage of the years, a depression, two world wars, a cold war, and the inescapable problem of mounting costs, the theatrical scene has changed almost beyond recognition. In the old days, it cost very little to put on a play. If it ran one hundred nights it was considered a success. Now production costs are dangerously high; it takes at least three months to recover them and, frequently, from six months to a year.

This means that unless a play is a hit and has a long run it is a financial loss. But the long run, while it means a profit to one playwright, means that there are fewer opportunities for the untried playwright. It means producers are hesitant about taking chances. It means that actors have little opportunity to diversify their rôles.

But there is another and an even more dangerous element of theatrical expense. This is the fact that tickets are largely in the hands of speculators, the prices are so fantastically high that the low-income groups cannot go to the theater, even if there were tickets available at the box office. What we are getting, instead, is the theater party, is the expense-account audience. What we are losing increasingly is lovers of theater itself.

Sitting in Schrafft's one day not long ago I overheard two young women talking. One of them said, "I haven't seen a play for three years. By the time I hire a babysitter and buy the tickets and commute to New York it costs me at least thirty dollars."

"It's the same with me," the other said. "We're saving our money for a television set because it will be cheaper than the theater in the long run. Still, it isn't the same, is it?"

"No," the first woman agreed, regret in her voice, "it isn't the same."

No one has done more for theater in the United States than Lawrence Langner. Its debt to him is beyond calculation. After the Washington Square Players came the Theatre Guild, in which he served as a director and co-director since its beginnings. Then, to implement his desire for a repertory company and for a place to try out new plays, came his Westport Country Playhouse which he built and operated with Armina Marshall, and which has transformed the whole picture of summer theater. Formerly, summer theaters featured stock companies and revived old Broadway successes. Lawrence reversed the process. The Westport Country Playhouse is a place where the young playwright can see his work in production and learn from the experience; it is a place where experimental plays and fare for limited audiences are given a hearing.

"All my clients," Lawrence said once, "have research departments to develop new products. The summer theater must serve the same function for new plays and for playwrights, for actors and technicians, for directors and stage designers." It is this theatrical workshop, this laboratory, that may contain the seed of future theatrical growth.

It was at Lawrence's Westport theater that I had my first experience as a director. It was also at the Westport theater that I made my one brief appearance in the rôle of an actress. Mine was a minor part in *Susanna and the Elders,* written by Lawrence and Armina, in which Uta Hagen was the lead. By sheer accident I acquired a momentary and quite undeserved fame when the critic from *Variety* got drunk and reported glowingly, "Theresa Helburn was dynamic in the leading rôle." A mistake which was soon cleared up. Though Robert Milton did warm my heart by writing me, "I hear you are better than Alexander Woollcott."

My husband, watching my performance, had only one comment to make: "Your petticoat was showing the whole time."

Another of Lawrence's successful projects in which Armina and I joined with him was the creation of the Shakespeare Festival Theater at Stratford, Connecticut, a lovely modification of the old Globe, set in beautiful surroundings. Here, as in Canada and in England, there is a theater and a company devoted entirely to bringing Shakespeare to the public. Last summer, before the regular season started, there was a period dedicated exclusively to presenting Shakespeare for school children, who were brought by bus from as far in the surrounding countryside and the neighboring states as was practicable. Watching the youngsters while they watched the stage, one knew that a generation of playgoers was in the making. That is part of the function of great theater.

And here is a curious sidelight on what theater can accomplish. We presented Paul Robeson in *Othello.* Robeson is a highly intelligent as well as a highly talented actor. One evening after a performance on the road I was talking to him.

"You know," he told me, "a number of the young men of my race were reluctant to go into the services. They felt that as long as they received no equality of treatment there was no justification for making them fight for a way of life they weren't permitted to participate in. But a lot of them came to tell me that, after seeing *Othello,* after hearing the warm applause of a white audience for a Negro's performance, they felt differently about the whole thing."

At Stratford, in the school of the American Shakespeare Academy, and at Westport in its apprentice system, there has been put into operation one of our enduring dreams, a place for actors to learn their art. Of the hundreds who apply only a couple of dozen are chosen by each group. They are taught some of the fundamentals of acting, which they can learn in few places today, and their theoretical training is bolstered and fortified by practical knowledge and experience on the professional stage.

Today, the summer theater everywhere is a growing factor in the training of young actors. As a rule, the theaters charge tuition. In some cases the young actors work at painting scenery, at carpentry, or whatever has to be done, while having a certain number of classes and lectures. At Westport, they give little shows at the end of the season. During the season they are cast in small parts in the regular performances, sometimes indeed in really good parts. The same is even more true at Stratford, where students and former students have played important rôles.

Here, as in auditioning for the professional theater, they

315

try them out first in order to weed out those without talent. You cannot get too much from such a reading, of course, but you can determine the quality of the voice, the diction, and something of the quality of the mind.

And this, incidentally, brings up a point which always interests me. We have frequently had radio actors come to us for auditions. They read extremely well. It took us a perceptible time to discover that an ability to act is unnecessary for radio, only an ability to read. Time after time, we have learned to our cost that this was all there was, they could not grow, they had never learned the rudiments of building a part.

People have often asked me, who is the finest actor? In my opinion, the crown must go to Sir John Gielgud. He is the greatest artist of them all. Sir Laurence Olivier runs him a close second; more human, perhaps, as Gielgud is more of a poet. Now and then, people complain that Olivier has a tendency to ham. That's an interesting point to me, because English audiences accept much broader characterizations than we do. American actors tend to underplay, and often English actors seem to us to overdo it. Certainly this must be a lot closer to the Elizabethan approach to theater. And there's another thing: here in the United States we've been moving closer and closer to the drawing room and shying away from the theatrical. But you simply can't defraud theater of the theatrical. It belongs there.

A play is the most ephemeral of all art forms. Only repertory can really keep plays alive for any length of time, except for the periodical revival of the masterpieces. Knowing how many fine plays the Guild had produced — and that, except for the couple of hundred thousand who had seen them both in New York and on the road, they were virtually unknown to the great bulk of the people — Lawrence, Armina and I began to turn over in our minds the possibility of doing some of our best plays and the best plays of other producers on radio where they could reach an almost completely untouched audience.

Archibald MacLeish had declared, "The peace can best be achieved if the peoples of the world share with one another their common inheritance of art, knowledge and skill." It became increasingly evident to us that before we tried to share our common inheritance of art with others we should first share it among ourselves.

At first the idea was received with horror. "The Theatre Guild is the kiss of death in radio," we were told bluntly. But then nobody but us had believed much in the aspirations of the early Theatre Guild.

However, our attorney, H. William Fitelson, became interested, and personally secured for us a contract with U. S. Steel to produce one-hour plays on radio. We organized a special department, operated by Armina, with Lawrence and me acting as supervisors; later on Armina became the executive producer and Bill the general manager of the program. Our radio programs were based on theater plays only, as we did not produce so-called "originals." We did not attempt to give people gangsters or cowboys, neither crime stories nor sentimental romances. We gave them the very best theater we could.

There were problems, of course. But we learned as we went along. And this new audience liked our plays, it wanted more of them. What's more, the Theatre Guild on the Air began to do for radio what the Theatre Guild had done for Broadway. It raised standards.

Later, when television began to come into use, we prepared a program of six plays for the National Broadcasting Company which set standards for the production of theater plays in television. And then, when our radio programs changed over into television, we began a series of television plays, some from the theater and some "originals." Other producers have followed our initial efforts; so that now, in the midst of gunshots and galloping hoofs, there is also a choice of fine plays — though perhaps not as many as are needed.

Television, which was regarded with foreboding by Broadway, much as the radio had been and the talkies before it, has proved in many ways to be a boon not only to playwrights but to actors. Its effect, it seems to me, has been to stimulate playwriting rather than to compete with it. The young playwright, who must often wait for months for production, and sometimes never gets it, now has an opportunity to express his ideas without the strain or uncertainty of waiting for Broadway production. As for the actor, he is enabled to do a variety of rôles, a thing which is impossible with the long-run play, thus increasing the scope and range of his technique.

When I got this far I thought: Well, that's pretty much the picture of the theater as I knew it in the past and the theater of today. But what of the theater of tomorrow?

One thing seems fairly certain. The present situation is growing more untenable every day. If we are not going to make the commercial theater completely impossible, we've got to change our methods.

I have my own particular dream of what the theater of tomorrow should be and how it could be attained. It should be a co-operative venture in which everyone — producers, actors, directors — go in at a minimum salary and then divide the profits. Everyone associated with the theater would gain by this, even those who normally expect to make the most money, because they are also the ones who take the risk and the big losses. By this system, risk is so minimized that it can almost be discounted.

How is this kind of co-operative system to be worked out? Not easily. Just at the start of the Second World War, I sat in at a meeting made up of all the groups in the theater; the purpose of the meeting was to find out what contribution the stage could make to the war effort. As it happened, I was the only woman present and I sat between the heads of the actors' union and the stagehands.

For some time we talked amicably. At last I said, "Look here, why can't we all get together? Why can't everyone go in for a basic minimum salary and a share in the profits, minimize loss and enable everyone to gain?"

They thought it over, because co-operation of any kind is an alluring picture. Then they shook their heads. No, they said regretfully, that would be impossible. Such a system would make them part of management, and then they would no longer be in a position to fight.

But what would there be to fight about, under the circumstances, I asked them. They had no answer to that.

And yet, without some such co-operative venture, how are we to have an opportunity to try out unusual wares, to experiment? Must we relinquish all this to the summer theater and the ventures coming up Off Broadway? Perhaps we must. But, personally, I'm ready to put up a fight.

I ought to explain that I don't think of experimental theater primarily as a classroom for the inexperienced playwright. I am thinking of it as an outlet for mature writing talent, which does not aim at mass appeals or smash-hit values. I've been beating the drum for this experimental theater on a co-operative basis for a long time. I'll go on beating the drum.

My idea is to go back to the Guild's original system of Sunday performances — where there is no problem of competing with the commercial theater; where playwright, director, producer, actors, everyone would go in on a minimum wage and then share the profits. Every director or actor worth his salt would jump at the opportunity to find new means of expression.

Nothing that is alive can stand still: it goes forward or it goes back. *Without experiment, theater cannot live, because it cannot grow.*

The obstacle, of course, stands out a mile. What do the union workers get out of such a project to compensate them for forgoing their union scale of wages? Because we've got to be fair: their scale of living remains the same whether they work for the commercial theater or the experimental theater. Now there is no getting around the fact that, human nature being what it is, the man on top is bound to take what advantage he can. In the pre-union days the stagehands and all the technicians around the theater were underpaid. Today, under union scales, they seem to me overpaid. The danger is that by making production too expensive they are threatening the very life of the theater itself, and so endangering their own jobs. There must be a happy medium somewhere, an equal pull so that no one gets on top. I call it co-operation.

But to get back to my major question: What does the union worker gain by this experimental theater setup for special Sunday performances? Well, the unhappy truth is that, temporarily, he does not gain a thing. He is working for less money than he could get in the regular theater. So? The only immediate solution I can see is that back payments at full union scale will take precedence, out of profits, even before the repayment of capital. And, honestly, where's the injustice in that?

So far as financing such an experimental theater is concerned, my dream would be to make the whole enterprise truly co-operative, under the sponsorship of the commercial theater as a whole, the industry paying a reasonably proportioned amount after each producer has covered his own production costs. I'd like to see the Dramatists Guild and the Actors Equity and the heads of the unions act as an advisory group for such an organization.

If we are to maintain a legitimate theater and the co-operative idea is not accepted, then there simply must be a new kind of approach to theater. I have always favored a national theater, *if it could be a free art theater, completely removed from politics, and run by free artists.* That would be the ideal from every standpoint. But, recollecting the public attempts at censorship of the federal theater during the war, I cannot be too sanguine.

Today, theater means Broadway. Tomorrow, I hope it will mean acting companies in all the great cities, just as there are orchestras in various cities or, where the city cannot maintain an orchestra of its own, there is at least an orchestral or operatic season financed by sponsors.

If commercial theater must mean only commercial entertainment, then I see no answer except that of sponsorship. Surely a city that can support sixteen weeks or so of fine music can support a comparable amount of good theater. With a repertory season, every actor would be kept constantly at work, the artistic monotony of the long run could be broken up, the actors could play a wide range of rôles.

Best of all, with the theater establishing its own indigenous character in Philadelphia and Boston, in Baltimore and Washington, in Chicago and San Francisco, in Houston and New Orleans, and so on and so on, more native drama could be developed, the Broadway pattern could be broken, and new live theater would take fresh life in the country.

Oh, if I had ten more years of active work ahead of me, how I'd love to try it!

TWENTY-ONE

In Search of Me

A FRIEND OF MINE, looking over these pages, asked, "But when do you get away from the theater? When do you live your own life?"

The only possible answer seems to be: The theater *is* my life. And yet that is not altogether true. It is true, of course, that never, in the past forty years, have I really escaped or wanted to escape from the theater. Until recently during the summers I have kept in close touch with the Westport Country Playhouse, where the Guild often produced experimental plays in which I participated. I also visited other summer theaters, sometimes in the hope of finding talented actors, sometimes to see the production of a play by a new playwright. Even when I visit the West Coast or Europe on vacations I am constantly on the lookout for new writers and actors.

But aside from technical knowledge in one's own field, sometimes I wonder how much anyone ever learns from living. I wonder to what extent any of us actually change as

323

people. Even now I'm constantly starting over, continually planning to reform my ways, earnestly attempting to take myself in hand and rebuild my character. One day I had to laugh at myself. I was at the Ritz in Paris, just back from buying dresses from Schiaparelli, with a full schedule of dinners and parties ahead with fascinating people. I'd gone as far as I could, with such abilities as I have, in my chosen profession. But there I was, earnestly reading *Wake Up and Live* and making solemn notes for my future guidance. And I was over sixty at the time!

With the years creeping up, getting so ominously close to the seventy that's supposed to be the terminus for the life span, I cleared the decks where I could and resigned from all clubs, except the National Arts of which I'm a life member and from which I could resign only by committing suicide, which isn't worth it.

Only for a few weeks each year have I lived comparatively remote from Broadway, enjoying my season in the sun, though the echoes follow me even to Terrytop, the house Oliver and I rebuilt at Westport. This was to be a place to rest in, to "get away from it all," to vegetate and invite the soul. Of course, it hasn't been like that. True, Oliver and I had more time for leisurely talk. The phone didn't ring so much — well, not all the time, at any rate.

Rarely, when work was slack and there were no plays in production, we were able to steal some time, even in the winter months, for Connecticut. I'd go walking in the snow with Blunder, our ninety-five-pound English sheep dog — and taking a walk without Blunder was like a stew without onions. Blunder, who went through life with the mistaken idea that he was a lapdog, once, to my pride and surprise, won a blue ribbon at the dog show. True, he was the only dog in his class, but that wasn't his fault. When I came home from one of these winter walks I wrote:

The sky is blue as Italy;
    The slender firs like cypress grow,
The snow burns hot against my cheek,
    Although the temp. is ten below.

Oh, sing away of southern climes,
    Twang your guitar until it splinters;
You cannot charm me with your rhymes —
    Give me Connecticut in winters.

My husband loved the country but he did not care for possessions or the burden of a house. He could have lived quite happily in a trunk or even a small Gladstone bag. But he was in love with trees. How often I have seen him nurse a burned tree back to health with infinite patience and stubborn loving care! He did not like to prune anything. Terrytop became known to our friends as "the Opdycke Wilderness."

Oliver did not even like to cut flowers. "One flower is enough," he would say, but in a kind of helpless tone. He had made his point but he knew there would be a lot of flowers cut anyhow.

After his death, when I began to have the place cleared and some of the trees cut down, I had an odd sort of pang, as though I were murdering his friends. Even when people said Terrytop had become "the Helburn Park" I wasn't sure I had done right.

Oliver, as I've said, disliked social life and I never planned to see people while we were in Westport. One of the friends whom he enjoyed seeing often, however, and against whom he did not feel the need to raise his usual defenses, was Ben Kaye, our lawyer. Ben's stanch friendship, his loyalty, and his thoughtfulness have been a continuing comfort to me. Actually I went out a lot. Westport has always seemed a little different from any other place. It would be hard to find another town of its size with so heavy a concentration of creative people. They are such extraordinarily good company that sometimes one forgets to consider whether they are good people. Or perhaps, sobered by a heart attack and the warning note it has sounded, I have come to look recently for values I never missed in the past.

"The trouble with us," Helen Gahagan Douglas once said, complaining of the superficiality of this group, "is that we have got too far away from the bed, the source of all energy."

But if there is an air of artificiality about Westport, there is also solid creative work coming from there, too. And whether they are brittle or not, malicious or not, they are some of the most entertaining people to be found anywhere, and I have been privileged to spend my life among them.

Westport in summer means a variegated group: Edna Ferber, always at odds with someone so you have to find out whom she's speaking to this week in planning a dinner party; John Gunther, very jovial; Beatrice Lillie, who pops up there as she does on ships to Europe and trains for Hollywood; the Lawrence Langners; Peter De Vries, writing brilliant, sophisticated books on exurbia but unexpectedly behaving like a solid citizen, carefully checking the license numbers of speeders in order to keep Westport safe for the forgotten pedestrian.

Summer was the time for tennis and more tennis. I say *was,* alas, because after the doctor ordered me to give it up at forty I finally — but reluctantly — got around to stopping it at sixty. And high time, too. But then most of my tennis partners, like myself, were falling into the sere and yellow. We would reach the court with a racket under one arm and a list of complaints on our tongue about stiff shoulders and aching backs, until I suggested we all bring hot water bottles with us. Tennis partners were usually Frank Adams, Kip Fadiman or Sig Spaeth. Frank Adams had been one of the founders of the Long Shore Country Club, which later, to his disgust, became anti-Semitic.

Summer was also the time for music. And, while music has never been the center of my life, I have met and enjoyed the company of most of the musicians of my day, from Irving Berlin, the Gershwins and Oscar Levant to Damrosch, Prokofiev, Honegger and Toscanini.

A wonderful evening that stands out in my memory was a dinner party at Edna Ferber's. Among the guests were Michael Arlen; Richard Rodgers and his wife; and Noel Coward — terribly attractive, witty, caustic, wonderful company, an egoist but with a right to it. After dinner, Noel sat at the piano and played and sang Dick's songs. He knew every one of them by heart.

Another musical evening that stands out was with the Chotzinoffs, Mrs. Heifetz and George Gershwin, whom I had first met when we produced *Porgy and Bess.* That night George talked for hours about his analysis. His constipation, he assured us solemnly, was the result of his earliest effort to show power over his parents. He also told us that, as a gesture of kindness, he had commissioned a Mexican painter to do his portrait. The painter, it appeared, liked to work on large canvases, so he had selected a wall space eight feet long by five feet high in George's apartment. He was going to paint George's head and shoulders, with his arms reaching out to the piano.

Ira Gershwin was overcome at the idea of his brother displaying such a huge portrait of himself and George was discouraged. He decided it would be better to have a picture of a crowded amphitheater with himself, somewhat reduced in size, sitting at the piano at one end. At this, his mother was shocked by his vanity — having a packed house listen to him. In disgust, George abandoned the idea and substituted for his own portrait one of a blond Stokowski. But after his analysis, he concluded triumphantly, he was going to have it changed back to himself.

Looking back after having lived among the Alexander Woollcott set with its biting wit, I feel that we did bad things to each other, that too many of the witty remarks were marred by malice.

But there's one person of whom that could not be said. I think it was through Cheryl Crawford that I met Mary Martin in Westport. She has the most loving quality of anyone I ever knew. Even the first time one meets her one is enchanted.

Mary has none of the superficial quality that one associates with actors. She has had genuine experience in life. She started in honky-tonks, where she was turned down by the astute impresario, Billy Rose, who told her firmly that she was in the wrong business. It was not until she introduced "My Heart Belongs to Daddy" — charming, sophisticated, appealing — that she made a hit.

Mary is outgoing and thoughtful as mother, wife and friend. She is real and simple, a musical comedy star who comes home to do her own housework if necessary and to look after her children whom she has worked hard to make simple and real.

Feminine as she is in quality, she has hardness and strength and an ability to shoulder responsibility that would stagger most men. I can remember seeing her in Chicago, where she was on tour with *Annie, Get Your Gun*. She was so ill she spent every moment in bed except when she gave her performances. She never missed a single one.

My husband rarely cared for theatrical people. They seemed unreal and artificial to him. But he fell for Mary. I can still see them the first night they met. Oliver and Mary were sitting a little apart from the rest of the group. Oliver was talking earnestly, and I wondered what common interest they had found to discuss. To my stunned surprise I discovered that Oliver was telling her about Gandhi. Mary, instead of being bored, was fascinated.

Later, after Oliver's death, I received a book from Mary which she had sent me from London. It was a life of Gandhi for which she had written the introduction. "Think," she wrote me, "of a little honky-tonk chorus girl writing an introduction to a book on Gandhi!"

Another warm and vital woman was Aline Bernstein, the

stage designer, plump and pretty, a free and rich soul, warm and loving and gay. I've never known anyone who was better fun than Aline. Aline the undefeated, always buoyant, charmingly self-satisfied, ingenuously boastful. She would tell you about her achievements as if she were reporting a great bit of news, generously shared; she discussed her own and her family's virtues as though she were letting you in on a delightful secret.

She was marvelous fun to go on a trip with. Summer was also the time, as a rule, for traveling. Whenever possible, I persuaded Oliver to go along. One of the trips which stand out most vividly I made with Oliver and Aline Bernstein and Philip Moeller. That year we went to Paris, Rome, Rapallo, Genoa, Pisa, Vienna and Carlsbad, where Aline and I went in strenuously for reducing.

That strenuous reducing has also been a part of my life. Periodically, I go on diets, or take treatments of one kind and another. I'm always about to reform my life completely. On the first of the year I start the neatest kind of accounts and for at least two weeks list every expenditure. Then I drop the whole thing. Ardent but sporadic — that seems to sum me up.

Aline had the same ardor. In addition, she had terrific vitality. While we were in Paris together, we would go sightseeing until four o'clock in the afternoon, at which point I would give up in exhaustion. Aline would fortify herself with a drink and then continue sight-seeing by herself.

A typical picture of Aline never fades from my mind. Very late one night we were walking in Paris. There wasn't a sound. On a deserted street corner stood a lonely young gendarme. We walked past. Then, on impulse, Aline turned back and handed him a single rose from a bunch she carried. He looked after her, completely charmed and delighted.

The love affair between Aline and Thomas Wolfe went on for years, as all the world knows now. Tom was a great talker with a terrific flow of words. (Somewhere in one of his great sprawling novels is a page describing me. I tried to find it to insert here, but I bogged down in Tom's prose.) His bitter anti-Semitism and the ruthless way he used it to inflict pain on Aline made it most difficult for me to like him.

Aline was generous and outpouring with whatever she had. She had that indefinable thing called charm. She would look up at people with wide, interested eyes and let them talk about themselves for hours. No one could resist it.

Charm, I think, consists largely of a sympathetic understanding of the other person. My husband gave this impression at first encounter but with Oliver it was, perhaps, less an actual interest in others than a defense of his own barriers. By keeping on the other person's terrain he succeeded in keeping his own inviolate.

It is curious that only once in over forty years of marriage and understanding and companionable friendship did my career and Oliver's ever meet. That was in 1952 when we both received honorary Doctor of Lit. degrees at Franklin and Marshall College at Lancaster, Pennsylvania. It's rather frightening how much we take for granted in the people we live with every day. In the last scene of *Our Town,* Thornton Wilder beautifully expressed how we never really see each other. This I felt particularly keenly after Oliver's death. We had both been busy with our secondary loves, I with the theater, he with English literature. Oliver, I think, put aside his profession more often than I. It's not that I haven't been willing to shut out the theater from time to time. I simply can't do it. Once, I recall, we were on a mountain road in the Pyrenees, crawling along the side of a precipice, skirting an abyss. A car, coming the other way, edged past us; and from the back seat a voice exclaimed, "Good God, there are some Theatre Guild people!"

Lawrence Langner has always preached at me that the sensible thing to do, however many irons are in the fire, is to go away occasionally and forget them. He wrote me in Paris, where I was trying unsuccessfully to follow his advice — because I was all churned up over some new plays and new techniques and new writers:

This letter is to stop you from worrying unduly and not to start you getting executive again. Nothing to worry about. Everything is going fine. We make a little money. We lose a little money. We get a little upset. We have a little fun.

Lawrence has a philosophy that works well for him. I have never formulated a philosophy for myself. It has seemed to me always that one's philosophy is implicit in the choice one makes. Only one's actions indicate what one really believes, and this brings us back to Spinoza: Men believe a thing when they behave as though it were true.

So many people claim, for instance, to have a religion, but I see comparatively few of them behaving as though it were true. I believe in the human comedy, in the need to live and to be aware of one's self and one's errors, even to laugh at one's self. But I grew up in a skeptical era, among skeptical people. I had no religion and I felt the need of none.

It is only with age that I have come to feel that everyone must find God if he is to find happiness. Many people accept a faith in God which comes to them from outside, but it seems to me we must find Him, each in our own way, each after our own difficult struggle. And so, lately, I've been pushing aside play scripts and turning avidly to books.

"Nature and Books belong to the eyes that see them," said Emerson. I have gone back to study his essays and draw on his belief in the dominance of Mind, the harmony of the universe, and man's lack of physical equipment to discern it; his conviction of the need for man's faith in himself.

I have become interested in the many religions of the world. I have read about Hinduism, its first great reform, Buddhism, and also Zen Buddhism. I've gone back to the Bible and read William James and Mary Baker Eddy. It has surprised me to see how close they seem to come together, if you put aside the ritual observances and superficial differences. I've been finding out, bit by bit, what I believe in, taking what I like best from each; taking more perhaps from the Quakers; concluding that each of us is a part of God, not separate from Him. There seems to me no need for religions to quarrel with each other. Up over the timberline, the trails must certainly meet. Somewhere in simplicity and loving-kindness and the Golden Rule there must be a link with God that will help me find Him.

333

I started to describe my quest for the theater and I end with my quest for God. Perhaps I have not gone so far afield. The theater, after all, began as a form of religious expression. With the present great religious revival, the wheel may come full circle. But this I know — in my bones if not in my mind: because it is the strongest, the most immediate emotional expression of all the arts, theater can never die.

What have I learned during all these years? Little enough, I suppose, though each step in the learning process was slow and painful.

I have learned that you cannot protect people from life. That is why censorship is senseless. Everyone must learn by his own personal experience. Children are not hurt by learning. What they don't understand doesn't hurt them; what they do understand won't hurt them. It is the understanding that counts.

I have learned that what matters most is doing whatever you do with all your heart. People worry such a lot about finding exactly the right career. But most people know almost nothing about their own strength and weakness. I wanted to be a playwright. I didn't really want the job I finally took. One's lifework, I have learned, grows with the working and the living. Do it as if your life depended on it and, first thing you know, you'll have made a life out of it. A good life, too.

Anything else? Well, yes, one more thing — I learned it in the theater: There are a thousand rules and theories about the theater and about life itself. None of them holds. Just take a long breath, dive off the cliff, and swim as hard as you can.

334

Index

343

Wertheim, Maurice, 15, 74–75, 81, 88–89, 94, 110, 170, 198
West, Mae, 130–131, 226
Westley, Helen, 57, 68, 69, 72, 73, 74, 81, 89–91, 94, 107–108, 109, 127, 208, 209, 225
Westport, Conn., 64, 326–328
Westport Country Playhouse, 85, 272, 313, 314, 315, 323
Wheelock, John Hall, 20
White, Miles, 284
Whyte, Jerome, 293
Widdemer, Margaret, 20
Wilder, Thornton, 239, 331–332
Williams, Hope, 131
Williams, Tennessee, 239, 249

Wine of Choice, 246
Winsor School. *See* Miss Winsor's School
Wolfe, Thomas, 331
Woman Suffrage Movement, 46–47
Woods, Al, 66
Woollcott, Alexander, 185, 208, 246, 314, 328
World War I, 43, 45, 55

You Never Can Tell, 215
Young, Marjorie, 11
Youngh, Mrs. Creena d', 29

ZURICH, 43